THE WORLD IS MY CLASSROOM

International Learning and Canadian Higher Education

Edited by Joanne Benham Rennick and Michel Desjardins

In today's knowledge economy, much attention has been focused on international education, and universities are key to creating successful programs for students learning abroad. *The World Is My Classroom* presents diverse perspectives on these experiential learning programs and ways of promoting global education in Canadian classrooms. The contributors examine topics related to global citizenship and service learning, shedding light on current ethical debates and practical approaches.

The World Is My Classroom is the first book to examine pedagogical questions about the internationalization and globalization of higher education from an explicitly Canadian perspective. It features students' reflections on their transformative experiences in learn-abroad programs, as well as a foreword by Craig and Marc Kielburger, founders of Free The Children and Me to We. Combining practical knowledge, theoretical perspectives, and personal insight, the volume is essential reading for university faculty and administrators concerned with developing, enhancing, and refining their learn-abroad programs, as well as students considering enrolling in such programs.

JOANNE BENHAM RENNICK is an assistant professor in the Department of Contemporary Studies at Wilfrid Laurier University.

MICHEL DESJARDINS is a professor in the Department of Religion and Culture at Wilfrid Laurier University.

The World Is My Classroom

International Learning and Canadian Higher Education

EDITED BY JOANNE BENHAM RENNICK
AND MICHEL DESJARDINS

UNIVERSITY OF TORONTO PRESS
Toronto Buffalo London

ISBN 978-1-4426-4775-6 (cloth)
ISBN 978-1-4426-1582-3 (paper)

Printed on acid-free, 100% post-consumer recycled paper with
vegetable-based inks.

Library and Archives Canada Cataloguing in Publication

The world is my classroom : international learning and Canadian higher
education / edited by Joanne Benham Rennick and Michel Desjardins.

Includes bibliographical references and index.
ISBN 978-1-4426-4775-6 (bound). –ISBN 978-1-4426-1582-3 (pbk.)

1. International education.   2. International education –
Canada. 3. Education, Higher – Canada.   4.Education, Higher –
International cooperation.   5. Education and globalization.   I. Desjardins,
Michel Robert, 1951–, editor compilation   II. Benham Rennick, Joanne,
1970–, editor compilation

LB2324.W67 2013   378'.016   C2013-902886-2

This book has been published with the help of a grant from the Canadian
Federation for the Humanities and Social Sciences, through the Awards
to Scholarly Publications Program, using funds provided by the Social
Sciences and Humanities Research Council of Canada.

University of Toronto Press acknowledges the financial assistance to its
publishing program of the Canada Council for the Arts and the Ontario
Arts Council.

University of Toronto Press acknowledges the financial support of the
Government of Canada through the Canada Book Fund for its publishing
activities.

For our students: you continually inspire us with your enthusiasm, vision, and ingenuity in your efforts to "be the change you want to see in the world."

—JBR and MD

Contents

Part V: Conclusion

Foreword

Candy.

That's one way we can tell that a group of well-meaning people have come before us to "help" a community in the developing world: we're surrounded by children clamouring for candy.

It's understandable: kids love candy. North American kids are handed candy at restaurants, the barbershop, and even the doctor's office. So travellers often bring small candies to distribute to poor children as a gift – a treat they rarely or never receive.

But this introductory gesture represents a relationship of giving and receiving – of dependency on generosity instead of partnership among equals. The kids take the candy and run, and the visitor rarely learns a name or understands what the child really needs, which is almost never candy. The children see foreigners as givers of temporary happiness, instead of as friends and partners who want to know them and work hand-in-hand to improve their life.

On the other hand, when visitors from afar arrive with a handshake and a smile, introduced by a permanent local guide, and they stay a week or more to build a friendship and participate in a project that puts the community first, that connection can truly change the lives of everyone involved.

Many will ask: "Do these trips really help? Why not just send the money you'll spend travelling there directly to the projects?"

Sure, any organization will welcome the cheque. But Canadians want to travel, and they will. So we say, instead of tanning on a beach, give them the opportunity to experience something that, if done well, will lead to a lifetime of contributions beyond a one-time donation.

Marc, for example, was a page in the House of Commons, on track for a career in law or politics, when a Member of Parliament (for whom

Marc was fetching a glass of water) challenged him to spend a summer volunteering in Bangkok. After the first sleepless night listening to pigs being slaughtered in the streets, Marc packed his bags to fly home. But that day, after a crash course in administering HIV drugs to terminally ill patients at a Thai hospice, he cradled a stranger as he died.

Marc stayed another six months, met orphans who didn't know their own birthdays, watched countless more people die in his care, and returned home to switch his major to international development. Marc still eventually studied law, but his focus was on human rights and non-profit management, and his career path led to social enterprise and charity instead of big firms or corporations.

Craig, meanwhile, was a connoisseur of the newspaper's comics section until he read of the death of Iqbal Masih, a freed child slave in Pakistan, which sparked the creation of Free The Children. Craig first travelled to South Asia at age twelve with his friend and guide Alam Rahman, where he met in person children weaving carpets, recycling used syringes, and living in garbage dumps, their families struggling to survive financially, and activists fighting sweatshop owners, governments, and economics.

The people and communities we've met on our travels have been formative influences on our perspective, our choices, and our paths. They've gifted us with innumerable, invaluable life lessons that we want to pay forward to others. Our stories echo those of students you'll encounter in this book, in their own words and those of the teachers who are equally passionate about global, engaged learning. The contributors address the need to think carefully, responsibly, about that type of learning.

Our thinking took a particular path. We started bringing along friends and other Free The Children members informally, and it grew into organizing trips for thousands of people, ages eleven to eighty, to Kenya, Nicaragua, Ecuador, Thailand, India, and Mexico. The best part about starting so young is that we knew that we didn't have the answers. So we asked a lot of questions of those who came before us, especially in the local communities. With their wisdom and from our own mistakes we've learned a lot.

We've learned that the volunteer trip, on its own, is insufficient. Its true utility is its lasting impact: the sustainable improvement to the life of the community, and the lifelong commitment of the participant to building a better world.

Like the authors of this book, we, too, found that, for the community, projects work best when driven by their needs and led by their members and when continued beyond the tourist season by permanent local development teams. Participants from North America ideally add needed extra hands to an existing project, such as raising a wall for a school or caring for children who would otherwise not receive much attention, rather than partaking in a make-work project or taking the place of paid local workers. If it's done well, your trip could actually create local jobs – from cooks and tour guides to drivers and security.

For the participants, we've found it useful to include programming before the trip about the communities they'll visit, to establish a base of cultural understanding and sensitivity; during the trip to explore the deeper social, economic, and environmental issues at play; and afterward to facilitate follow-up action. Workshops and discussions with host community members on culture, trade, aid, and development promote a deeper, more genuine understanding of their experience.

The objective is an enduring impact on their future decision making about consumer choices, charitable actions, and in their professional life. We don't want every participant to switch majors to international development; on the contrary, ideally participants continue their career track in medicine, business, science, or other fields, and make decisions in those positions that reflect the values and realities they've learned through the program.

That is why we are writing the foreword for this book – we recognize that the perspective developed on these journeys can be life changing. If tomorrow's CEOs, politicians, engineers, and trades people know and understand global issues such as poverty and inequality, imagine how different their decisions will be. If tomorrow's parents pass their awareness and sensitivities about these issues on to their children, we raise a new generation committed to a better world.

We end most of our trips with an activity called "Into the Fire." Participants are given ten pieces of paper and asked to jot down, on each, one of the ten most important things in their lives: family, boyfriend, school, iPod, and so on. One by one, they throw one of the papers "into the fire," starting with the least important. The last piece of paper – what they have decided is most dear to them – is placed in an envelope with a note they write to themselves. The package is mailed to the participant several months later – a reminder of their values once they've returned to their everyday lives. Reading their self-addressed letter, they recall the experience and their determination to make a difference. We've heard countless stories of changing jobs, changing majors, changing boyfriends. Changing lives.

Our most important lesson from fifteen years of leading overseas trips is that the trip is just the beginning – for both the volunteers and the community they visit. You'll find the same realization in this book, among university educators and students. They acknowledge the profound pedagogical value of international learning experiences, and insist on quality, reciprocity, and humility. Any time we interact with other cultures, and any time we endeavour to partner with people in communities that aren't our own, we must tread carefully and respectfully.

By sharing experiences, challenges, and successes, we can enhance the effects of volunteer-abroad programs on the students who participate and the communities they meet.

We sincerely hope that this book helps build a volunteer-abroad movement where the travellers bring, not candy, but friendship.

Craig and Marc Kielburger
Founders, Free The Children and Me to We

Acknowledgments

As with all labours of love, this book has been inspired and supported by many individuals, including our spouses and families, colleagues and students, and teachers whose dedication to learning have been constant reminders that education always deserves our full attention. We hope they all see some of themselves in the pages that follow.

We are thankful for a project grant from the Wabash Center for Teaching and Learning that allowed us to organize our two-year Good Global Citizenship Think Tank, which set the stage for this book. The funding enabled us to bring staff, faculty, and students together from across Canada for workshops to discuss the topic of global citizenship in relation to programming in higher education. *The World Is My Classroom* is a key outcome of those discussions. We are also grateful to Wilfrid Laurier University for its award of a Book Preparation Grant that has helped bring this manuscript to press.

Not all people who participated in these workshops prepared chapters for this book, but their ideas – as well as discussions with colleagues and feedback from others at academic presentations for the Canadian Association for International Development, the Canadian Society for Studies in Higher Education, and the International Society for the Study of Teaching and Learning – influenced the nature of this book. We are grateful to all of them.

The academic dean and vice-president of St Jerome's University in the University of Waterloo during those two years, Myroslaw Tataryn, could not have been more supportive of our project. So too were our student assistants, Nicholas Shrubsole and Cathleen DiFruscio, who not only participated actively in the discussions but also ensured that the workshops ran smoothly.

Students in fact breathed life into this project from the very start. We think in particular of the courage and openness of those who participated in the volunteer-abroad programs we independently managed, those who shared their stories during our workshops, and those who took up our challenge to contribute directly to the book.

The other contributors to this book also worked hard to revise and refine their arguments in light of comments by others and in the context of a series of deadlines. Writing is always challenging, and a collective writing project of this nature in particular requires patience and commitment. We consider ourselves fortunate to have developed a book with them.

We are delighted that Marc and Craig Kielburger share our concerns about many of the issues examined in the book and agreed to take time out of their busy schedules to prepare a Foreword. Their vision and dedication to global education continue to inspire Canadians.

The University of Toronto Press – in particular, its acquisitions editor Douglas Hildebrand, our copy editor Barry Norris, and managing editor Anne Laughlin – were invaluable. Press feedback, especially from the anonymous readers chosen to review the manuscript, enhanced the quality of the book. We are also grateful to the various journal editors who allowed us to reproduce material that has been previously published in part elsewhere.

PART I

Introduction

1 Towards a Pedagogy of Good Global Citizenship

JOANNE BENHAM RENNICK AND
MICHEL DESJARDINS

I am not trying to "save the world." I do, however, see it as my duty to leave the world a better place than when I entered it. This is me, stepping up, with hopes of being joined by others in my generation, so that together we can create a better future that we all want to be a part of. So often I feel restless, seeing the gap between my vision and the current reality, but for now, I am working hard to do what I can and creating a path that is the most suitable for me.

–Ruby Ku, alumna of the Beyond Borders program,
http://www.ac4d.com/home/people/students-and-alumni/ruby-ku/

1.1 Introduction

If you drill down to the core of this book you will find a concern for values, embedded in reflections on global learning programs that are offered to Canadian university and college students – particularly those who choose to participate in international service or volunteer programs. Before discussing the book's contents, we would like to take you back to two components of its genesis: the questions that emerged for us when we managed international university service learning programs, and the workshops we organized in 2010 and 2011 with educators and students from across Canada to discuss "good global citizenship" and all its inherent complexities and tensions.

We are passionate about teaching. The emerging focus on "global" in Canadian post-secondary education, coupled with growing demand by students and faculty for opportunities to learn abroad, offers significant possibilities for bringing about positive change in the lives of Canadians and others around the world. That is to say, the issues addressed in this book matter, not only to those of us engaged in university life, but also to individuals and communities throughout the world. The student who spends three months volunteering in an Ecuadorian orphanage – or takes a summer course in Prague, or does a four-month work internship for a multinational company in New Zealand, or volunteers in a multi-ethnic, multiracial women's shelter in Saskatoon as part of a credit course – will have her horizons expanded. So, too, one hopes, will the people she encounters. As educators we encourage and support these learning opportunities, and as editors we hope that this book can contribute to their improvement.

1.2   Managing International Service Learning Programs

The pedagogical challenges associated with these learning opportunities took on renewed urgency for the two of us in 2008–09 when we each assumed responsibilities for an international service learning program at our respective universities: Joanne with Beyond Borders, at St Jerome's University, federated with the University of Waterloo, and Michel with the Global Studies Experience in the Department of Global Studies at Wilfrid Laurier University. Both programs had numerous students who sang their praises, and both fell squarely within their university's renewed mission statements. As we would later discover, we each proceeded incrementally in roughly the same way to strengthen our programs.

What makes international service learning experiences so pedagogically challenging and exhilarating are their multiple vantage points. Students, teachers, and program recipients – or participants, Freire (1970) would insist – all have distinct responsibilities. One might ask, therefore, what it is about service learning that makes it such a valuable learning experience for students, and such a valuable pedagogical tool for educators as well, and also what is actually gained by the people with whom students come in contact abroad. All three of these constituencies – and there are more – are also implicated in everyday university teaching and learning, but when student learning extends outside the classroom, outside the country, into parts of the developing world, those realities are more acute.

In trying to ensure that our two programs were as pedagogically sound as possible and that their goals were clear and transparent, we independently sought advice from various quarters within our universities, including our students, then turned to the scholarship on teaching and learning for guidance. We found students highly supportive, though understandably nervous about taking up international opportunities. Still, we are convinced that a far larger segment of the student body would take up the opportunity to learn abroad if increased financial and program supports were forthcoming. Senior administrators were also supportive, while also hoping, not surprisingly, that most of the work could get done without additional strain on their tight budgets. Some faculty members raised red flags – Are we not simply supporting forms of volun[teer]tourism? How can we assess quality when students learn outside the classroom? Do we have adequate resources to ensure that this sort of teaching is done well? – but the vast majority of our colleagues were enthusiastic. Few, however, had any experience with this form of teaching, and almost none had any familiarity with the accompanying pedagogical literature.

The relevant scholarship on teaching and learning is predominantly US-centred, and it is also not extensive. The turn to "global" is so recent, and learning abroad programs are increasing at such a rate, that the literature lacks a broad base and simply cannot keep up with the realities on the ground. Experts on teaching and learning, however, are certainly aware of these global extensions to teaching, and are highly supportive of them. The Canadian Society for Teaching and Learning in Higher Education, for example, identifies learning abroad experiences as those most likely to draw students to programs, keep them engaged in their learning, and leave them satisfied with their education after they graduate. The most influential US academic organization dedicated to teaching and learning, the American Association of Colleges and Universities, also strongly supports this form of pedagogy, for similar reasons. We were heartened to have our experiences as program managers confirmed in this way, and we were also motivated to contribute more Canadian content to the discussion.

When we turned from the scholarly literature to other international service learning program coordinators across Canada, we discovered something else: many people developed their program with minimal consultation. Study abroad programs have a long history in Canadian universities, and are often well supported. So, too, are co-op work and research programs, though the international connections here are less well established. But service or volunteer learning, both international and local (and both now have global concerns), is not as developed. There is also little communication between these Canadian learning abroad programs – at times even between those within the same institution. Instructional development officers on Canadian campuses meet regularly across the country, as do deans, presidents, and staff who run international offices. But the people who develop and run learning abroad programs – and those who run local service programs that aim to encourage students to become more globally conscious – do not often or ever talk with one another.

In 2009 we came together and compared notes, then proceeded to seek funding to invite like-minded individuals from across Canada to join us in Waterloo to share their experiences and ideas. In a post-secondary context where "global" is now *de rigueur* and university presidents talk about educating good global citizens, we thought that here would be the place to start to reflect more deeply on what we do as teachers across this country.

1.3   The Good Global Citizenship Workshops

Funding from the Wabash Center for Teaching and Learning allowed us to establish a two-year, interdisciplinary workshop to examine the problems of pedagogy surrounding programming intended to develop good global citizens. Two dozen students, staff, and faculty members joined us from across Canada, twice in person (January 2010 and January 2011) and other times in virtual space, to share information, identify key challenges and successes, and consider what might be possible in the best of possible worlds.

Although most workshop participants were concerned primarily with international learning experiences, some faculty and staff were involved in programs whose students learn, both inside and outside the classroom, to develop increased sensitivity to global concerns, but they do so only domestically. This cross-fertilization of local and international, both focused on the global, turned out to be highly productive for our discussions. So, too, were the varied perspectives that came from conversations among a mix of students, staff, and faculty members. The contributions by students who had recently participated in international service learning programs were particularly instructive.

Our workshop objective was to move "towards a pedagogy dedicated to good global citizenship." Our purported goal, though, immediately became an issue when, as a group, we challenged one another with the different meanings we ascribed to "global," "citizenship," and "good." We also debated a variety of questions: Whose idea of good should we consider? Is there more harm than good in these initiatives? Who is on the receiving end of the so-called good? What is the difference between a "good" global citizen and a "bad" one? Our seemingly straightforward objective of moving "towards" anything was quickly made more complex by our responsibility, specifically within the Canadian context, to examine the parameters of education that purports to be global.

We also pursued a general definition of "global citizenship." Workshop participants suggested several possibilities and identified a number of tensions within the phrase itself, including questions about who was using it, whether or not it was tied to economic or political goals, and who really belongs to (or considers themselves members of) a global society. Our discussions turned to various ideas about good and bad forms of global citizenship, conversations that were naturally grounded in the individual and institutional values participants carried with them. One prominent theme was the appreciation that, by immersing themselves in a different culture, language, or region of the world, students might find new ways to embody knowledge and increase their capacity for understanding diverse human experiences.

Without ignoring the contentious nature of "global citizenship" and cognizant that the phrase is likely to convey very different meanings to many different people, group members ultimately concurred that the more general language of Oxfam's definition was helpful for guiding our discussions about international learning opportunities in higher education: "Global Citizenship is about understanding the need to tackle injustice and inequality, and having the desire and ability to work actively to do so. It is about valuing the Earth as precious and unique, and safeguarding the future for those coming after us. Global Citizenship is a way of thinking and behaving. It is an outlook on life, a belief that we can make a difference" (Oxfam 2007).

This definition, too, is value laden. Values – and attempts to define them – always come with heavy cultural baggage. The critical task is to identify them and to recognize that one person's deeply held values are not necessarily someone else's.

Oxfam's description is echoed by Michael Byers, Canada Research Chair in Global Politics and International Law at the University of British Columbia, who has argued in favour of a definition of global citizenship that promotes the empowerment of all people to be fully engaged in decisions and processes that affect their lives, while also enjoying a quality of life that ensures human dignity (2005). Christian liberation theologians, including Gustavo Gutierrez, Paolo Freire, and Enrique Dussel, have long argued in favour of a society that places human experiences above social and corporate demands. Paul Farmer, founder of Partners in Health, also insists that the "structural violence" identified by liberation theologians continues to exist, particularly concerning issues of health care for the poor, and must be addressed through "good global citizenship" that gives agency and recognition to the world's marginalized peoples (2004). Taken together, these ideas suggest a context of human solidarity, rather than one of political affinity, and are prominent themes in the chapters that make up this volume, even as they remain points of tension and ambiguity for educators and students alike.

In defining global citizenship, we counted ourselves among the wealthy elite able to obtain a higher education, act with our own agency, and impose ourselves both physically and psychologically in the international domain. Naturally, this raised for us the uneasy spectre of our potential to be counted among the oppressors – the "bad global citizens." Indeed, in our individualistic and commodity-driven culture, there is a real risk that, as with current concerns about education in general, international learning experiences might develop into "trophy" courses where students get to take a trip, avoid much critical thinking, and have an exotic experience to talk about later.

As proponents of higher education keen to increase the quality of their programs, the directors, staff, and faculty in our workshops acknowledged the fine line between supporting narrow institutional goals and exploiting global partners. Although numerous types of international learning experiences are available, the more contentious involve global partnerships with vulnerable populations, rather than peer-to-peer or university exchanges within similar cultural milieux. This is what makes it so important to develop sound international service learning programs. Questions about how much good we are really doing with these programs caused all of us to squirm on more than one occasion.

At the same time, there was broad recognition among educators and students alike that, when done well, these experiences bring extraordinary perspective and understanding of ourselves and the Other. Program directors spoke passionately about how their own experiences abroad had been the impetus to raise awareness of global concerns and involve themselves in meaningful opportunities for student learning. Students described being motivated to reframe their careers in the context of "giving back" or "making a difference." All around the room, participants referred to the continuing relationships that started with their time abroad and the lasting impact the experience had on them. Physically absent from our discussions, however, were the community members with whom the students had lived and worked abroad; our dream workshop would include them.

Workshop participants also agreed that the institutions and individuals involved in these programs should do much more than simply provide an opportunity for students to learn abroad. We cannot emphasize enough that, without ongoing reflection and debate on the ethical implications of sending students abroad, we run the risk of establishing a new form of structural violence that disempowers, undermines, and rejects the agency of the very groups we are simultaneously claiming to "help" – not to mention giving the participants a simplistic, at times misguided, view of international development and cultural differences.

1.4   What Lies Ahead in the Book

We are acutely aware of the dearth of Canadian pedagogical models, best practices, and continuing opportunities for dialogue within and between institutions offering international learning programs. There are a number of US studies on internationalization and higher education (Bhandari and Laughlin 2009; Gürüz 2011 [2008]; Lewin 2009; Salmi 2009; Shaw, Sharma, and Takeuchi 2009; and Stearns 2008), and several on pedagogy, education research, and assessment (Alred, Byram, and Fleming 2006; Arcaro and Haskell 2009; Brewer and Cunningham 2009; Byram 2006; and Hellstén and Reid 2008). The significant differences between US and Canadian culture, however, as well as current ideas about internationalization and higher education, make exclusive reliance on these resources problematic for our purposes – particularly in the context of national identity and cultural ideas about "the common good." What follows, then, is a discussion that speaks to Canadian culture, values, and concerns, in the voices of Canadians, including students, who are engaged in these activities. This book provides a balance between theory and practice while examining international learning programming and ideas about good global citizenship at different Canadian universities.

Because international experiences are developing on a variety of trajectories – including skills-specific opportunities (for example, in engineering or health care) and social justice initiatives – several different approaches, applied in a wide range of departments and programs, are being employed across Canada. Our hope is that this book will lay the foundation for greater collaboration within, between, and across

and how we might carry them out with the greatest degree of effectiveness and sensitivity. Maureen Drysdale, a psychologist at St Jerome's University and the University of Waterloo who specializes in developmental and education psychology; her colleague Nancy Johnston, former director of Co-operative Education at Simon Fraser University; and research assistant Caitlin Chiupka present models for preparing and supporting students through learning abroad experiences with the goal of developing their knowledge and understanding as global citizens.

Two other chapters present case studies of programs in which students' experiences start or remain at home but still allow them to engage with global realities. Communications, Culture, and Information Technology program director Tracey Bowen writes about student experiences in a fourth-year internship program at the University of Toronto. Jackie Eldridge and John Smith, who have coordinated the Concurrent Teacher Education program and internship program at the Ontario Institute for Studies in Education in Toronto, examine a second-year course intended to prepare future teachers for the diversity they increasingly will experience in their classrooms.

International experience alone does not suffice – contextualization and critical analysis are essential components of the greater learning experience. Pairing the local with the global, as Bowen, Eldridge, and Smith do, adds opportunities for students to experience some of the struggles of a new social environment and to become aware of the values and assumptions they carry into their learning. Creating multiple occasions for students to reflect on their experiences amplifies the learning.

Our authors agree that, as educators and participants in an increasingly interconnected and in many ways increasingly fragile world, we are responsible for preparing students to participate in this world as effectively and sensitively as possible. Our own experiences point to the difficulty of preparing our students adequately for some of the challenges they will face while working, studying, or volunteering abroad, while also equipping them on their return with the resources they need to interpret their international experience in ways that are relevant to their broader life goals. Institutional goals and faculty objectives can trump student concerns, and typically there are insufficient opportunities for students to reflect on and evaluate their experiences. Yet, some of the most valuable insights will come from student participants, and we need to listen to them.

We have taken this mantra seriously. At every step along the way, students have played an integral role in our reflections. They quickly became the focal point of our gatherings as they gave poignant insights from their lived experiences as they prepared to undertake their international learning or having recently returned from abroad. Their participation was crucial for helping us all reframe our thinking and reconsider our pedagogical approaches. Student viewpoints are also prominent in this book. These include short reflections by University of Waterloo students Conor Brennan, Jessica DeBrouwer, Cathleen DiFruscio, and Nevena Savija, and Wilfrid Laurier University students Stephany Lau, Lynn Matisz, and Clara Yoon. Their thoughts have helped frame the themes highlighted in this volume. The students tell their stories in their own way, but their narratives are also typical of what we and our colleagues have heard from other students across the country. Moreover, one additional chapter co-authored by DiFruscio examines the cognitive dissonance so many students experience on their return, as they bring together the experiences they had abroad with their Canadian lives and values.

We close this Introduction by reflecting more about values. As workshop facilitators and editors, we are now increasingly cognizant of some of the tacit assumptions, conflicting or uncertain values, and ethical challenges embedded in promoting and pursuing international experiences in higher education. Administrators, program coordinators, and students need to have an explicit understanding of the values that inspire the projects in which they engage, and those values need to be embedded in Canadian cultural contexts. Overarching ethical and moral principles should contribute to students' capacity to empathize, understand, and become concerned for the experiences of others – particularly those living in the developing world.

Enhanced dialogue between program coordinators and teachers across Canada, and shared knowledge about these programs, can go a long way towards helping those who are running these programs and to making the programs more effective, responsible, and sustainable. Our hope is that this book will start a new kind of discussion about the purpose, responsibilities, and best practices for international learning programs in Canadian higher education. By collaborating with stakeholders from different programming levels, we have identified some of the broader challenges inherent in creating and maintaining meaningful experiences for our students. The challenge now is to continue this dialogue in productive ways and to engage more stakeholders to join the discussion. Already, our "Good Global Citizenship" project has established a pan-Canadian community of colleagues with whom we can confer and collaborate about our international learning programs. It has also provided an unusual – and, we think, progressive – forum for egalitarian collaboration among faculty, staff, and students.

As we move further into the twenty-first century, we face significant new challenges surrounding issues of human health, global security, the environment, human rights, inter-religious tensions, economic uncertainty, and population movements. The international perspective gained by students who engage in global learning will enable them to better understand and engage with these challenges. At the same time, such students need opportunities for intentional, focused re-examination, ongoing reflection, and dialogue if they are to reflect meaningfully on their experiences and face the future with a sense of clarity about their Canadian identity and purpose. Continuing, meaningful discussion among educators, student participants, and host communities is fundamental to these objectives. We offer this book as a step forward in that ongoing process.

NOTE

1 Some of the material in this volume was also presented in two panels at the Congress of the Canadian Federation for the Humanities and Social Sciences, Fredericton, New Brunswick, May–June 2011.

REFERENCES

Alred, G., M. Byram, and M. Fleming, eds. 2006. *Education for Intercultural Citizenship: Concepts and Comparisons.* Bristol, UK: Multilingual Matters.

Arcaro, T., and R. Haskell, eds. 2009. *Understanding the Global Experience: Becoming a Responsible World Citizen.* Upper Saddle River, NJ: Allyn & Bacon.

Bhandari, R., and S. Laughlin, eds. 2009. *Higher Education on the Move: New Developments in Global Mobility.* New York: Institute of International Education.

Brewer, E., and K. Cunningham. 2009. *Integrating Study Abroad into the Curriculum: Theory and Practice across the Disciplines.* Sterling, VA: Stylus Publishers.

Byers, M. (2005). "Are you a global citizen?" Speech given at the University of British Columbia, Vancouver. Available online at http://thetyee.ca/Views/2005/10/05/globalcitizen/.

Byram, M., ed. 2006. *Living and Studying Abroad: Research and Practice*. Bristol, UK: Multilingual Matters.

Farmer, P.E. 2004. *Pathologies of Power: Health, Human Rights, and the New War on the Poor*. Berkeley: University of California Press.

Freire, P. 1970. *Pedagogy of the Oppressed*. Hammondsworth, UK: Penguin.

Gürüz, K. 2011 [2008]. *Higher Education and International Student Mobility in the Global Knowledge Economy*, 2nd ed. Albany: State University of New York Press.

Hellstén, M., and A. Reid, eds. 2008. *Researching International Pedagogies: Sustainable Practice for Teaching and Learning in Higher Education*. New York: Springer Publishing.

Lewin, R., ed. 2009. *The Handbook of Practice and Research in Study Abroad: Higher Education and the Quest for Global Citizenship*. New York: Routledge.

Oxfam. 2007. "What is global citizenship?" Available online at http://www.oxfam.org.uk/education/global-citizenship/what-is-global-citizenship; accessed 13 June 2012.

Salmi, J. 2009. *The Challenge of Establishing World-class Universities*. Washington, DC: World Bank Publications.

Shaw, R., A. Sharma, and Y. Takeuchi, eds. 2009. *Indigenous Knowledge and Disaster Risk Reduction: From Practice to Policy*. Hauppauge, NY: Nova Science Publishers.

Stearns, P. 2008. *Educating Global Citizens in Colleges and Universities: Challenges and Opportunities*. New York: Routledge.

STUDENT INTERMEZZO
What draws students to go abroad?

Planting little seeds

JESSICA DEBROUWER

In my second year of university, I left the comforts of the world around me – having the ability to take cold, warm, or hot showers at a moment's notice and benefitting from the instant availability of clean laundry in less than an hour – to go abroad into the world of chicken buses, heat waves, lack of Internet, and an unreliable water source. With both the financial and emotional support of my friends and family, I removed myself from my safe little bubble of Mitchell, Ontario, to spend three months in a town I had never heard of, in a country I knew little about.

May 4, 2009, my two feet landed in Estelí, Nicaragua, and my summer away from home was about to begin. I went to Estelí in hopes of changing the world a little and making a positive impact in someone else's life. With Costa Rica to the north and Honduras to the south, Nicaragua is right in the heart of Central America, and that is where I dove into a culture I didn't understand, a language I couldn't speak, and a place that certainly did not feel like home – at least not straight away. At one time, I was told, Nicaragua was not a name that evoked thoughts of poverty, illiteracy, sickness, or extreme difficulty. With government corruption and civil war, Nicaragua has now become the poorest country in Central America, wracked with social problems and oftentimes with little hope for growth or change.

Living in Estelí was much different than visiting or just stopping through. Living there gave me an appreciation for the way of life – as well as toughened me up to catcalls and freezing cold showers! While in Estelí, I worked at a centre called Los Pipitos, which translates into "little seeds." It was designed as a safe haven for children, youth, and adults who were born with mental or physical disabilities. Disabilities are not socially acceptable in the Nicaragua I encountered. Los Pipitos is supposed to reproduce the structure of a regular school while making the students feel accepted by their peers.

While working at the centre, I was able to meet one of the women who founded the organization and graciously answered all my questions.

Los Pipitos is a not-for-profit organization that operates on donations as well as different materials that are made and sold by the students. There are many different activities for those students at Los Pipitos, anything from arts, crafts, candle and wax flower making, cooking, woodworking, and agricultural work. They make fertilizer, cultivate fruits, and sell hand-made puzzles, cards, and dolls. All proceeds from these projects go directly back into the centre and into the programs for the students.

Spending the majority of my time at Los Pipitos opened my eyes to the seriousness of discrimination against those with disabilities. When members of a society see a person as something outside their own restricted view of "normal" and "acceptable," those who already suffer due to a disability are made to feel even worse.

When Father's Day came around, I saw first-hand how difficult the home lives were for many of these children. There were approximately fifty children, youths, and adults at Los Pipitos, and only four fathers came to the celebration, leaving many children disappointed during a party that was supposed to lift their spirits. That day I learned a little bit more about the culture around me and the stigmas I was trying to fight. This is an example of "ignorance is bliss" because I soon learned that many of the kids had been abandoned by their parents in one way or another, leaving them to live with older siblings, distant relatives, or simply on their own. Many of the parents had died, moved away, or plainly turned their children away because of their disability. Many fathers wanted nothing to do with children who reminded them of weakness and failure. The implications of this point of view were too staggering for me to absorb. All I wanted to do at that moment was somehow take all their pain (and mine) away and have them play and live like kids are supposed to, untouched by the pains of reality for at least a little bit longer.

At Los Pipitos I not only worked at the centre itself; I also completed home visits with my supervisor. We interviewed parents and checked on their living situation, the possibility of violence, availability of food, and other basic concerns. This was another difficult moment in Estelí as their living situations were rough, to say the least.

The week of these home visits was a great learning opportunity, even though I found it tough to be there while the parents and guardians spoke of their hardships. The first visit began the series of difficult moments. We went to visit a young teenager whom I'll call Martha, who had been frequenting Los Pipitos for many years. She lived in a single-parent family that literally shared a cement room with a few chickens and little else. Martha's mother washed other people's clothes for a living. Sometimes they had food to eat, at other times they didn't. My boss assured me this situation, which seemed to me difficult, wasn't too bad: "at least there appeared to be no violence"! Once again I wanted to bring out the fairy dust, sprinkle it all over the place, and free them of their misfortune, be it disability, violence, poverty, or illiteracy. My feeling of helplessness and the pain I felt for others again generated in me a wish to make everything better in one fell swoop. I also realized that here was an opportunity for me to incorporate into my own life their constructive response to life: I wished I could pocket some of their optimism in times of personal despair.

There were other lows. In late June, the small group of Canadians I lived with and an American journalist ventured into the capital, Managua, to spend the day in Central America's biggest garbage dump, also known as La Chureca, or the Gates of Hell. One day here was more than enough to really show me the struggles of everyday life for those on the outer margins of Nicaraguan society. La Chureca, we were told, houses more than four hundred families, and many of these individuals have never set foot outside the dump. Children as young as four frequent the mounds of garbage looking for anything recyclable, reusable, edible, or of any kind of value. These children, like most of their parents, are refused education and often experience the trauma of sexual, physical, and emotional abuse. La Chureca was a particularly devastating day because the conditions were something straight out of my world's constructed images of hell: with an odour that burns your nostrils and makes your eyes tear up, rotting animals, spontaneous combustions, and huge numbers of people physically fighting over different piles of trash. Once again this day showed me what strength some people possess even in the worst of circumstances.

Not all of my time was spent abroad doing work, and certainly not all of Nicaragua is bleak. Central America is big on siestas, relaxation, and taking it easy. Throughout my three months there, I was able to visit the majority of the country, always leaving my own mark behind in one way or the other. During our time away, I and some other students who were also volunteering in the region improved our navigational skills, climbed volcanoes, kayaked around monkey islands, zip lined over the rain forest, swam in the bluest of waters, and watched sea turtles lay their eggs.

The whole time abroad led me to new opportunities and to new experiences I could never forget. In the beginning I thought this trip was all about poverty awareness and experiencing a different culture; however, I learned more about myself than I ever expected. Three months took me on a roller coaster of emotions, tested everything I knew, and challenged me in ways I would have never expected. With all that said and done, I am a little closer to discovering the true me, and I would return to those same chicken buses, heat waves, and unreliable water sources in a heartbeat.

PART II

Historical and Pedagogical Contexts

2 Canadian Values, Good Global Citizenship, and Service Learning in Canada: A Socio-historical Analysis[1]

JOANNE BENHAM RENNICK

2.1 Background: Whose Values?

The federal Department of Foreign Affairs and International Trade states that Canada "has been a consistently strong voice for the protection of human rights and the advancement of democratic values" (Canada 2011). In fact, volunteer initiatives based on social justice, social welfare, and a missionary and "civilizing" agenda have a long history in Canada. They are tied to nationalistic values growing out of a Christian heritage concerned with mutual responsibility and the interrelatedness of human and divine concerns. Even as Canadian society becomes progressively more secular and more sensitive to religious diversity, and as religion becomes increasingly privatized, much of our foreign policy is still strongly linked with Christian concerns for solidarity and recognition of the Other.[2]

At the same time, Canadian proximity to, and extensive collaboration with, its US neighbour have resulted in the adoption of certain American national values, which include neo-liberal economic policies affecting military, foreign affairs, and trade activities. These values are further linked to modern bureaucratic models of "efficiency" and "progress" that elevate the system above human needs, thus shifting the "Canadian social welfare" model to that of a corporate oligarchy focused on prosperity, security, and protection of Canadian national interests.[3] These various influences are also identifiable in other Canadian institutions, including health care and the military.

The result is a complex cross-current of values and purposes that infuses discussions about national identity[4] and creates uncertainty about the intent behind phrases such as "Canadian values" and "global citizenship." This generic labelling allows human, economic, and hege-monic interests to be alternately promoted, demoted, or abandoned according to public or political interests while retaining "this warm fuzzy feeling that Canada is a caring country" (Michaud 2007, 347). In my own experience as the director of an international service learning program at St Jerome's University in Waterloo, Ontario, I encountered this confusion of values and meaning in the interchange that occurs between institutional goals to target new student markets while also toeing the economic bottom line and avoiding liabilities, along with student objectives to participate in a service learning experience that will allow them to "help" and "make a difference." Although none of these goals is objectionable on its own, together they present a con-text in which neo-colonial practices of exploitation and subjugation can occur – ironically, in the name of creating "good global citizens."

My purpose in this chapter is not to establish one set of values over another, but rather to insist that values can be interpreted in a number of ways and must be made explicit, particularly in contexts involving vulnerable populations and marginalized groups. More extensively, I intend to show that the religious ideals that helped shape Canadian society retain significant influence on Canadian concerns with solidar-ity and recognition of the Other.

I start with an examination of religion, identity, and culture in Canada. Then I consider their relation to later movements towards multiculturalism, pluralism, religious freedom, and policies of recogni-tion. I show how religion, even in diffuse and informal forms, contin-ues to shape individual, regional, and national ideas about Canadian identity through concerns with social justice, mutual responsibility, and recognition. I then go on to examine the continuing embeddedness of Christian values in Canadian institutions of higher education. I chal-lenge the idea that "Canadian values" are shared values, and question the way that terms such as "the common good" and "global citizen-ship" are understood and employed by Canadian government depart-ments, collaborating institutions, and students themselves. Although my examination could be applied to a number of Canadian institu-tions,[5] my particular interest here lies with institutions of higher educa-tion and their engagement in international service learning activities.

2.2   Religion, Identity, and Canadian Values

Religion's role in Canada today is quite different from that of the early days of European settlement, when French and British colonizers established their religious institutions in the New World in the midst of a rich array of aboriginal forms of spirituality. Religion in sixteenth- and seventeenth-century Europe was sufficiently integrated with all aspects of state and society that the colonizers naturally imposed their religious values on their colonies' cultural, political, economic, and social institutions. As a result, from the 1700s to the late 1800s, Canadian institutions were clearly defined by the Christian values of those in authority. In regions under French control, Catholicism dominated; in the English-speaking territories, the Church of England was granted state-sanctioned authority that lasted until the mid-1800s (Murphy 1996, 113, 184–8). Ultimately, however, established church rule failed in Canada because, unlike in the home countries of France and Britain, church authority in the new territories suffered from lack of resources, competition with one another and with other, smaller sects, and the difficulty of ministering to a widely dispersed population that was not always warmly inclined to church governance of their frontier lifestyles (Clark 1948). Nonetheless, the *idea* of a Christian Canada remained significant in both anglophone and francophone regions. In the decades following Confederation, Christian pluralism in English Canada increased with the arrival of groups such as the Mennonites and Doukhobors, as well as Orthodox Christians from northern and eastern Europe during the late 1800s (Grant 1988 [1972], 33, 119; Murphy 1996, 137).[6]

Canadian and US religious developments during this period were similar in that believers in both countries understood religious, civil, and national goals to be inextricably linked. Unlike the dynamic evangelicalism that fostered American millennialism, however, the power and influence retained by French Catholics in Quebec and Acadian New Brunswick ensured that no "unified vision of Protestant purpose" of establishing God's "dominion from sea to sea"[7] ever developed in Canada (Martin 2000, 29; Noll 1992, 246). Moreover, unlike Americans, Canadians retained their ties to the Old World, and found themselves culturally *situated* somewhere between the United States and the founding European nations (Noll 1992, 246).

The resulting Canadian culture was one that favoured an openness to change, a distrust of ruling elites, and a deep concern for questions of diversity and justice. Furthermore, divided loyalties and the unwillingness of Canadian politicians to retain an established church (or churches) after 1854 stopped any group from exercising a religious monopoly. Nevertheless, in Quebec, numerous social services remained under the official jurisdiction of the Roman Catholic and Protestant churches until the 1960s, and churches of both denominations continued to operate what David Martin calls "shadow establishments" that heavily influenced society through "a social gospel of international good works" (Martin 2000, 26, 29).

2.3   Pluralism and Compromise

Census figures show that, between 1871 and 1911, almost 90 per cent of Canadians were affiliated with Christian denominations, the largest being Roman Catholic (estimated at 39–42 per cent), Methodist (15–18 per cent), Presbyterian (15–16 per cent), and Anglican (13–15 per cent) (O'Toole 2000, 43). The integration of religious and political values fostered a strong sense of national duty and situated the objectives of "nation building" in religious terms (42), thus becoming an important project of the churches during the nineteenth and early twentieth centuries. The ensuing milieu was one in which previously distinct religious bodies and ethnic groups could find objectives on which to collaborate. Protestant assemblies in particular exerted influence on matters of national interest by speaking and voting as a collective,[8] and they exercised strong political influence through social gospel and evangelization initiatives that led to even greater opportunities for Protestant collaboration (Clarke 1996, 322).

In this environment, civic-minded groups took on various forms of faith-based activism to improve the conditions of others. Temperance and other social reform movements became part of a general effort "toward the improvement of the worth of the human being through improved morality as well as economic conditions. The mixture of the religious, the equalitarian [sic], and the humanitarian was an outstanding fact of the moral reformism of many movements. Temperance supporters formed a large segment of movements such as sabbatarianism, abolition, woman's rights, agrarianism, and humanitarian attempts to improve the lot of the poor" (Gusfield 1955, 222–3).

Nellie McClung, an active and influential member of the Methodist Church of Canada, provides us with an example of the types of social and moral reforms Christian men and women embraced during the early twentieth century. McClung was an advocate of temperance, education, health services, seniors' pension programs, women's rights, and better conditions for factory workers, among other things (Hallett et al. 1993). In Catholic circles, movements such as farming cooperatives, youth groups, institutions dedicated to health and education, and labour unions such as the Federation of Catholic Workers of Canada, sought social justice reforms (Lemieux and Montminy 2000, 27–40; Linteau et al. 1986, 94–9).

The surprising success of these religious movements was not to last in the face of the hardships and uncertainty imposed by the First World War and the Depression of the 1930s. Nonetheless, the church-based leadership of the time, both Protestant and Catholic, established social welfare services for all as an important Canadian value, and continued to influence the character of the nation (Baum 2000, 150; Van Die 2001, 4). Following the Second World War, optimism buoyed by a thriving economy, low unemployment, rising wages, and the return of thousands of military personnel resulted in both an economic boom and a religious revival. Ever-increasing numbers of immigrants fed Canada's growing economy with their needs and their contributions, while the public sector churned out new social programs. The federal government during this period shifted responsibility for social welfare projects from the churches to the Canadian people as a whole, and laid the foundation of the secular welfare state by initiating old-age and job security programs (Clarke 1996, 355). At the same time, the healthy economy and a renewed interest in religious values increased charitable donations for Christian social projects.

Increasing individualism, rapid social change, the rise of the interventionist state, and continuing social concerns following the war years ultimately required new responses from Canadian churches. The opportunities introduced by Vatican II's Decree on Ecumenism[9] would find special significance for Canadian Catholics and Protestants alike who were determined to create opportunities for dialogue and exchange, first between Christian communities, and eventually with other religious traditions from around the world.

It is during this era that we see the beginning of the development of international experience programs in Canada, mostly under the enduring framework of missionary objectives, but also in response to growing awareness about human rights violations and political abuses of power around the world. I return to this issue after a brief examination of the unique situation that developed in Quebec.

2.4 A Revolution in Quebec and New Values for Canada

While the ecumenical spirit of the 1960s and 1970s was creating new opportunities for growth for most of the country, modernizing influences were having a different effect in Quebec, where the rapidity of change frequently seemed overwhelming. *La révolution tranquille* (the Quiet Revolution) is widely understood as the movement of Quebec society during this period away from its traditional religious past and into the secular, modern context. This complex era was marked by three significant changes: the secularization of Roman Catholic social institutions such as health care, social services, and education; the undermining of religious certitudes by pronouncements of Vatican II; and the development of new communications technologies that increasingly exposed *Québécois* to international affairs and North American consumer culture (Lemieux and Montminy 2000, 54–5). The radical changes that occurred across Quebec society during this period moved the Church in Quebec from the centre to the margins of society.

Meanwhile, the struggle for greater national recognition of Quebec's uniqueness, the identification of the contributions of ethnic minority groups in Canada, and increased immigration contributed to special protection for minority groups and helped set the stage for a more liberal democratic society, one that fostered the values of religious pluralism and multiculturalism alongside elements of the welfare state (Baker 1997, 3–4). In that mix, long-held Catholic ideals concerning social justice and care for others, both at home and abroad, endured – so, too, in Quebec and across the rest of Canada, did the broader Christian desire to make a positive difference in the life of others. We find this Christian influence in all walks of life, including notions about service learning, to which I now turn.

2.5   Service Learning in Canada

University and college mission statements from across the country identify institutional objectives aligned with civic duty, global responsibility, and service. These, I would argue, are inherited from Canada's Christian past, though rarely is that link now explicitly acknowledged by our publicly funded secular institutions.[10] For example, the University of Guelph's motto is "Changing Lives, Improving Life," while the University of British Columbia promotes a learning environment that "fosters global citizenship, [and] advances a civil and sustainable society" (University of British Columbia 2011). The University of New Brunswick promises that its "graduates will be prepared to make a significant difference – creating opportunities for themselves and for others" (University of New Brunswick 2011). In addition to being a "centre of excellence dedicated to the service of the people of

Saskatchewan and Canada," the University of Saskatchewan aims to "help society become more just, culturally enriched, and prosperous" (University of Saskatchewan 2011). Many other examples shed light on institutional values and assumptions that point back to Christian values of service, solidarity, and concern for the marginalized.

In some instances the links to Christianity have direct historical roots. Many of Canada's oldest colleges and universities started as parochial schools to train religious leaders and lay people of the two nationally established religious groups, Roman Catholicism and Anglicanism. Canada's oldest institution of higher education, Université Laval in Quebec City, was originally established as the Séminaire de Québec in 1663 (Université Laval 2011).[11] In English Canada, Loyalist Anglicans established the University of King's College in Nova Scotia (now affiliated with Dalhousie) in 1789, the first university in British North America (University of King's College 2011). King's College, the Anglican precursor to the University of Toronto and the first university in Upper Canada, was established in 1827 (University of Toronto 2011). Other Catholic and Anglican universities were established across the country and are the founding colleges of larger secular universities today.

In other regions of the country, Protestant groups such as Baptists, Lutherans, Episcopalians, and Presbyterians also made significant contributions to higher education. The values underpinning these institutions remain identifiable in mottos and coats of arms, when not directly in their mission. For example, the University of Alberta, founded in 1908 by the first premier of that province, Alexander Cameron Rutherford, a Baptist lawyer from Ontario (Babcock 1989, 1–4), retains as its motto *quaecumque vera*, meaning "whatsoever things are true," taken directly from the New Testament (Philippians 4:8) (University of Alberta 2011). Similarly, Memorial University of Newfoundland, established in 1925 under the headship of John Lewis Patton, the son of a Congregationalist minister and a man described as someone who "regarded his vocation as fundamentally a religious calling" (Carew 1968), describes its coat of arms thus: "The Arms of Memorial University have as their central element a cross, a symbol of sacrifice. Its anchor-shaped ends signify the hope that springs from devotion to a good cause. The wavy bars allude to our maritime setting, and the three books signify our educational role. White and claret, derived from the Cross of St. George, are the colours of the Royal Newfoundland Regiment: red for courage and sacrifice, and white for purity. Gold is associated with nobility and generosity. The colours remind us that courage tempered with mercy may be enlisted in the service of noble causes" (Memorial University of Newfoundland 2011). Let me refer briefly to one more example. McGill University, one of Canada's most prominent secular institutions of higher education, nonethelesst retains the heraldic crest of its founder, James McGill, that includes an open book with the words *Domino Confido* (In God I trust).

In the same vein that mission statements of institutions of higher education are founded on the social context out of which they developed, so Canadian goals for international engagement are also inspired by our cultural past. Louis St-Laurent, then Canada's first secretary of state for external affairs, explained this context in the Duncan & John Gray Memorial Lecture at the University of Toronto on 13 January 1947:

> No foreign policy is consistent [or] coherent over a period of years unless it is based upon some conception of human values. I know that we live in an age when it is fashionable to speak in terms only of hard realism in the conduct of international affairs. I realize also that at best the practice of any policy is a poor approximation of ideals upon which it may be based. I am sure, however, that in our national life we are continually influenced by the conceptions of good and evil which emerged from Hebrew and Greek civilization and which have been transformed and transmitted through the Christian traditions of the Western World. These are values which lay emphasis on the importance of the individual, on the place of moral principles in the conduct of human relations, on standards of judgment which transcend mere material well-being. They have ever influenced our national life as we have built a modern state from east to west across this continent. I am equally convinced that on the basis of this common experience we shall discern the same values in world affairs, and that we shall seek to protect and nurture them. (St-Laurent 1947)

St-Laurent's successor at external affairs during the infamous Suez Crisis of 1956 was Lester B. Pearson. The crisis was headed off by the creation of the first United Nations Emergency Force designated to keep the peace between Israel and its Arab neighbours. In fact, this moment is widely attributed as seminal in Canada's strong support for and involvement in peacekeeping activities. David Bercuson writes that, during this era, peacekeeping became so integrated in Canadian military operations that civilians "tended to forget that armies exist to fight wars" (1996, 58–60). This value persists in what some have called "Canada's national myth." Eric Wagner goes so far as to argue that

"Canada's image of itself as a peacekeeping nation has been cemented into the national consciousness. In the popular imagination, Canadian soldiers do not fight wars, they fight war itself" (2007, 46–7).

This idealized national identity stems from the political views of the Liberal Party of St-Laurent, Pearson, and Pierre Trudeau, which wanted to establish Canada as a "soft" or "middle" power between other highly militarized nations, using diplomacy and policing rather than raw force (Morton 1990, 240–2, 254–5). Apart from its clearly political agenda, this project continues to highlight Canada's religious subtext. For example, St-Laurent saw Canada's participation in the North Atlantic Treaty Organization (NATO) as based on "the common belief of the North Atlantic union in the values and virtues of Christian civilization" (233).

Still, even as churches were losing their influence and Canadians were opening themselves to alternatives, Canadian national values remained distinctively framed by Christian values. Thus, as social movements inspired action around the world, we see Canada taking its place as a distinctively Christian nation, publicly supporting perceived Christian goals – including peace building, aid, and service work as a form of global solidarity. Eric Morrison describes the result as "human nationalism" based on "ethical responsibilities towards those ... who are suffering severely and live in abject poverty" (1998, 2).

As with institutions of higher education and government, international service learning programs in Canada followed a missionary agenda, starting in 1958 with the Jesuit-founded Centre d'études missionnaires (CEM) in Quebec,[12] which trained Catholic lay and religious people to serve as missionaries abroad. On the secular side of things, by 1960 Canada had an External Aid Office and by 1968 the Canadian International Development Agency (CIDA) was expanding aid to much of the developing world (Bergbusch 1999). The same year, following the great *laïcisation* that occurred in Quebec as a result of the Révolution tranquille, CEM secularized, changed its name to the Centre d'étude et de coopération international (CECI), and joined forces with CIDA.[13] Today CECI is a "not-for-profit organization fighting poverty and exclusion in the developing world." It describes itself thus: "As a pioneer of Canadian cooperation, CECI has broken new ground in many areas. For example, CECI laid the first foundations for international cooperation in Québec, integrated human rights concerns into the bilateral programs of ...CIDA, and instituted such important programs as Women's Rights and Citizenship in West Africa, Leave for Change, and Uniterra – Canada's biggest international volunteer program" (CECI 2011).

World University Service Canada (WUSC) has a similar Christian heritage. In 1920 in Switzerland, the World Student Christian Federation initiated the International Student Service (ISS), geared to helping students cope with turmoil in Europe. Students and faculty at the University of Toronto established the first Canadian chapter of ISS in 1939. In 1950, as the focus spread to other causes and regions of the world, ISS was renamed World University Service International; the Canadian chapter, WUSC, was established in 1957 (World University Service 2007; WUSC n.d.).

Another example is Canadian University Service Overseas (CUSO),[14] described as the first secular organization for international development in Canada (Benning 1969; Brouwer 2010). In describing CUSO's evolution, however, Elizabeth Cobbs Hoffman gives insight into the thinking that inspired it, relating how one of the founders, Lewis Perinbaum, believed Canada had a "unique role to play as a 'city set on a hill' " (1998, 81). The reference is from Matthew 5:14–16: "You are the light of the world. A city set on a hill cannot be hidden. Neither do people light a lamp and put it under a bowl. Instead they put it on its stand, and it gives light to everyone in the house. In the same way, let your light shine before others, that they may see your good deeds and glorify your Father in heaven." Another of CUSO's founding members, Keith Spicer, took his inspiration from Canadian missionary Donald Faris's book, *To Plow with Hope* (Hoffman 1998, 84). Despite the infusion of these ideas, CUSO was not linked to a religious or missionary agenda. In fact, like their American counterparts rushing to join the Peace Corps, in an era of decolonization and human rights numbers of Canadian young people intentionally chose CUSO as a non-religious response to injustices around the world – in the words of Grace Davie's book title, they were "believing without belonging" (1994). Ruth Compton Brouwer, writing about the United Church of Canada, says:

> Despite the church's decidedly non-evangelistic approach to missions in this decade, globally minded young Canadians were not won over: they overwhelmingly chose to express their interest in development work through secular organizations like CUSO, even when ... they had had a traditional church upbringing and sometimes youthful dreams of a missionary career ... Indeed, when circumstances brought development-minded volunteers their way as would-be missionaries, the church's missions officials frequently referred them to organizations like CUSO, viewing such organizations as acceptable alternatives for expressing a Christian

compassion in the developing world. This perspective was not recipro-
cated. CUSO's organizers were prepared to accept practical, start-up help
from the missions community, but like the majority of their volunteers
they were anxious to avoid the taint of the *M* word and the distasteful
associations with proselytization and colonialism that it evoked. (Brouwer
2010, 622–3)

Nonetheless, Benning writes that "some of the traditional volunteer
image, which includes sacrifice and personal hardship and the idea
of service in remote villages, is still retained by CUSO" (1969, 529).
Indeed, as some chapters in this volume attest, numbers of the young
people who participate in these programs, and the institutions that host
them, continue to be inspired by religious values.

2.6 Diversity and Recognition

Protestant anglophones and Roman Catholic francophones are not, of
course, the sole authors of Canadian identity today. What started as a
dual hegemony of English and French Christianity has developed over
time into a cultural, linguistic, and religious mosaic. Canadian regard
for recognition of diversity and difference is the direct result of the
determination to preserve religio-ethnic differences even as individuals collaborated (and competed) to establish an overarching national
identity. These interests are both sustained and challenged by the very
values and subsequent laws that Canada's founders established to preserve their own identity.

The large numbers of British immigrants who arrived after the
Second World War ensured the continuation of the empire in English-
speaking regions of Canada. In Quebec, however, where birth rates
dropped sharply in the 1960s, no such influx of French nationals
occurred. As a result, many in Quebec voiced growing concerns about
the protection of the French language and culture (Linteau et al. 1986;
McRoberts 1997). As nationalist foment in Quebec drew political attention to francophone protests for greater provincial autonomy and the
promotion of *Québécois/es* in the economy and government offices, the
federal government struggled to quell rising discontent in the province while pursuing the goal of national unity.[15] In this process, Pierre
Trudeau's Liberal government placed importance on protecting human
rights, including language rights (McRoberts 1997, 142). As a means
to achieving that goal, the Liberals initiated the Royal Commission on

Bilingualism and Biculturalism, whose initial findings resulted in the Official Languages Act (1969), which addressed discrimination against francophones outside Quebec (Fontaine 1995, 1042).[16]

Ironically, however, the Royal Commission also discovered the existence of numerous ethnic groups in enclaves across Canada (Fontaine 1995, 1042) and, in recognition of this ethnic pluralism, in 1971 the federal government created an official policy on multiculturalism that attempted to ensure official status for English and French and equal status for different cultures; bilingualism had paved the way for multiculturalism. The original intention of this project was to check Quebec nationalism; the perhaps unintentional result was the embedding of multiculturalism and freedom of religion, in *all* its forms, as Canadian national values (McRoberts 1997, 159–71). In 1967, Canada's immigration policy was changed from a racist system based on ethnicity to one based on accumulated "points" attributable to more neutral qualities, including education, French- and English-language acquisition, and occupational skills and the immigrant's potential to contribute to Canadian society (Boyd 1976, 83; Kalbach 1987, 82–110). Immigrants then began to arrive not only from traditional European sources but from around the world – 1.5 million between 1960 and 1972, with the highest numbers coming in the 1966–68 period (Statistics Canada 2003).[17] Yet, even as the majority of immigrants continued to come from at least nominally Christian countries, the growing presence of individuals from non-Christian groups was becoming noticeable, particularly in some larger centres.

In 1982, the Canadian Charter of Rights and Freedoms was enshrined in the Constitution Act. The Charter ensured the protection and promotion of human rights, established the value of multiculturalism as an important aspect of Canadian society, and addressed the matter of fair treatment of minority groups, which would be translated by the courts and human rights councils as necessary. This is the moment when the national values of social justice, concern for the marginalized, and mutual accountability, which had been encouraged and promoted by the churches, were embedded in public policy, law, and Canadian institutions – including those focused on education.

Pauline Côté suggests that influences on Canadian society by minority groups fostered the current Canadian value of tolerance, including tolerance of religious pluralism. She states that "very early in the *Charter* era, the [Supreme] Court elected to balance individual rights against public values and societal needs. By so doing, it seems to have developed a kind of civic ethos that might have replaced 'common Christianity' as the public culture of the land" (2004, 430). Of course, tolerance for cultural and linguistic diversity had been hallmarks of Christian groups in Canadian society long before Confederation – the civic ethos Côté describes reflected religious values of social justice and solidarity that the churches had promoted for more than a century.[18] What had changed was not core values of solidarity or social justice but how Canadians understood and identified the Other. Côté suggests (2004, 434) that Canadians' attitudes towards visible and religious minorities changed from one of discrimination to one of acceptance and, in the best of times, even of appreciation.

Predominating today in the public sphere is an unspoken secularism that does not exclude religion – at solemn celebrations such as Remembrance Day, religious leaders are often invited to take part – but does not promote it either. Yet Christian privilege remains embedded in our culture through statutory holidays associated with that tradition and the assumptions that underlie purported "Canadian values." Roger O'Toole insists that Canada remains a society where Christian traditions with historical roots in Britain and western Europe dominate the demography of religious identity from Newfoundland to British Columbia (2000, 45). Fully 77 per cent of Canadians continue to identify themselves as Christians of one sort or another. More important, values associated with various forms of Christianity still influence our thinking, and certainly our rhetoric, in ways that are not always appreciated in the public sphere (elsewhere, similar values are sometimes embedded in other religious and non-religious ideologies). These values continue to inform the ways that Canadian organizations and institutions operate and interact with others around the globe. Yet, increasing numbers of Canadians come from non-Christian traditions or identify themselves in censuses as having "no religion," a change that requires us to imagine Canadian values, as expressed in international work and study, in more complex ways.

2.7 Conclusion

The influence that Canada's Christian heritage has had on social projects, national institutions, and the ways in which Canada engages with the rest of the world is not just a historical by-product of one belief system or one social context. In fact, from the very beginning, the intersections of linguistic, religious, ethnic, and cultural diversity have refined and shaped religio-nationalistic ideas about the kind of country Canada should be, including its relations with other peoples and nations – now including First Nations. David Lyon, in his introduction to *Rethinking Church, State, and Modernity*, writes that religion in Canada is "channeled and filtered by distinctive Canadian cultural and historical experiences" (2000, 18). Of course this relationship is reciprocal, and many Canadian institutions continue to reflect and promote, if only tacitly, the values upon which they were established.[19]

Ideas about education, volunteering, and Canada's role in the world are a reflection of broader trends occurring in Canada and elsewhere. These trends are founded on the changing tides of modernity, which allow for a greater interchange of ideas through the movement of people and access to information through the media. As with the cultural shift that has occurred in recent decades, particularly in Quebec, there is now a shift of certain values long held as religious to the secular context. Although a sense of individual and collective belonging to a shared set of values is maintained through what Danièle Hervieu-Léger (2000) describes as a religious "chain of memory," the context and application of these values are embedded in personal experience and infused with a number of other possibilities and alternatives for engagement.

With the international development movement, an attempt is being made to extract the values of charity, service, aid, and solidarity from its neo-colonial and missionary framework and reshape it into the language of "development." If we return to Davie's concept of "believing without belonging," we can see a number of similarities between what is happening in Canadian churches and in international development projects: many of the values remain the same but the projects, language, and context change.[20]

Service learning in Canada is strongly tied to values based on historical Christian principles of service, responsibility, social justice, and accountability. Yet much of the learning at the post-secondary level occurs without recognition of the deep religious and cultural roots that have nourished – and continue to nourish – the demand for such involvement. This amnesia, coupled with a growing unease about religion, has led some to look for models established elsewhere – particularly the United States – for international learning. Much of the research that frames Canadian service learning and international experience programs thus is taken from the US system of higher education, which, not surprisingly, is embedded in US religious and national values that do not always reflect the Canadian situation.[21] Such foreign models only add confusion to the objectives and purposes of Canadian service learning opportunities and make it more difficult for Canadian institutions to turn out students who can carry Canada's national values into the world.

We also need to acknowledge the mixed nature of the religious roots of service learning. These carry elements many Canadians now find progressive, while promoting ideals that are no longer in accord with current principles. The late-modern tendency to subjectivize interests while picking and choosing one's values from an array of consumer-style options makes highly problematic the assumption that all stakeholders will share an understanding of terms such as "Canadian values," "global citizenship," and the "common good." Those of us who work in international programs in higher education are caught between the quasi-religious aims of "doing good" and "making a difference," and the corporate-style institutional goal of the internationalization of education, the national aim of promoting Canada in the world, and the personal objectives of students.

As other chapters in this volume show, unclear assumptions about values can do considerable harm to our partners, our students working abroad, and our credibility as institutions of higher education committed to preparing the next generation of Canadians. More important, unless we establish and embed particular and explicit values in our programming, we are likely to perpetuate a neo-colonial agenda that carries a subtext of "saving," "helping," and even "civilizing" partners in what is now sometimes called the global South. Such an approach flies counter to Canadian constitutional concerns for human rights and recognition. All international experience programs for Canadian students, in my view, should clarify, in succinct and explicit language, their goals and purpose. Vague language, such as "global citizenship," needs to be re-examined in light of the various projects that promote and employ it – the phrase is not only imprecise; it suggests a number of possible approaches to engaging in the international forum while presupposing primary loyalty to some form of polity. Encouraging Canadian students to act as global citizens is nothing more than a late-modern form of cultural hegemony that is inappropriate and dangerous.

I propose instead "global solidarity" as a more appropriate term for the objective behind service learning programs in Canada. By "global solidarity," I mean a reclaiming of the objectives of mutual responsibility and interrelatedness of purpose on a global scale, but with the acknowledgement and acceptance of difference and diversity. This definition allows one to make a distinction between economic, nationalistic, and corporate interests and an agenda based on a collaborative commitment to a range of concerns affecting human rights and our planet.

Furthermore, despite current debates over the commodification of education, it is far more appropriate for Canadian institutions of higher education, as places of learning and critical thinking, to employ apolitical language around our international programming. Our intention, actually, is not to produce "good global citizens," but "good Canadian citizens" with global focus and values that promote global solidarity in the face of highly complex and contentious twenty-first-century challenges.

For most of Canada's history, the national project has been missionary in nature; it is now under challenge both in public forums and in the courts. Nonetheless, the underlying Christian values that inspired the Canadian project laid the foundation for important new national projects tied to social justice, social welfare, openness to diversity, acceptance of difference, and a culture of national reflexivity and re-evaluation. As universities and colleges face the challenge of corporatization and pressure to conform to political mandates, educators have an opportunity to consider what we really want to achieve with international experience programs. Similarly, everyone – students, faculty, and staff – involved should be encouraged to identify the assumptions and values they bring with them to such programs. To use a classic Christian expression, we can at least hope we are approaching a new horizon leading to true global solidarity, rather than another chapter of domination, exploitation, and discrimination, which is also a legacy of our religious past. But if we are to pursue that objective, we must appreciate our national roots, elucidate our values, and clarify the terms of engagement so that we can meet our global partners on equal terms.

NOTES

1 An earlier version of this chapter appeared in the *Journal of Global Citizenship and Equity Education*; see Benham Rennick (2012).
2 Some scholars argue that Canada has already failed in this regard; see, for example, Cohen (2004) and Welsh (2004).
3 For a discussion of the Canadian development and usage of the phrase "global citizenship," see Trilokekar and Shubert (2009).
4 This topic continues to be hotly debated on a number of levels in Canada; see, for example, Bouchard and Taylor (2008); Brown (2006); Kymlicka (2007); and Stein et al. (2007).

5 Elsewhere I have looked at this question as it relates to Canada's military forces. For more about the role of "Canadian values" in the Canadian Forces, see Benham Rennick (forthcoming).

6 Minority groups, including many belonging to non-Christian religions, were present in Canada before this time. Jews were in Canada as early as the seventeenth century, Japanese Buddhists and practitioners of Chinese religions were present from the mid-1800s, and Muslims, Sikhs, and Hindus arrived in the early 1900s. Furthermore, these groups organized many of their own social welfare programs based on their religious values. For a full discussion of the history and contributions of the largest religious minority groups in Canada, see Bramadat et al. (2005).

7 In 1867 Leonard Tilley, a Methodist politician, used Psalm 72:8 to describe the relationship Christianity was to have in the new nation according to the Protestant vision.

8 Catholic groups during this period were somewhat less effective at mobilizing nationally, as local bishops tended to retain greater influence over regions; see Grant (1988, 222).

9 Pope John XXIII described the goal of the Second Vatican Council as the *aggiornamento*, or the bringing up to date, of the church; see the Decree on Ecumenism, *Unitatis Redintegratio*; and John XXIII (1964).

10 In fact, higher education throughout history attests to these concerns. Starting with the Platonic Academy of ancient Greece (fourth century BCE), the tradition of groups of educated citizens thinking and learning together continued among religious orders from a number of faith traditions and eventually established itself as the "modern" university, beginning with the University of Bologna in 1088; see Pedersen (1998).

11 Laval was not chartered as a public university until 1852.

12 Missionary-type projects were occurring in Canada before this time. Churches sent "missionary chaplains" to fight and support Canadian soldiers in both World Wars, for example, but this project was the first training centre for such activities. For more on wartime missionary activities, see Crerar (1995).

13 This alliance was possible due to CIDA's non-governmental organization division, which for the first time allowed collaboration and funding opportunities between government and private agencies; see CIDA (1986).

14 CUSO's Web site states that, in 1961, the organization was founded "at McGill University in Montreal. Many university presidents attended, along with representatives of 21 organizations including COV, CVCS, WUSC, UNESCO and the Student Christian Movement" (CUSO 2010).

15 There is extensive literature on this topic; see, for example, Clift (1982); McRoberts (1988); and Quinn (1979).

16 This project was initiated by then-prime minister Pearson and continued later under Prime Minister Trudeau.

17 My own parents and siblings arrived in Canada during this time. My mother fondly recalls sailing past the Expo '67 pavilions in Montreal as she arrived in what was to become her new home on 1 July, Canada Day (then called Dominion Day).

18 None of this is to suggest that Canada is innately more "tolerant" of differences than any other society; simply, recognition and the protection of minority rights (originally intended to identify French Catholics) are constitutionally, and therefore legally, protected.

19 Furthermore, because the Constitution Act decrees that higher education be administered at the provincial level, we must also consider the sociohistorical development of the provinces in attempting to understand the values and assumptions embedded in Canadian university and college objectives.

20 For a detailed discussion of how CUSO developed in relation to Canadian goals for internationalization, see Brouwer (2010).

21 For more on the US context, including a chapter providing a Canadian comparison by Roopa Desai Trilokekar and Adrian Shubert, see Lewin (2009).

REFERENCES

Babcock, D.R.C. 1989. *A Gentleman of Strathcona: Alexander Cameron Rutherford.* Calgary: University of Calgary Press.

Baker, M. 1997. "The Restructuring of the Canadian Welfare State: Ideology and Policy." *SPRC Discussion Papers,* ed. T. Eardley. Sydney: Social Policy Research Centre.

Baum, G. 2000. "Catholicism and Secularization in Québec." In *Rethinking Church, State, and Modernity: Canada between Europe and America,* ed. D. Lyon and M. Van Die. Toronto: University of Toronto Press.

Benham Rennick, J. 2012. "The New Mission Field? International Service Learning in Canadian Universities." *Journal of Global Citizenship and Equity Education* 2 (1): 91–107. Available online at http://journals.sfu.ca/jgcee/index.php/jgcee/article/view/56/39.

Benham Rennick, J. Forthcoming. "Value Clash, Value Confusion: Understanding the Role of Values in Canadian Military Operations."

In *Religion in the Military Worldwide,* ed. R. Hassner. New York: Cambridge University Press.

Benning, J.A. 1969. "Canadian University Service Overseas and Administrative Decentralization." *Canadian Public Administration* 12 (4): 515–50.

Bercuson, D. 1996. *Significant Incident: Canada's Army, the Airborne, and the Murder in Somalia.* Toronto: McClelland & Stewart.

Bergbusch, E. 1999. "Development Odyssey Revisited: How CIDA Evolved." *Behind the Headlines* 56: 24–7.

Bouchard, G., and C. Taylor. 2008. *Building the Future: A Time for Reconciliation.* Report of the Commission de consultation sur les pratiques d'accommodement reliées aux différences culturelles. Quebec City: Government of Quebec.

Boyd, M. 1976. "Immigration Policies and Trends: A Comparison of Canada and the United States." *Demography* 13 (1): 83–104.

Bramadat, P., et al., eds. 2005. *Religion and Ethnicity in Canada.* Toronto: Pearson.

Brouwer, R.C. 2010. "When Missions Became Development: Ironies of 'NGOization' in Mainstream Canadian Churches in the 1960s." *Canadian Historical Review* 91 (4): 661–93.

Brown, W., ed. 2006. *Regulating Aversion: Tolerance in the Age of Identity and Empire.* Princeton, NJ: Princeton University Press.

Carew, S.J., ed. 1968. *J.L.P. – A Portrait of John Lewis Paton by His Friends.* St John's, NF: Memorial University. Available online at http://www.mun.ca/memorial_history/bios/Foreword_Paton.html; accessed 2 May 2011.

CECI (Centre d'étude et de coopération international). 2011. "History of Ceci." Available online at http://www.ceci.ca/en/about-ceci/history-of-ceci/; accessed 29 April 2011.

CIDA (Canadian International Development Agency). 1986. *CIDA's NGO Division: Introduction and Guide.* Ottawa: CIDA.

Clark, S.D. 1948. *Church and Sect in Canada.* Toronto: University of Toronto Press.

Clarke, B. 1996. "English-Speaking Canada from 1854." In *A Concise History of Christianity in Canada,* ed. R. Perrin and T. Murphy. Toronto: Oxford University Press.

Clift, D. 1982. *Quebec Nationalism in Crisis.* Montreal; Kingston, ON: McGill-Queen's University Press.

Cohen, A. 2004. *While Canada Slept: How We Lost Our Place in the World.* Toronto: McClelland & Stewart.

Côté, P. 2004. "Public Management of Religious Diversity in Canada: Development of Technocratic Pluralism." In *Regulating Religions: Case Studies from Around the Globe*, ed. J.T. Richardson. New York: Kluwer Academic/Plenum.

Crerar, D. 1995. *Padres in No Man's Land: Canadian Chaplains and the Great War*. Montreal; Kingston, ON: McGill-Queen's University Press.

CUSO (Canadian University Service Overseas). 2010. "Our History." Available online at http://www.cusointernational.org/about-cuso/ our-history; accessed 11 March 2013.

Davie, G. 1994. *Religion in Britain since 1945: Believing without Belonging. .* Oxford: Blackwell.

Canada. 2011. Department of Foreign Affairs and International Trade. "Canada's International Human Rights Policy." Ottawa.

Fontaine, L. 1995. "Immigration and Cultural Policies: A Bone of Contention between the Province of Quebec and the Canadian Federal Government." *International Migration Review* 29 (4): 1041–8.

Grant, J.W. 1988 [1972]. *The Church in the Canadian Era*. Vancouver: Regent College Publishing.

Gusfield, J.R. 1955. "Social Structure and Moral Reform: A Study of the Woman's Christian Temperance Union." *American Journal of Sociology* 61 (3): 221–32.

Hallett, M., et al. 1993. *Firing the Heather: The Life and Times of Nellie L. McClung*. Saskatoon: Fifth House.

Hervieu-Léger, D. 2000. *Religion as a Chain of Memory*. New Brunswick, NJ: Rutgers University Press.

Hoffman, E.C. 1998. *All You Need Is Love: The Peace Corps and the Spirit of the 1960s*. Cambridge, MA: Harvard University Press.

John XXIII. 1964. "Decree on Ecumenism *Unitatis Redintegratio*." The Second Vatican Council. Rome: Vatican Archives.

Kalbach, W.E. 1987. "Growth and Distribution of Canada's Ethnic Populations, 1871–1981." In *Ethnic Canada: Identities and Inequalities*, ed. L. Driedger. Toronto: Copp Clark Pitman.

Kymlicka, W. 2007. *Multicultural Odysseys: Navigating the New International Politics of Diversity*. New York: Oxford University Press.

Lemieux, R., and J.-P. Montminy. 2000. *Le catholicisme québécois*. Quebec City: Les Presses de l'Université Laval.

Lewin, R., ed. 2009. *The Handbook of Practice and Research in Study Abroad*. New York: Routledge.

Linteau, P.-A., R. Durocher, J.-C. Robert, and F. Ricard. 1986. *Le Québec depuis 1930: Histoire du Québec contemporain*. Montreal: Boréal Express.

Lyon, D. 2000. "Introduction." In *Rethinking Church State and Modernity: Canada between Europe and America*, ed. D. Lyon and M. Van Die. Toronto: University of Toronto Press.

Martin, D. 2000. "Canada in Comparative Perspective." In *Rethinking Church, State, and Modernity: Canada between Europe and America*, ed. D. Lyon and M. Van Die. Toronto: University of Toronto Press.

McRoberts, K. 1988. *Quebec: Social Change and Political Crisis*. Toronto: McClelland & Stewart.

McRoberts, K. 1997. *Misconceiving Canada: The Struggle for National Unity*. Toronto: Oxford University Press.

Memorial University of Newfoundland. 2011. "History." Available online at http://www.mun.ca/memorial/history/; accessed 7 June 2011.

Michaud, N. 2007. "Values and Canadian Foreign Policy-Making: Inspiration or Hindrance." In *Readings in Canadian Foreign Policy: Classic Debates and New Ideas*, ed. D. Bratt and C.J. Kukucha. New York: Oxford University Press.

Morrison, D. 1998. *Aid and Ebb Tide: A History of CIDA and Canadian Development Assistance*. Waterloo, ON: Wilfrid Laurier Press.

Morton, D. 1990. *A Military History of Canada*. Edmonton: Hurtig Publishers.

Murphy, T. 1996. "The English-Speaking Colonies to 1854." In *A Concise History of Christianity in Canada*, ed. R. Perrin and T. Murphy. Toronto: Oxford University Press.

Noll, M. 1992. *A History of Christianity in the United States and Canada*. Grand Rapids, MI: Eerdmans.

O'Toole, R. 2000. "Canadian Religion: Heritage and Project." In *Rethinking Church, State, and Modernity: Canada between Europe and America*, ed. D. Lyon and M. Van Die. Toronto: University of Toronto Press.

Pedersen, O. 1998. *The First Universities: Studium Generale and the Origins of University Education in Europe*. Cambridge: Cambridge University Press.

Quinn, H.F. 1979. *The Union Nationale: Quebec Nationalism from Duplessis to Lévesque*. Toronto: University of Toronto Press.

St-Laurent, L. 1947. "The Foundations of Canadian Policy in World Affairs." Duncan & John Gray Memorial Lecture. Toronto: University of Toronto, Department of External Affairs.

Statistics Canada. 2003. "Canada's Ethnocultural Portrait: The Changing Mosaic." *Analysis Series: Ethnocultural Portrait*. Ottawa, 28 October. Available online at http://www12.statcan.ca/english/census01/products/analytic/companion/etoimm/canada.cfm; accessed 6 November 2006.

Stein, J.G., et al. 2007. *Uneasy Partners: Multiculturalism and Rights in Canada*. Waterloo, ON: Wilfrid Laurier University Press.

Trilokekar, R.D., and A. Shubert. 2009. "North of 49: Global Citizenship à la canadienne." In *The Handbook of Practice and Research in Study Abroad*, ed. R. Lewin. New York: Routledge.

Université Laval. 2011. "History." Available online at http://www2.ulaval.ca/en/about-us/a-brief-overview/history.html; accessed 7 June 2011.

University of Alberta. 2011. "Fast Facts." Available online at http://why.ualberta.ca/ualbertafacts/fastfacts; accessed 6 March 2013.

University of British Columbia. 2011. "Vision and Values." Available online at http://www.ubc.ca/about/vision.html; accessed 7 June 2011.

University of King's College. 2011. "History." Available online at http://www.ukings.ca/history; accessed 7 June 2011.

University of New Brunswick. 2011. "UNB Mission Statement." Available online at http://www.unb.ca/aboutunb/mission.html; accessed 7 June 2011.

University of Saskatchewan. 2011. "The University of Saskatchewan Mission Statement." Available online at http://www.usask.ca/university_secretary/policies/contents/uofs_missionstat.php; accessed 7 June 2011.

University of Toronto. 2011. "History and Traditions." Available online at http://www.utoronto.ca/about-uoft/History___Traditions.htm; accessed 7 June 2011.

Van Die, M., ed. 2001. *Religion and Public Life in Canada: Historical and Comparative Perspectives*. Toronto: University of Toronto Press.

Wagner, E. 2007. "The Peaceable Kingdom? The National Myth of Canadian Peacekeeping." *Canadian Military Journal* 7 (4): 45–54.

Welsh, J. 2004. *At Home in the World: Canada's Global Vision for the 21st Century*. Toronto: HarperCollins.

World University Service. 2007. "The WUS International: How It Began." Available online at http://wusromania.home.ro/began.htm; accessed 13 June 2011.

WUSC (World University Service Canada). 2012. "Our History." Available online at http://www.cusointernational.org/about-cuso/our-history; accessed 13 June 2011.

3 An Experiential Pedagogical Model for Developing Better Global Citizens

NANCY JOHNSTON, MAUREEN DRYSDALE, AND
CAITLIN CHIUPKA

3.1 Introduction

Helping learners develop the knowledge, skills, and attributes necessary for their successful contribution to society has been of interest to philosophers of education throughout the world for centuries. With the meaning of "society" expanding to include the "global village," this task requires that educators explore new pedagogies that encompass a multiplicity of cultures, ways of knowing, and ways of doing. Universities have a particular role to play in the delivery of this education, which increasingly includes teaching courses on global citizenship, conducting research in the area, integrating global citizenship issues into existing courses, and providing diverse "opportunities to engage in relevant, meaningful activities that enhance students' global perspectives and help them to contribute to a more peaceful, environmentally secure, and just world" (Shultz and Jorgenson 2008, 1). Some of these "opportunities for engagement" are categorized under the umbrella of "experiential education" and include such programs as international field schools, cooperative education, internships, and exchanges. These experiential programs offer students situated learning environments that allow for deep engagement with the issues while immersed in the context in which the issues seem most relevant.

This chapter provides a brief overview of some of the Western philosophical underpinnings of experiential learning, outlines select international experiential programs within the Canadian post-secondary education system that contribute to education for global citizenry, and suggests ways to make those programs more effective. Many classroom-based programs currently exist to address the development of global

citizenry, and many post-secondary institutions use internationalization as a strategic measure to develop what some call "global citizens."
We understand global citizens to be individuals who are comfortable
on the world stage – that is, they are aware of what is happening and
have enough travel experience to make their way confidently around
the world – and are engaged with political, environmental, economic,
religious, and social realities outside their own country.

We begin with a historical Western perspective of experiential education, with specific references to the development of citizenry. We then
move from historical to contemporary perspectives regarding the complex relationship between theory and practice. Here, we present specific
formal international pedagogies common to many systems of higher
education that play a significant role in the development of global
citizens. Next, we present a model of experiential learning in post-
secondary education that includes both formal and informal learning
opportunities and programs. We end with pedagogical considerations
for preparing and supporting students in international experiential
learning opportunities such as international field schools, cooperative
education, internships, service learning, and exchanges.

3.2 Experiential Learning

Experiential programs are seen as a relatively new phenomenon, yet
Western educational theorists have long valued the notion of learning
through practice. Unable to reason their way to "truths," a reaction-
ary group of philosophers known as the Sophists emerged in Greece
in the fifth century BCE, determined to focus on the teaching of useful
skills with less regard for finding some abstract truth. They worked
with young boys, teaching them the art of argument – "an especially
valuable skill, because eventually those boys would, as heads of house-
hold, have to speak in public forums that constituted Greek democracy" (Reed and Johnson 2000, 5). These early teachers were in essence
teaching for citizenship.

The Sophists were not alone. In contrast to the Platonic view of education, which focused mainly on the intelligible, Aristotle (fourth century
BCE) included what he called "practical wisdom" as part of the ratio-
nal component of the psyche. In Plato's view, however, the development of a "well-socialized" individual adept at contributing to society,
as Aristotle promoted, was a sacrifice of the proper use of the mind to
the "lesser good" of practical action. Here we see the emergence of two

different classical views of the primary purpose of education: "learning through inner reflection" and "learning for, and through, participation," each intended to produce engaged citizens.

Fast forward two thousand five hundred years and we see that, although these two divergent perspectives persist in the minds of many in higher education today, the development of "educated *and* engaged global citizens" increasingly is cited as a key graduate outcome by many institutions. The practical wisdom imparted to young Greek male citizens (this world was not available to women or non-citizens) foreshadowed the need for a theory-practice continuum, and it is within this framework that we later discuss the role of experiential education in the post-secondary system with respect to the development of global citizens. Aristotle's notion of practical wisdom and Roman architect Vitruvius's treatise "On Architecture" (first century BCE), which called for the union of theory and practice, provide very early introductions to this idea, which has become a recurrent theme, in various forms, throughout the history of Western philosophy and education.

In the seventeenth century René Descartes returned to the role of experience in education. He largely rejected the role of the school, believing that "true education must be done by the individual alone, outside of history, outside of tradition, outside of school" (Garber 1998, 127). In the international education context Descartes' rejection of the communal classroom raises the question of the extent to which learning is an individual activity, decontextualized in nature, yet readily transferable to new situations. Recent research on both the social nature of learning and the transfer of learning (Bandura 1977; Detterman and Sternberg 1993) challenges Descartes' idea of the solitary nature of learning; nevertheless, his assumptions represent an example of the rejection of the academy and the classroom as the main, or only, places where valuable learning occurs.

The take-away message for us, then, is that the idea of extending one's "formal education" beyond the school walls pre-dates by several hundred years current experiential education models that include field schools and international cooperative education. Current models are also the basis of many earlier forms of experiential learning, including guild and craft apprenticeships and professional internships. Were we to extend this cursory overview to other parts of the world, including China and India, we would find countless examples of extracurricular learning activities that could form part of broader pedagogical strategies.

Some contemporary educational researchers (such as Lave and Wenger 1991; Schön 1983) contend that all meaningful learning is situated, and therefore it can occur *only* in the full context of where it is ultimately to be applied – usually beyond the classroom, and increasingly beyond language, cultural, and geographic borders. Situated learning theory underpins the learning models we discuss in this chapter, and it is instructive to note that this theory, while described only relatively recently by Lave and Wenger (1991), is deeply rooted in early Western educational philosophy and age-old models of professional and practical education.

Returning to Descartes for a moment, it bears noting that practical application of knowledge, or praxis, is a critical component of his educational strategy, as it enables learners to liberate knowledge from its past, internalize it, and take action for themselves. Descartes' strategy pre-supposes the Platonic view that wisdom – or intuition – resides within an individual and, through habitual reflection will emerge and become self-evident. Descartes noted the value of reflective practice, an idea that much later emerges as a central theme in the research on professional and practitioner education (Schön 1983), and transformative learning (Mezirow 1991). He also rejected the transmission model of education, and believed that knowledge without experience was not knowledge at all.

Both these notions, reflection and active engagement of the learner, in our view, should be critical elements of international global education curricula. For learners to move effectively from "knowers" to "knowledgeable performers" or "engaged citizens," they must have the opportunity to practise or reconstruct what they know and can do in urban and rural environments with actual problems. This is the very argument many put forward for the inclusion of experiential programs in contemporary post-secondary curricula. The premise is that there is often a wide gap between knowing something, or about something, and being able to understand, interpret, and translate that knowledge into practice. We all know that an A+ accounting student does not necessarily make an A+ accountant; in the same way, learning about "fair trade coffee" in a classroom can be entirely different from learning about it immersed in the very community where the beans are harvested. Indeed, gaining meaningful experience *in situ* provides the context Descartes noted as a pre-requisite for discovering new truths through the interplay between theory and practice. It might be fair to suggest that any education for global citizenship should necessarily include an opportunity for the learner to experience personally some aspect of that education outside the confines of the educational institution.

Students learn best when they are able to engage fully with the material at hand. Those who undertake studies abroad learn better when they are presented with many experiences upon which to reflect. Many such students find themselves in contexts that are foreign to them, where little if any of their recently acquired "school" knowledge or "lived" knowledge appears applicable – that is, they lack any theoretical or experiential framework within which to interpret their new experiences, some of which could transform their understanding of the world. In contrast to the lockstep views on learning of Aristotle and Descartes, however, this kind of learning does not necessarily follow an orderly pattern. Experiential learners talk about learning that emerges from phenomena they have observed or events they have lived, and as learners they often have to work backwards, or deductively, to make meaning of those experiences. They must start at the end point that has been given through their experience and discover the building blocks that help them understand that end point, through reflection and deliberation on their related experiences *and* theoretical knowledge. Similarly, it is not always the case that the experiential "problems" they encounter are clearly defined and presented in an orderly manner, as they might be in school; rather, they often need to be discovered and defined while they are being lived. The nature of international experiential learning is very much a part of this cycle of concrete experiences, reflection, meaning making, and subsequent testing of that meaning in a new experience. This process is iterative and can be complex. It is enhanced by curricular mediation and support from the post-secondary institution.

Central to learning in this way is the idea of making connections between known ideas and those to come. Seventeenth-century philosopher John Locke, while critical of the concept of innate truths, suggested that new truths are learned through connections to knowledge already possessed by the learner. This "connection making" is central to current research on the transfer of learning, which strongly promotes "metacognition" as a critical tool for enhancing skills transfer. Through reflective techniques, learners begin to ponder their own thinking and are better able to see the shared general principles underlying apparently very different problems. With this reflective insight, two apparently different problems can begin to share some underlying similarities, prompting the learner to access and apply strategies and knowledge used in a previous experience to the new context. This type of learning is especially powerful when the learning contexts are culturally new, as is the case in many international learning experiences.

Twentieth-century American educational theorist and philosopher John Dewey (1859–1952) is perhaps the most cited when it comes to experiential education. Dewey's educational pragmatism – in particular, his notion of anthropological epistemology – provides a strong educational rationale for international experiential learning models such as field schools, cooperative education, service learning, internships, and exchanges (Dewey 1938). The notion that people learn what they need to in order to succeed in the situation in which they find themselves is at the heart of Dewey's pedagogical reflections. Like Descartes before him, Dewey elaborated the notion of helping learners build connections between current knowledge and new knowledge, suggesting it as a "fundamental principle in the development of a theory of experience" (Reed and Johnson 2000, 105).

Dewey wrote about the difference between experiences that lead to growth versus those that do not, and the importance of understanding the role of environmental factors and how they interact with the individual to form the overall experience – or, as he called it, the "situation" (Dewey 1938). In contrast to more traditional education carried out in classrooms and laboratories, where objective conditions can be relatively controlled, Dewey called on experiential educators to "become intimately acquainted with the conditions of the local community, physical, historical, economic, occupational, etc., in order to utilize them as educational resources" (Reed and Johnson 2000, 109). He was also concerned about the narrow notion of citizenship being taught in conventional schooling, and cautioned against patriotic "indoctrination" of students, especially with a singular reference to the dominant culture or political regime. This plea to move beyond the classroom foreshadows the cultural approach to curriculum studies advocated nearly a century later by Joseph et al. (2000).

Although international learning educators are often aware of these varied environmental conditions, few changes have been made to the curriculum to examine ways in which this cultural knowledge can be used more intentionally as an educational resource. This requires recognition of the different skills and knowledge that educators who design and deliver such programs need. Field school instructors, co-op coordinators, and faculty who incorporate service learning into their classes all need to understand the different requirements for learning in an experiential, international setting. Furthermore, institutions need to recognize and support staff and faculty who develop and manage these non-traditional pedagogical approaches.

As noted earlier, chief among Dewey's criticisms of traditional education was the decontextualized nature of learning and the subsequent difficulties learners have in transferring their knowledge to a new situation. In some cases, Dewey noted, learners seem to need to relearn or even unlearn skills from school in order to make progress in a new environment (Dewey 1938). The same can be said for students who attempt to live and learn in a different country and culture. That successful students are often unable to mobilize their skills and knowledge in new or different environments points to a gap in the contemporary curriculum – in particular, it indicates a critical need for transition-related pre-departure and re-entry content for students participating in international learning experiences.

The transformational potential of the learning opportunities presented through international education programs is powerful, largely because learners are experiencing the problems, challenges, and excitement of living abroad as they learn about issues and subjects relevant to that experience. This potential is of critical importance to the mission of developing citizens with heightened global sensitivity, as such efforts typically ask learners to question their many assumptions about issues of, for example, power and justice, and to examine how culturally embedded these assumptions are. Education that is transformative – as experiential and international educational opportunities often are – requires careful consideration and skilled leadership, as the process can be very unsettling for learners placed in new contexts. Such programs, with their mix of opportunities and challenges, require support beyond what might be found typically in traditional classroom situations.

Dewey (1938) and another important contemporary theorist, Brazilian educator Paulo Freire (1921–97), believed strongly in a project- or problem-driven approach to learning, for its ability to engage learners fully with their world, and in so doing transform them both. Problems, they contended, create purpose and motivation within learners, allowing them to build upon what they might already know in new ways. Problems require learners to participate actively in their learning, thereby changing the typical power structure inherent in transmission models of education. Project-based pedagogies embedded in community-based and service learning projects provide very real opportunities for students to engage with issues that transcend a particular community, and often serve as a vital step towards their development as individuals who are more aware not only of their own biases and social contexts, but also those of others. Immersion programs such as international field schools, exchanges, and co-op placements offer opportunities for even deeper engagement – especially when appropriate educational support activities are provided before, during and after the experience.

In sum, historical perspectives of experiential and international learning remind us that the tension between theory and practice has deep roots and often reflects very different worldviews regarding the goals and purpose of education. Rather than impeding the development of theories of learning, this tension instead has served as a force for the exploration of new perspectives and ideas of how theory and practice might interact. History reminds us that, while valuable learning has always occurred outside the academy, learners need help in making the connections between their various learning environments. It also reminds us that the notion of learning in order to contribute more effectively to society has long been an objective of educational theorists; it is now becoming apparent that an increasing number of people around the world share that pedagogical goal.

The problems the international community faces are large and complex, but their solutions are more attainable with the help of people working on them around the world. This is the context in which "citizen" becomes "global citizen." Although conceptualizations of learning have changed over the centuries, certain features have endured, including the critical role of reflection and metacognition, the value of both theory and practice, the motivation afforded by working with real problems and projects, and the importance of intentionally supporting all aspects of the learning environment. These basic tenets underpin the experiential pedagogies we discuss next.

3.3   International Experiential Opportunities for Developing Global Citizens

In this section, we describe seven types of international experiential learning programs common in post-secondary institutions in North America and elsewhere. Although each provides students with both domestic and international experiences, we focus on the latter while recognizing that, as Eldridge and Smith clearly show elsewhere in this volume, one does not have to learn abroad to become more attuned to global and personal issues. We do not recommend one particular type of program over others; each has its merits for educating students beyond the traditional classroom, depending on the goals of the student and institution. We begin with community-based service learning, followed by cooperative education, work exchanges, research assistantships, dual degrees and so-called 2+2s, field schools, and program/ course exchanges. We then show how the seven programs fit into our model of experiential learning in post-secondary education.

International community-based service learning is an experiential pedagogy whereby the student applies knowledge and problem-solving skills to issues in the community. It combines service activities with academic learning objectives, ideally to benefit both the community and the student in meaningful and valuable ways (Holland and Robinson 2008). The service is often in the form of a project carried out by the student that fills a specific need in the community and that integrates specific learning objectives from an academic course or program. The overall benefit – in addition to the meeting of community needs – is that the student is given an opportunity to engage in critical self-reflection and self-discovery, develop civic responsibility, enhance practical skills, develop an appreciation for collaborative effort (Lake and Jones 2008), and reflect more deeply on values and social justice. Such an opportunity can give the student direct, hands-on experience with respect to environmental factors, health and welfare issues, and social services. Furthermore, the student reaps such benefits in an international community development setting where he or she learns about global issues directly from the environment in which the impact is felt. The student thus gain the opportunity to view a variety of world issues through different lenses. Examples of international service learning projects and placements with which we are familiar include housing in Peru, sustainable development in Costa Rica, HIV/AIDS support in Uganda, children's rights in Swaziland, and literacy in Kenya.

International cooperative education integrates academic studies with paid relevant and practical work experience that is related to the student's academic program and career interests. The premise is that learning new and different things in both the classroom and workplace – including experience with interpersonal relations, conflict management, values, and attitudes – enhances the student's studies and   subsequent transition from school to workplace. Cooperative education involves a collaborative partnership between the student, the educational institution, and the employer. In such co-op programs, the student has more than one work experience – many have up to five – and academic terms alternate with work terms. In international co-op programs, the student chooses one or more work terms outside the country in which he or she is obtaining post-secondary education (Johnston 1996). International placements generally occur in high-demand fields such as business, computer science, computer engineering, systems design, architecture, and actuarial science.

International work exchanges, with groups such as the International Association for the Exchange of Students for Technical Experience (IAESTE), aim to enhance technical and professional development. International exchanges provide post-secondary education students with the opportunity to engage in technical experience relevant to their studies, while simultaneously offering employers well-qualified and motivated employees. In addition, organizations such as IAESTE promote international understanding and cultural enrichment for students, academic institutions, employers, and the wider community. Programs are based on a balance of trade – that is, an agreement established with each country that indicates how many international students it is willing to accept. The student submits a non-specific application to the hosting organization, which is then responsible for distributing applications to employers in participating nations, communicating with them, and arranging necessary international work documents and, in many cases, the student's accommodation. In contrast, when international employment is arranged through the student's home government, it is the student's responsibility to find a job, obtain the necessary documents, and make other pertinent arrangements. Examples of international work exchanges include placements in veterinary science in Sri Lanka, pharmaceuticals in Ireland, media studies in Germany, and environmental engineering in Montenegro.

International research assistantships are designed to support the research and teaching responsibilities of an academic institution, while providing the student with professional development opportunities. Research must be relevant to the student's field of study and be of academic value, and is overseen by a supervisor or principal investigator. Although research assistants most often are employed at the graduate level, honours thesis undergraduates also may be helped with their research. Research assistants may be employed at a local institution or organization, or internationally to aid with research outside the home country. The international research assistant must arrange appropriate travel and work documents to be eligible for a research apprenticeship in the host country. Research assistantship opportunities are available in several fields, including psychology, engineering, business administration, and international policy management.

Dual degrees and so-called 2+2s offer the student the opportunity to gain two credentials through study at two different partner institutions (often in different countries). Dual degree programs are also known as double degree, combined degree, co-joint, or simultaneous degree programs. In such a scheme, the student spends two to three years in each degree program and, after completing all the requirements for both programs (usually in four to five years), is awarded two degrees. These programs are available at both the undergraduate and graduate levels in many countries, and interest in them is growing, as they are seen to enrich the student's education while enabling him or her to make the transition to the labour market more easily. 2+2 programs offer the student the opportunity to study at one level at one institution, then proceed directly to the next level of credential at another with fully articulated credits and a seamless continuation of learning. For example, the student could complete a two-year associate degree at a community college, then transfer those credits to a partner university to study for two more years and earn a baccalaureate degree. Increasingly, 2+2 (and sometimes 2+1) programs are offered between countries – for example, Simon Fraser University offers a dual-degree computing science program in conjunction with Zhejiang University in China, while American University in Washington, DC, offers law students the opportunity to acquire additional degrees from associated university campuses in Australia, Canada, France, and Spain.

International field schools can be described as extended field trips in which courses are delivered, either as group study tours or as the off-campus delivery of the institutional curriculum. They typically deliver the academic curriculum in the context most relevant to the subject matter – an archaeology course on a dig in Fiji, an art and design course in Milan, or a contemporary arts course on drumming in Ghana. Educational theorists such as Lave and Wenger (1991) have described this *in situ* learning as the only way "real" learning can occur, as it takes place and is practised in the context in which it would be used. Typically, field schools are full-term programs in which the students undertakes formal courses, assignments, and fieldwork that is integrated with the location of the school. Several Canadian and international universities offer international field school programs, most of them during the summer.

International program or course exchanges promote scholarly and global learning through a worldwide network of academic institutions. Student education is enhanced through the promotion of international relations and understanding that offer learning opportunities in new environments. Agreements may be established between participating institutions and a central organization such as International Student Exchange Programs (ISEP) or International Student Exchanges (ISE) or directly organized by a student's home institution. Fees paid to the student's home institution incorporate tuition and other student-related fees, and sometimes also accommodation and meals. Participating institutions makes similar arrangements for incoming hosted students, creating a "place" and a set of benefits for them. Students typically are responsible for arranging their own travel documents, including passports and international visas. Exchanges can be arranged for a minimum of one academic term to a maximum of one cumulative calendar year.

3.4   Pedagogical Considerations

Each of the programs we have just described has its own terms of structure, method of delivery, and outcomes; however, each can also be classified within a single framework of experiential learning in post-secondary education. We determined the classification after completing an exhaustive review and analysis of the many experiential pedagogies currently implemented around the world. We devised a comprehensive model to accompany the base framework (Figure 3.1) that ranges from informal learning opportunities (such as participation in a student club or a museum visit) through more formal experiential education programs (such as a co-op or research assistantship).[1] As well, we differentiated between learning that occurs primarily on campus and learning that takes place off campus, although all opportunities included in this model are mediated to varying degrees by the institution. Within our model, we constructed a specific category of work-integrated learning in higher education that we call the *taxonomy of work-integrated learning* (TWIL; see Drysdale, Johnston, and Chiupka 2012). This model will require continuous updating given that new pedagogical approaches are being developed in response to emerging opportunities afforded by technology, increased mobility, labour market demands, and the need to differentiate educational offerings in the increasingly competitive global education marketplace. For the purposes of this chapter, we also identified the relevant international experiential opportunities.

Figure 3.1. A Model of Experiential Learning in Post-Secondary Education
with the Taxonomy of Work-Integrated Learning

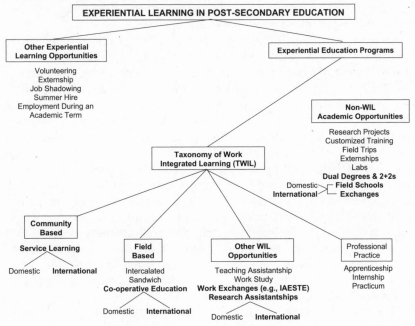

Source: Adapted from Drysdale, Johnston, and Chiupka (2012), reprinted with permission.

The various philosophies and theories of experiential learning can usefully inform our understanding of the powerful transformational learning that often occurs through international experiential education programs. To harness the potential of such programs fully, the institution, through its various curricula, needs to support this learning in specific ways that acknowledge the differences between learning on campus and learning abroad.

We identify three separate but related curricula as critical for international experiential learning programs: first, a school-based preparatory and follow-up curriculum (courses or programs) intended to prepare students for, and support them through, their transition from school to the new culture they are about to enter (including the workplace in TWIL opportunities), then to give them an opportunity for serious reflection after they return; second, the traditional course-based curriculum designed for each class that is to be delivered; and third, an

experiential-based learning curriculum that emerges as students negotiate their new international learning environment. Each curriculum is
important in preparing students for, and supporting them through and
beyond, the overall international learning experience.

In most institutions, the first curriculum focuses on pre-departure
information and typically is designed around risk management and
cultural integration themes. These themes are important, but missing
from this curriculum are preparation for the ways in which the learning
environment will change and a sophisticated follow-up. Students could
benefit from a curriculum that allows them to know themselves better
as learners, to appreciate other ways of knowing, and to develop some
flexibility to adapt their learning behaviours – ultimately to develop
themselves better as self-directed learners. They could also benefit
from better understanding how to transfer their skills and knowledge
between the many contexts they will experience – country to country,
school to workplace, and so on. In addition, learning in this type of curriculum typically is limited to student preparation for the international
opportunity, and fails to continue substantially throughout the learning period or to assist after students re-enter the traditional learning
environment. Also often missing are substantially more rigorous and
sustained post-experience sessions.

The second, course-based curriculum may be provided both prior
to and after an experiential activity or in the new environment – in
field school, for example. Field school courses typically are on-campus
courses tailored by the instructor to take advantage of the new environment. Such an approach might be more effective, however, if it were
integrated more fully with a pre-departure preparatory curriculum.
Courses specific to global citizenry are also part of this curriculum,
designed and delivered by faculty, often in preparation for an experiential learning opportunity. Typically, such courses focus on topics such
as defining citizenship and global citizenship, exploring the notion of
global ethics, examining key challenges to global citizenship, power
and global citizenship, the role of media and communications, and
the exploration of topical issues such as the environment, civil society,
human rights, and peace promotion.

The emergent third curriculum is less controllable than the other two
as it results from the interaction of learners with their new environment; it is therefore adapted to each student, unpredictable in many
instances, yet potentially the most powerful. The best we can do is to

prepare learners to be flexible and responsive to whatever might unfold. This would be done through the first curriculum by highlighting specific ways in which international experiential education programs differ from classroom learning. These differences include cultural particularities regarding the value of information, the roles of learner and teacher, types of instruction and assessment, and ways of knowing and learning. For programs – such as international cooperative education placements, service learning, or research assistantships – that are embedded in the international workplace, considerations beyond cultural ones further differentiate a classroom-delivered curriculum from one that emerges in the workplace (adapted from Chin, Munby, and Hutchinson 2000):

- differences in the role and value of declarative (school) and procedural (workplace) knowledge;
- differences in information dissemination – dividing lessons into smaller units in order to increase the points of contact (in the workplace) versus loading content at the start of the process to provide an effective learning base (at school);
- differences in the type and amount of instruction (much less of the transmissive approach in the workplace);
- differences in the nature of assessment (exams versus performance evaluations or other success indicators such as meeting deadlines or securing a contract);
- differences in ways of learning (passively accepting and reproducing information in school versus actively engaging with problems, observing, and being absorbed into the workplace culture);
- differences in the origins of the curriculum (set by the school or emerging from the work situation); and
- differences in curricular goals (content mastery in school versus performance mastery in the workplace).

Clearly, preparing students for and supporting them during and after international experiential learning opportunities requires serious pedagogical consideration. It is not sufficient to develop such opportunities, place students in them, and simply expect learning to occur. The differences between on-campus and off-campus learning sites are often too great for learners to be expected to negotiate on their own. Institutions that wish to harness fully the tremendous potential of such opportunities to develop engaged global citizens need to attend to all three curricula noted above: first, pre-, para-, and post-preparation and support of the learner that focuses on self-direction and optimizing the experience; second, appropriate revisions to the traditional course curriculum to take advantage of *in situ* opportunities; and third, for those opportunities that are work integrated, specific content (some of which would be delivered in the first curriculum) that acknowledges the significant differences between classroom-based and workplace-based learning environments.

3.5 Conclusion

Educating global citizens has become an explicit goal of many post-secondary institutions that wish to prepare their graduates to be able to contribute effectively to the world in which they live. Creative international learning experiences are also in high demand by high school students and their families when choosing post-secondary institutions. Such education might best be realized through traditional classroom approaches complemented by periods of experiential learning in relevant international contexts. This combination of theory and practice helps learners make meaning of what they know and how they come to know it, and is vital if we are to meet the transformational goals of twenty-first century Canadian post-secondary education.

Several existing experiential programs in post-secondary education, with enhanced curricular attention, are well positioned to develop informed citizens who are more self-aware and globally connected. Further conversations are needed about how such programs might be leveraged more to help meet this agenda. Educators also seriously need to consider changes to curriculum and practice that ensure learners are prepared for the experience, know how to learn in multiple contexts, have some theoretical understanding of relevant issues, and are supported throughout their experience before, during, and after their return to campus.

NOTE

1 The impetus for this model came from an invitation-only research symposium held in Victoria, British Columbia, in June 2009, organized, hosted, and sponsored by the Centre for the Advancement of Co-operative

Education at the University of Waterloo and by Co-operative Education and Career Services at the University of Victoria. Additional financial support was provided by the Cooperative Education and Internship Association, the *Journal of Cooperative Education and Internships*, the Canadian Association for Co-operative Education, the World Council and Assembly on Cooperative Education, the National Commission for Civic Education, and Simon Fraser University.

REFERENCES

Bandura, A. 1977. *Social Learning Theory*. Englewood Cliffs, NJ: Prentice-Hall.

Chin, P., H. Munby, and N. Hutchinson. 2000. "Meeting Academic Goals." In *Working Knowledge: Conference Proceedings*, ed. Colin Symes. Sydney: The University of Technology.

Detterman, D.K., and R.J. Sternberg, eds. 1993. *Transfer on Trial: Intelligence, Cognition, and Instruction*. Norwood, NJ: Ablex.

Dewey, J. 1938. *Experience and Education*. New York: Simon & Schuster.

Drysdale, M., N. Johnston, and C. Chiupka. 2012. *Experiential Learning in Post-Secondary Education: A Proposed Model*. Manuscript in preparation.

Garber, D. 1998. "Descartes, or the Cultivation of the Intellect." In *Philosophers on Education: New Historical Perspectives*, ed. A.O. Rorty. New York: Routledge.

Holland, B., and G. Robinson. 2008. "Community-based Learning for Adults: Bridging Efforts in Multiple Sectors." In *Linking Adults with Community: Using the Tools of Community-based Learning to Promote Civic Engagement*, ed. S.C. Reed and C. Marienau. San Francisco: Jossey-Bass.

Johnston, N. 1996. "The Nature of Learning in Co-op Education." Master's thesis, Simon Fraser University.

Joseph, P.B., et al. 2000. *Cultures of Curriculum*. Mahwah, NJ: Lawrence Erlbaum.

Lake, V., and I. Jones. 2008. "Service-learning in Early Childhood Teacher Education: Using Service to Put Meaning Back into Learning." *Teaching and Teacher Education* 24 (8): 2146–56.

Lave, J., and E. Wenger. 1991. *Situated Learning: Legitimate Peripheral Participation*. Cambridge: Cambridge University Press.

Mezirow, J. 1991. *Transformative Dimensions of Adult Learning*. San Francisco: Jossey Bass.

Reed, R.F., and T.W. Johnson. 2000. *Philosophical Documents in Education*. New York: Addison Wesley Longman.

Schön, D.A. 1983. *The Reflective Practitioner: How Professionals Think in Action.*
    New York: Basic Books.
Shultz, L., and S. Jorgenson. 2008. "Global Citizenship Education in Post-
    Secondary Institutions: A Review of the Literature." Available online at
    http://www.uofaweb.ualberta.ca/uai_globaleducation/pdfs/GCE_lit_review.
    pdf; accessed 23 February 2011.

4 Culture Shock, Cognitive Dissonance, or Cognitive Negotiation? Terms Matter in International Service Learning Programs

CATHLEEN DIFRUSCIO AND
JOANNE BENHAM RENNICK

4.1 Introduction

The concept for this chapter largely developed from my own experiences[1] as an international service learning (ISL) program participant and from my desire to further understand the frustrations and challenges I faced during my experiences both in Canada and abroad. I began my involvement with an ISL program in 2009. The program, affiliated with the academic institution I was attending, involved a year-long commitment that included the completion of three one-term development- and ethics-related courses. Two of these courses consisted of community-based placements, one pre-departure in my community of residence, and the other abroad.

Before participating in ISL, I was involved with social justice initiatives that gave me a number of opportunities to interact with individuals from a wide range of backgrounds and experiences. Through my work in such projects, I became familiar with some of the common discourses, frameworks, and philosophies in use – most often in the more informal and grassroots social justice circles – when negotiating interactions both on an individual basis and as part of a collective. Anti-oppression theory, queer theory, post-structuralism, and post-modernism (used largely in a feminist theory context) became the foundation of my situated knowledge, and they strongly influenced the lens through which I viewed the world and my interactions with it. Anti-oppression theory, in particular, became instrumental in my personal understanding of spaces, the power dynamics that govern them, and my ability to navigate them in a manner that would preserve the physical, emotional, mental, spiritual, and intellectual safety of those spaces for all parties involved.

This, then, is the context in which I approached my experience as an ISL participant. These theories provided the framework that I used to deconstruct many of the ethical issues I saw as central to gaining a deeper understanding of my position of privilege and the role it played in shaping my experiences and interactions with others. Further, I considered this deconstruction to be a fundamental step in the application of an effective harm-reduction strategy that targeted systems of oppression during my interactions in the communities from which I was learning, and from which I continued to learn, in a service context.

Although this approach seemed clear to me, I found that, in many ways, it conflicted with my understanding of ISL program objectives and how I perceived the learning objectives of fellow participants. This inconsistency became particularly problematic after I completed my placement abroad, when I felt most in need of safe intellectual space in which to facilitate unpacking the immense complexity of my experiences – a process I saw as necessary to meet the program objectives I had for myself and felt were expected of me as an alumna of an ISL program. The use of terms and phrases such as "culture shock" and "global citizenship" contributed greatly to these perceived expectations, largely because their unclear and inconsistent use reached beyond the confines of the ISL community. Moreover, in a post-structural context, these terms were multilayered and had meanings inherently embedded in them (whether intentionally or not) that influenced my understanding of them and that shaped the ways in which I and others understood our ISL experiences.

Culture shock was a term fellow students, program facilitators, peer groups, and ISL resources used frequently during my time as an ISL participant. I understood from these various sources that I would experience culture shock during my placement abroad, that it would be a negative experience, and that one of my goals would be to overcome it. Eventually, when my ISL placement experiences did not correspond with my understanding of the term, this disjunction created an environment that I felt was not conducive to maintaining safe intellectual space. The result was an enormous hurdle for me in terms of my intellectual development and creating meaning from my placements, especially since the avenues for support at my disposal (fellow students, facilitators, peer groups, ISL resources) did not generally use the same anti-oppressive framework in which I functioned to deconstruct the specific experiences I had had during placements – the "ISL experience" in the larger sense. Thus, my peers and facilitators were unable to engage with why "culture shock" was such a source of friction for me.

The more I examined the term, the more I saw problems with the way it has been used and understood by some in the ISL community. In what follows I highlight the potentially problematic elements of the understanding of student experiences – if only for a moment in our intellectual development – that stems from the use of colloquial terminology in the ISL community, and that can create unsafe intellectual spaces and contribute to the oppressive nature of our interactions with others, particularly in the host communities with which we engage.

Since the mid-1980s, as others also note in this book, there has been a significant movement to introduce service learning programs in institutions of higher learning, particularly in the United States (CACSL 2011b). More recently this growth in experiential education has been seen in Canadian colleges and universities, with a focus on internationally based placements. Although there are clear variances in service learning programs in terms of historical context, current mission statements, and expected outcomes, in both Canada and the United States and across institutions (see Benham Rennick, Chapter 2, in this volume), the connection between outreach and "hands-on" education remains a central component of all these programs (Che, Spearman, and Manizade 2009, 101).

When examining the stated aims of ISL programs in institutions of higher learning, what emerges is a clear emphasis on shaping students into more self-aware and globally minded individuals through educational experiences that exist outside the traditional classroom setting (Che, Spearman, and Manizade 2009, 100–1). Despite this common emphasis, the exact interpretation of these objectives and how they manifest themselves on a programmatic level are far less clear. This point is highlighted by the presence of colloquial terminology – including "global citizenship" and "culture shock," which have varying definitions in the ISL community – to describe various concepts relevant to ISL programs and the ISL experience. This lack of clarity and consistency in terminology is significant, because it creates challenges when one attempts to derive meaning from the aims and outcomes of these programs and to determine the means of developing these outcomes – and, by extension, the effectiveness of these programs and their effects on institutions, students, faculty, and community partners abroad.

Further exploration of ISL terminology and associated concepts, although it would facilitate useful commentary on the effectiveness of experiential learning, lies outside the scope of this chapter. Instead I use the stated aims of international exchange programs and the hypothesized process of development that students ideally undertake during experiential learning abroad – as Che, Spearman, and Manizade (2009) identify – as the starting point for addressing some of the obstacles that could prevent current ISL programs from meeting these aims and objectives, at least as I have come to see it. Drawing on my own experiences as an ISL program participant and on the experiences, recorded on Internet blogs and Web sites, of other students in similar programs, I intend to show, through the application of an anti-oppressive framework and discourse analysis, that commonly used ISL terminology, specifically the term "culture shock," prevents the formation of safe intellectual space in which to facilitate intellectual development. The result is an obstruction of ISL program mandates, inadequate support for student learning and intellectual development, and disservice to community partners.

4.2   The Aims of Service Learning Programs in Institutions of Higher Learning

To assess the value of service learning programs for their various stakeholders – including facilitators, students, community partners, and associated organizations – there must be a way to measure the effectiveness of such programs. One place to start might be to examine the stated aims of ISL programs and those of their affiliated institutions or organizations, as they outline the expectations of participating factions and desired outcomes upon program completion. The failure of a specific program to meet these aims can raise questions about its effectiveness, but the failure of several programs to do so leads to more complex concerns about the value of ISL programs for their stakeholders – including the relevance of pedagogies and frameworks that shape these aims and are common to several service learning programs.

ISL programs commonly are run through institutions of higher learning and other independent organizations. Those offered by postsecondary institutions can be classified according to their method of placement provision and their purpose (see Johnston, Drysdale, and Chiupka, Chapter 3, in this volume). An individual program may use staff, faculty, or students to establish its placements directly or employ the services of a third-party organization (see Peacock, Chapter 9, in this volume). The latter have their own mandates to fulfil as independent organizations and businesses, and are an additional consideration when discussing stakeholders involved in ISL programs; this chapter, however, deals only with the former type of programs.

The relationship between educational institutions and ISL programs is symbiotic in nature in that the operation of each entity is designed to be mutually beneficial (Gemmel and Clayton 2009, 6–7). Colleges and universities that create opportunities for students to participate in ISL programs clearly support, in some capacity at least, the objectives of such programs, which, when met, also meet the mandates of these educational institutions on some level. The parameters of the involvement of educational institutions and ISL programs in this mutually beneficial relationship differ, to be sure, given that their mission statements and stated aims are not identical. However, a number of commonalities emerge that are significant in terms of assessing the effectiveness and value of these programs for the many parties involved.

For stakeholders, the desired outcomes of individual service learning programs differ, but a significant consensus exists in the service learning community about general expectations. Students typically expect "to make meaning from their community experiences, to connect experience outside of the classroom to more theoretical study, and to develop as individuals in relation to their values, their sense of social responsibility, and their leadership skills" (CACSL 2011a). In short, students expect to develop personally, socially, and intellectually. For their part, institutions "benefit through enhanced teaching and learning opportunities, increased student engagement and retention, co-generation of new knowledge and ideas, research opportunities, and enhanced institutional reputation" (Gemmel and Clayton 2009, 37). Communities and community partners, meanwhile, expect to "generate enhanced understanding of community issues" through the integration of student and faculty knowledge with the expertise of those in the community, and build "collective capacity to address them, resulting in short term benefits and long term transformational change" (37).

Che, Spearman, and Manizade confirm these apparent service learning outcomes in an international context. In their analysis of study abroad programs and their role in student development, the authors find that the primary educational goal is to "improve or increase students' understandings about themselves, the world, or their particular area of study" (2009, 100). The mission statements of most institutions of higher education, they argue, include the domains of scholarship and teaching, and adding a service learning component extends the relationship between those two institutional goals to the domain of outreach.

For students to increase their awareness of themselves and the world around them, they must exhibit "intercultural maturity," or the ability to "respect differences in ethnic, religious, and political perspectives while still maintaining a strong sense of self identity." Students should not only "appreciate other cultural viewpoints, but also come to more critical understandings about their own, personal cultural backgrounds" (Che, Spearman, and Manizade 2009, 101). Over the course of their participation in an ISL program, students ideally undergo what is generally referred to as a "transformative learning experience" that results in increased intellectual, social, and personal development, and that is central to the desired outcome of participation in such a program. What constitutes a transformative learning experience is not always clear, but Che, Spearman, and Manizade use the concept of cognitive dissonance to explain how this development is attained and thus how desired student outcomes are met. In addition, the direct relationship between the post-secondary institution and the host community means that the transformative learning experience of students also fulfils desired outcomes for both the institution (increasing knowledge, outreach to the community, and so forth) and the host community (knowledge exchange and positive development).

4.3   Cognitive Dissonance as a Catalyst for Transformative Learning

For some theorists, the concept of cognitive dissonance is a key foundational element for experiential and transformative learning. Cognitive dissonance was theorized originally as "the existence of nonfitting relations among cognitions, where cognitions include any knowledge, opinion, belief about the environment, about oneself, or about one's behaviour" (Festinger 1957, 3).[2] When one experiences cognitive dissonance, there is a strong internal motivation to "resolve the inconsistency between discrepant cognitions" (Egan, Santos, and Bloom 2007, 978). This can happen by valuing the new at the expense of the old – for example, those who convert to a new ideology might ridicule their former way of thinking to ease the tensions that naturally arise from their choice.

Cognitive dissonance is an aversive experience; accordingly, people will attempt to avoid situations where such discrepancies might occur (Elliot and Devine 1994, 382). It is expected, for example, that students in an international placement will encounter many things that conflict with their existing cognitions, as the host community is likely to differ from their own not merely in geographical location but also in language, social values, and the physical and cultural environments. From these conflicts in cognitions arise internal feelings of perturbation and disequilibrium. Che, Spearman, and Manizade use the work of Jean Piaget on cognitive structures to explain that disequilibrium occurs when one becomes aware of contradictions or inconsistencies in one's schemes, resulting in "dissatisfaction or discomfort with the inadequacies of one's current state" (2009, 103). Piaget notes that these feelings of disequilibrium are "the most influential factor" in the process of acquiring knowledge and intellectual development. To resolve this disequilibrium the individual develops new knowledge structures, causing the reorganization of cognitive schemes, in turn enabling one to engage differently with one's surroundings and environment.

What makes international placements in economically challenged regions of the world so conducive to causing this dissonance is that not only will students have experiences that are significantly distinct from their own, while not being totally removed from their own situated knowledge and perspectives, but the intensity of those experiences will be magnified by the economic disparities between the students' own country and their overseas placement. Poverty can be found everywhere, but Canadian students participating in service learning programs in Sweden, for example, will not see the same disparities they would in India. Indeed, it is this tension that allows for points of connection necessary for growth. To facilitate the creation of new knowledge structures, students must experience this disequilibrium in a social setting that provides a "safe space" for them to explore the roots of the dissonance and that supports cognitive risk taking and "outside-the-box" thinking (Che, Spearman, and Manizade 2009, 103).

Cognitive risk taking allows students to interact with and understand the environment of their host community in a manner that exists outside generally accepted social narratives, to the extent that students can become more cognizant of their role in contributing to and maintaining the complex structures of domination and oppression that shape their negotiation and interactions abroad. Regardless of the categories and identity labels they adopt, everyone participates in the subordination of others and in some capacity is subordinated themselves (Schüssler Fiorenza 2009, 9).[3] Moreover, although it is generally difficult to "recognize, feel, and openly acknowledge the inadequacies in one's cognitive structure[s]" (Che, Spearman, and Manizade 2009, 103), the provision of a safe intellectual space by ISL program facilitators and other participating students creates an environment where this process is best facilitated. In essence, students need to feel safe expressing things they do not know, asking questions, and taking intellectual risks where they will be cognitively challenged but not judged (103). When this safe space is not present or accessible, there is a significant risk that students will dismiss prematurely the ideas and experiences responsible for causing the disequilibrium and, due to feelings of frustration and fear, will be inhibited from engaging in a transformative learning experience (Houser 1996; Levykh 2008). Given a safe space, however, the disequilibrium becomes constructive and can be used as a means to build new cognitive structures that better allow students to understand themselves and their relationship with their experiences.

The safety of spaces can be characterized in a multitude of ways, including environmental factors, physical and psychological well-being, supportive relationships, clear and consistent structures, opportunities for belonging, and ethical practices, the absence of one or more of which has the potential to make a space unsafe. Many of these factors are conveyed through the use of words or phrases, including slurs and profanity, that generally are accepted as oppressive or that a particular individual or group might interpret as problematic or oppressive.

Thus, systems of oppression highly influence our use, understanding, and interpretation of language, and create scenarios where seemingly innocuous statements – including the use of terms such as culture shock – might be oppressive, regardless of intent, and diminish the safety of intellectual spaces for some individuals.

4.4   Problems with Current Terminology

Cognitive dissonance is sometimes used to understand transformative learning that takes place during ISL experiences. The concept is rich in possibilities, but its complexities are often lost on those in the ISL community who use it colloquially and superficially. The switch from abstract terminology to informal and accessible language, I find, alters the intended meaning. More strikingly, the shift from cognitive dissonance to culture shock loses that concept's explanatory force. More problematic still is that the deviation in meaning of these terms from academic and theoretical models can serve to reinforce the underlying neo-colonial and xenophobic foundations of ISL programs.

Let me consider the term neo-colonialism as a means to unpack oppressive frameworks; I then discuss the dangers inherent in using terms such as culture shock. Although "neo-colonial" can mean various things, I follow Kwame Nkrumah's (1965) usage: previously colonized communities and nations that appear to have sovereignty and political, economic, and social systems no longer touched by foreign hegemonic powers, but where foreign powers continue to exercise a great deal of power both to the detriment of those communities and to the benefit of the foreign powers, often under the guise of service.

Neo-colonialism occurs, although on a much smaller scale, among ISL program facilitators and students and in the marginalized or poverty-stricken communities in which many ISL placements occur. Indeed, the very essence of many ISL programs is to send people of significant privilege – when considering factors such as monetary wealth and access to human rights, education, and security – to destinations with colonial roots, where individuals and communities are significantly less privileged. From an anti-oppressive standpoint, although communities abroad do benefit in some capacity from hosting ISL students, the benefits to students, such as relevant job experience and school credit, are usually more tangible and consistent. The result is a power imbalance between students and host communities that can create problems apart from the potentially exacerbating effects that certain attitudes and perspectives held by student participants can produce (see Ladouceur, Chapter 10, in this volume). Add to that imbalance a sense of cultural superiority inferred by the notion of culture shock, and you have the conditions for recreating neo-colonial and xenophobic contexts for oppression.

Of specific concern for me here is that culture shock is used in a variety of ways outside ISL programs and discussions of international or long-range travel, which focus on better global citizenship or transformative experiences. In an ISL context, "culture shock" is generally used synonymously with the more helpful "cognitive dissonance," in the sense that it conveys the sense of disequilibrium when one comes in contact with a culture that is unfamiliar or in juxtaposition to one's own. Where the two terms deviate is in their inherent assumptions, biases, and underlying implications. The intersection of the two translates into significant differences in the way some students interpret the experiences they expect to have abroad and their perceived presence of safe intellectual space that affects the facilitation of their intellectual development. My argument, as should now be clear, is that the term culture shock is problematic because it includes notions of superiority, and thus it sustains oppression.

4.5   Culture Shock Deconstructed

To deconstruct the embedded meanings of "culture shock," let me first examine the words "culture" and "shock" separately. Culture means quite different things to different people.[4] Robert Prus offers a helpful overarching definition, describing culture as "an inter-subjective or community-based essence that derives its existence from the development of shared meanings or the abilities of people to attend to one another, to convey understandings to the other and to acknowledge the viewpoint of the other." Prus also includes in his definition "people's language, definitions of 'objects', techniques and modes of acting towards objects ... styles of relating to others and oneself ... [and when] people do things ... in the course of engaging in meaningful activity" (1997, 38). In many ways this definition points to the use of "culture" as a catch-all word to describe the commonalities present in human patterns of behaviour and association. Although it is impossible to comment on how the term is understood by individuals involved in ISL programs, Prus's definition suggests that, for some at least, "culture" refers broadly to patterns of behaviour and ways of life. This is the understanding I employ here.

The ambiguous catch-all nature of "culture" creates three distinct and problematic biases when one compares the cultures of the host and home communities. First, using the term to describe how those in a different country or community live creates a dichotomous division between the host and home countries by reinforcing the notion of the host country or community as the Other. In this sense, the two cultures are framed as being isolated and uninfluenced by one another, rather than interrelated yet distinct. The implied creation of the Other then creates a larger division between the existing structures of hegemonic power and the subaltern, or people outside that power structure, and provides a platform for neo-colonial influences to mark interactions between students and those in the host community.

Second, when "culture" is used to refer to manifestations of material poverty, there is an underlying assumption that poverty is a cultural value, which fails to recognize the responsibility of hegemonic powers for creating and maintaining many of the structural elements that result in the continuation of material poverty in their own countries as well as the more extreme poverty that exists in host countries. The underlying neo-colonial framework of ISL programs is reinforced, as the focus becomes helping the Other address its "self-created plight," rather than addressing the complex nature of poverty and creating a dialogue of accountability.

Third, "culture" in a very broad sense is often presented as a geographically homogenous entity when it is used to refer to the reality of an entire country or community. This is a vast oversimplification of how culture manifests itself in different countries and communities. It also fails to recognize sub-groups in these communities that have their own associated cultural identities. Read in this way, "culture" suggests that the host country, including its communities and people, is simple and unidimensional whereas the home country is complex and multi-dimensional. The division of power between hegemony and subaltern is once again reinforced through the suggestion that the home culture is in some way more evolved, or at the very least simply disjointed from the host culture. This oversimplification and misrepresentation of "culture" in turn creates an environment where the safety of more nuanced and productive intellectual spaces is at risk.

Let me turn now to the other component of culture shock – namely, "shock," a seemingly innocuous word and not generally the subject of much debate in academia. The problem lies in the combination of the straightforward negative meaning of "shock" with the complexity and bias of "culture." Shock is commonly associated with severe physical and emotional trauma – as in "shell shock" (now characterized as post-traumatic stress disorder) or "to go into shock" (in the medical context). Historically, those suffering from "shell shock" faced a high degree of stigma due to misconceptions surrounding mental illness. As such, "culture shock" can be read in a manner that is characteristic of a more inconspicuous – yet no less problematic – form of xenophobia, regardless of the intention of those using the term.

Identifying a culture as shocking, or as something that induces shock, implies two things: first, that there is something rather unpleasant about the host community's culture capable of initiating significantly negative feelings; and, second, that there is something innately inaccessible or dissimilar about the culture of the host community compared to that of the students' home community – so much so that a negative emotional response occurs, making the students incapable of drawing connections to their own situated knowledge. The xenophobic reading of the term stems from framing the host community as a foreign entity that will cause psychological disturbance to students who enter it, rather than imagining the experience as a form of cognitive dissonance, or disequilibrium resulting from the students' internal debate about the limits of their own situated knowledge. The division between hegemony and the subaltern is again reinforced. The concept of "normal" culture (ours) and its perceived inversion (the host community's) is a constructed reality based on one's situated perspective, rather than on the Otherness of the host community. Following this line of thinking, culture shock is then read as a singular experience to which one falls victim, rather than an internal dialogue that calls attention to the bias of perceived norms.

"Culture shock" as a singular entity, then, is greatly influenced by the subtextual meanings of "culture" and "shock," and, I argue, is a skewed understanding of the sister term "cognitive dissonance." Many in the ISL community, as I have come to know it, understand culture shock as a guaranteed outcome of any successful ISL placement abroad. And although different cultural elements can be responsible for this shock, the stimulated emotive response is understood to be quite negative and psychologically troubling. It is ironic that those who do not undergo this type of reaction, or who are not able to convey it within certain parameters, are considered generally to have had less significant, less meaningful, and less reflective experiences – an appreciation that in many ways is also indicative of cultural exotification. This holds true both for how some students view their peers and how they view themselves.

Consider the following statements taken from my personal reflections written during my time abroad as an ISL participant:

What is the point?! The point of this pain, hunger, poverty and suffering. Not only that but what is the point of what people are trying to do here? Why ... am I even here? I just can't compute really: what is it all for?! And more importantly how do you make sense of it all. I think I should feel horrible heartbreak and sadness. I feel like I should want to cry. But none of that is happening. I want it to hurt really bad[ly] but it doesn't. I feel anger and frustration, but even then I feel as though that response stems from my inability to process the things I am seeing around me. But processing implies understanding and I don't understand why things happen here the way they do ... it all just seems so pointless. (DiFruscio 2010)

Although I do not mention the term culture shock, it is clear that I associate experiencing extremely emotive and negative feelings with the ability to be introspective about many of the realities of the placement community and to engage in the process of intellectual development. Further, I suggest that these feelings are indicative of a true ISL experience. Ultimately the focus of my statements, which I made while still abroad, is on the significance of the emotional response, not on what it meant to gain a deeper understanding of complex social issues and my involvement in the oppressive structures that contribute to their existence.

Beyond students' understanding that they simply need to overcome culture shock and adapt by exhibiting cultural competency is a further problem: students are understood as successfully adapting to another culture if they show a particular kinship for it, regardless of whether or not this kinship has roots in cultural exotification. During my own ISL placement I struggled with the concept of authenticity on many occasions, and played into similar romanticized narratives that exotified the culture of my placement country. The following statements taken from my personal reflections during my time abroad echo similar neo-colonial undertones:

> I feel like the typical mzungu[5] who is just here to take some photos, buy some jewellery and traditional clothing and then go home and talk ... about how I have experienced the real world. I really wish that is not the case, and that we aren't viewed that way by the locals here, but when I look at all the other tourists here, that's all even I can see. [These visitors] are the same ones who refuse to tour the local village or see the local school. They are also the ones who ... can't see they are in the middle of Earth's natural wonders, surrounded by Indigenous peoples who have managed to live off the land for generations. How can you just sit there and not want to be part of it? (DiFruscio 2010)

These statements clearly highlight my confusion surrounding idealized ISL experiences and what it means to demonstrate cultural competency. In particular these thoughts, I later came to understand, reflect the misguided notion that to demonstrate cultural competency is to reject all aspects of one's own culture, as if the two cultures were completely dissimilar. It is not enough simply to act the part through the commodification of cultural artefacts; one must participate fully in "authentic"

ways of life. In addition, through my desire to be the "exceptional visitor," I attempt to separate my inherited racial and national identity
from the oppressive narratives that influenced my interaction with the
host community's culture and residents.

My own understanding of culture shock was certainly marked by
feelings of confusion, frustration, and marginalization, both during service learning placements (local and abroad) and after I completed the
program. I wrote the following personal reflection in the days following my departure from my placement country.

> My goal isn't to use the experience to make myself into a better global
> citizen. It wasn't just a cultural exchange for me. I lived there: establi-
> shed a life there, found my own work there, made my own friends there,
> picked up hobbies there. I lived my life there how I would in any new city
> I would move to. And perhaps that is why I feel disconnected from the
> "[ISL] experience," because ultimately [it] was a different experience. I feel
> like the [other students] had their world flipped upside down, like they
> saw things they never expected and changed their opinion about certain
> things. That wasn't the case for me. Nothing really changed for me, except
> the fact that I felt comfortable in my own skin ... I was hoping to find a
> world that allowed me to feel comfortable as me ... and that's what I found.
> (DiFruscio 2010)

There is a clear sense of frustration and alienation stemming from the
disconnect that existed between my lived experience and the experience I felt was expected of me as an ISL participant. In my frustration,
I worked hard to separate my experiences from those of my fellow ISL
participants (rightly perceived or not) and to reconcile the expectations I felt the program had of me, which created a narrative in which I
existed as the exceptional student and my peers represented the mono-
lithic "norm" with undesirable experiences. This is problematic in its
own right, but what is most significant is that experiencing feelings of
comfort and belonging abroad was not something I associated with an
authentic ISL experience. Instead, I assumed that significant dissonance
should occur, that it would be a negative experience, and, moreover,
that this dissonance would occur when I was faced with the difference
between my culture and that of the host community. Ultimately, my
expectations of what my experiences would be like were heavily influenced by my reading of the culture shock model, and they created a
great deal of confusion and frustration as I attempted to make meaning

from my time abroad. This confusion also inhibited my ability to process my experiences, and likely inhibited my ability to participate in my own intellectual development.

4.6 Cognitive Dissonance as the More Helpful Term

"Cognitive dissonance," it seems to me, is the central foundational element from which transformative learning develops. The concept is inextricably linked to the process of intellectual development, and thus must be viewed as part of the larger experiential process if it is to have significant meaning in the ISL context. Viewing cognitive dissonance as part of a larger process serves to create a framework for personal development in which individuals can participate equally, regardless of their situated knowledge or experiences abroad, so long as these experiences are outside their individual points of reference.

What makes cognitive dissonance particularly applicable and useful to students in ISL programs is that there is no suggestion that an emotional response should result when a state of disequilibrium occurs; merely that the conflicting ideas, images, and experiences should in some capacity elicit a response of internal reflection. Simply to recognize that an experience abroad differs from one's point of reference is a form of internal reflection. Often, internal reflection during experiences abroad can be characterized by feelings of discomfort and perturbation, which can be deeply emotional, but this is not necessarily true for all participants (Che, Spearman, and Manizade 2009, 102–3). This more nuanced understanding is not reflected in the inherently negative associations that exist in various readings of "culture shock."

The focus of cognitive dissonance as a process is on the disequilibrium caused by internal forces that are triggered upon encountering certain external forces, rather than the external forces that victimize an individual through the production of emotional turmoil. Using this frame of reference, students, it seems to me, can more easily become accountable to their own intellectual development. What is significant are the subsequent steps they take to resolve the dissonance, rather than the particular emotions they experience. Thus, all students, no matter what their initial emotive response to the external forces, are able to confront their preconceived notions of the world and how these relate to and interact with those of the host community and the individuals who reside there. Cognitive dissonance also maintains its inclusivity in that there is no insinuation that one cognition or the other that is present during a state of dissonance is more or less correct; simply, in some capacity, there is a discrepancy between the two.

This reframing of the experience, I argue, creates a safe and more neutral environment in which ISL program participants can deconstruct the origins and significance of the discrepancy in a non-judgmental capacity that, potentially at least, includes all perspectives. The goal is to promote intellectual development, whether collaboratively or independently. Not only does framing cognitive dissonance in this context recognize the ability of all students to participate in the process of intellectual development in a safe space; it also serves to alleviate the neo-colonial and xenophobic undertones present in some aspects of ISL pedagogy, as the cognitions are not framed in the traditional hierarchical power structure of hegemony and subaltern in which the preconceived notions of students are considered somehow superior or the standard.

4.7   Cognitive Negotiation: An Updated Model for Facilitating Transformative Learning

Cognitive dissonance then, is a model that is in many ways more inclusive, supportive, and conscientious of anti-oppressive discourse than the culture shock model. The co-authors of this chapter thus propose an updated model we call cognitive negotiation that is accessible, yet still conveys the key concepts behind cognitive dissonance and the process of intellectual development. The framework we propose facilitates – although, to be sure, does not guarantee – an intellectually safe space for both students and facilitators, and provides students with a means to apply their intellectual development outside their international placement, while also facilitating the transformative learning desired by ISL programs.

We define cognitive negotiation here as a process by which one approaches a situation – both during and after – where one faces an idea, value, way of living, or physical or social environment that lies outside one's own situated reality. The process of cognitive negotiation involves contextualizing the significance of one's own privilege in any given interaction with another individual or group (or, in some cases, a physical and social environment). This occurs by creating connections between one's own situated reality and that of another, and subsequently attempting to minimize the power dynamics in the encounter (and future encounters), with the end goal of empowering the self and reducing the oppression of others. The term "negotiation" conveys an intrinsically motivated yet dynamic exchange between the two parties. It shifts the focus from the significance of the emotions experienced to how these emotions are processed and understood by both parties.

This process requires a high degree of personal accountability, and operates best when there is a shared goal to create more equitable and inclusive interactions, as all parties are implicated in modes of oppression and act in intersecting roles of subordinate and superordinate. If cognitive negotiation were introduced into ISL pedagogy, facilitators and students alike could work more openly and consistently with host communities towards the same goal of more equitable and inclusive interactions. Having a shared goal that is met largely through personal reflection creates a space where all could explore the complex relationship between self and oppressive forces, a process that cannot occur independently given that individuals have access only to their own situated knowledge. The cognitive negotiation model has an advantage over the cognitive dissonance model, which does not specify how "safe space" can be set up through an integrated learning environment, because dissonance can be understood as more of an individual experience that is provoked by an initial external stimulus.

The basic notion is quite simple. When one encounters an idea, a value, a way of living, or a physical or social environment that lies outside one's situated reality, an initial emotional reaction takes place that is not crucial to the process of cultural negotiation. Whether one feels guilt, sadness, shame, anger, frustration, curiosity, joy, or nothing at all, these are all manifestations of being faced with one's own privilege and are indicative of a general state of disequilibrium. Some internalize these feelings, others feel uncomfortable and attempt to maintain the status quo, and still others simply are unable to understand. Ultimately it is not the initial reaction that is determinative; rather, what matters is how one comes to understand the response and resolve the "inadequacies in one's cognitive structures" through the process of cultural negotiation (Che, Spearman, and Manizade 2009, 103).

One's ability to engage in the process of cognitive negotiation can be reflected on a never-ending continuum with a fixed point of origin or, rather, multiple continuums of the same structure. Our subjective experiences place us on these "continuums of learning" in different locations. Each continuum represents different systems being negotiated. To gain a better understanding of self and surroundings, one must move forward on the continuum. Forward movement can be accomplished through internal reflection and coming to understand, in increasing complexity, the multitude of ways in which one contributes to the superordination of self and the subordination of others, and vice versa.

For instance, one continuum might correlate to one's understanding of issues relating to race, another to one's understanding of issues relating to gender identity; where these particular continuums intersect represents the depth of one's understanding of the intersectionality of race and gender identity. These continuums do not run parallel to one another because oppression is not a linear system, according with the complexity of lived experience and the process of intellectual development. An individual can be farther along on one continuum and yet much behind on another, a mixed movement that might indicate the individual's blindness to certain systems of oppression despite having a multidimensional and comprehensive understanding of other subsystems. To imagine these continuums is to create an inclusive environment for all students – and for the host community, to the extent that its members are willing to participate in this process. It does not matter where students initially are placed on the continuums; what matters is that they move forward. And moving forward will always be an option given an infinite number of situated kinds of knowledge and lived experiences to inspire a state of disequilibrium.

In an ISL context the nature of power dynamics is vastly more complex than many interactions students find themselves negotiating on a regular basis in their home country. Accordingly, ISL experiences require a greater degree of support and guidance from facilitators and fellow students to help participants reflect on the nature of the dissonance and to promote intellectual development. Since the process of cognitive negotiation applies to all interactions, and thus has the capacity to continue even upon return to the home country, students constantly build on their newly acquired intellectual development to better understand their relationships and experiences abroad as well as future encounters in their daily lives.

This sort of intellectual and personal development directly correlates with the aims and desired outcomes of ISL programs on three fronts. First, students acquire a greater knowledge base by framing their learning experience through the lens of cognitive negotiation, which is theoretically more conducive to creating safe intellectual spaces. Second, in turn, through this lens students become more open to alternative perspectives they might encounter abroad, which could help them resolve dissonance in a more constructive manner. As well, institutions can support and facilitate student learning by teaching cognitive negotiation and providing safer spaces for intellectual development. They can also create more positive relationships with community partners if they send students abroad who are more apt to approach scenarios in an anti-oppressive manner. Finally, community partners can benefit more from the presence of students who are equipped with a model that allows them to engage more equitably with the host community, in an anti-oppressive framework, and to support existing endeavours to address challenges in the community. What is negotiated, after all, requires the engagement of all participants in an ISL experience, including when possible the host community.

4.8   Conclusion

ISL programs justifiably face criticism, particularly in the development community, in part because of the many complex ethical and pedagogical issues they raise. Regardless of these criticisms, institutions of higher learning in Canada and many other countries continue to support ISL programs and need to address their drawbacks.

ISL programs are neither constructed nor do they occur in a vacuum. They are built on and support the same oppressive structures upon which society as a whole is founded, and they involve individuals and structures that are products of the same system. The types of oppression we have addressed – including the presence of narratives in the ISL community that ultimately sustain hegemonies and the subordination of the subaltern, across intersectional planes, and on both a global and national level – are often built into these programs and are not likely to disappear in the near future. As well, the problematic nature of certain colloquial language – particularly the term culture shock, with its implicit and explicit connections to neo-colonialism, xenophobia, and exotification – prevents the creation of safe, productive intellectual spaces through the marginalization of experiences and by hindering the use of other, more effective, narratives. Ultimately students need safe, rich, and open intellectual spaces to resolve their dissonant experiences from participating in ISL programs, and to use these experiences to move forward in their personal development.

Although the cognitive negotiation model we propose here is not perfect and is likely to face its own criticisms, it has the potential to resolve dissonance in a way that is less damaging to the self and others, for as one's cognitive structures expand, renegotiation is always possible. It also offers a platform on which to build further discussion of the complex ethical issues that emerge when students are sent abroad to learn in communities that are susceptible to the detrimental effects of oppressive forms of interaction. These discussions need to continue to ensure that there is less disconnect between the stated mandates of ISL programs, their means of implementation, and actual outcomes. Students and communities place their trust and, at times, their live-lihoods in the hands of ISL programmers; accordingly, all those who participate in such programs have a responsibility to aim for the high-est ethical and pedagogical ideals. To do anything less is to contribute to the normalization of already-prevailing structures of oppression that are shaping the current landscape of our world.

NOTES

1 The first half of this chapter was prepared mainly by Cathleen DiFruscio and uses her voice; the alternative model was developed together by Cathleen.DiFruscio and Joanne Benham Rennick.

2 Emile Durkheim (1952) describes a similar version of cognitive dissonance in his work on suicide and industrialization. "Anomie," as he refers to it, is the tension or conflict that results from the absence or mismatch of per-ceived norms, or from norms that are too rigid. Durkheim explains this conflict as occurring particularly during times of social unrest or transi-tion; see also Slattery 2003, 22.

3 Schüssler Fiorenza develops the term "kyriarchy" (from the Greek *kyrios*, or lord) as a label for the "complex pyramidal system of intersecting multi-plicative social and religious structures of superordination and subordina-tion, of ruling and oppression" (2009, 9). Although originally conceived in the context of Christian feminist theology, the term has since been adopted and reconceptualized more broadly in social justice circles and other aca-demic fields to account for the complex and multidimensional intersec-tionality of class, race, gender, ethnicity, empire, and other structures of discrimination, in experiencing oppression and granting privilege.

4 The understanding of the term "culture" is influenced by a number of fac-tors. For instance, in nineteenth-century Britain, culture was understood as "a whole way of life, material intellectual and spiritual" (Masuzawa 1998, 72). In Germany, culture was taken to mean "cultivation of the mind and spirit," while in France, culture referred to civilization as a whole (76).

5 *Mzungu* is a Swahili word commonly used by locals to refer to foreign visi-tors, usually whites from Europe nations or North America but also visi-tors of any race with perceived national identities outside Africa.

REFERENCES

CACSL (Canadian Alliance for Community Service-Learning). 2011a.
"Goals." Available online at http://www.communityservicelearning.ca/en/
about_goals.htm; accessed 31 May 2011.

CACSL. 2011b. "Historical Timeline in the United States." Available online at
http://www.communityservicelearning.ca/en/welcome_history_usa.htm;
accessed 31 May 2011.

Che, S.M., M. Spearman, and A. Manizade. 2009. "Constructive
Disequilibrium: Cognitive and Emotional Development through Dissonant
Experiences in Less Familiar Destinations." In *The Handbook of Practice and
Research in Study Abroad: Higher Education and the Quest for Global Citizenship*,
ed. R. Lewin. New York: Routledge.

DiFruscio, C. 2010. Unpublished fieldnotes.

Durkheim, E. 1952. *Suicide: A Study in Sociology.* London: Routledge.

Egan, L.C., L.R. Santos, and P. Bloom. 2007. "The Origins of Cognitive
Dissonance: Evidence from Children and Monkeys." *Psychological Science*
18 (11): 978–83.

Elliot, A.J., and P.G. Devine. 1994. "On the Motivational Nature of Cognitive
Dissonance: Dissonance as Psychological Discomfort." *Journal of Personality
and Social Psychology* 67 (3): 382–94.

Festinger, L. 1957. *The Theory of Cognitive Dissonance.* Stanford, CA: Stanford
University Press.

Gemmel, L.J., and P.H. Clayton. 2009. "A Comprehensive Framework
for Community Service-Learning in Canada." Ottawa: Canadian
Alliance for Community Service-Learning. Available online
http://www.communityservicelearning.ca/en/documents/
AComprehensiveFrameworkforCSL.pdf; accessed 31 May 2011.

Houser, N.O. 1996. "Negotiating Dissonance and Safety for the Common
Good: Social Education in the Elementary Classroom." *Theory and Research
in Social Education* 24 (3): 294–312.

Levykh, M.G. 2008. "The Affective Establishment and Maintenance of
Vygotsky's Zone of Proximal Development." *Educational Theory* 58 (1):
83–101.

Masuzawa, T. 1998. "Culture." In *Critical Terms for Religious Studies*, ed.
M.C. Taylor. Chicago: University of Chicago Press.

Nkrumah, K. 1965. *Neo-colonialism: The Last Stage of Imperialism.* London:
Thomas Nelson & Sons.

Prus, R. 1997. *Subcultural Mosaics and Intersubjective Realities: An Ethnographic
Research Agenda for Pragmatizing the Social Sciences.* Albany: State University
of New York Press.

Schüssler Fiorenza, E. 2009. "Introduction: Exploring the Intersections of Race, Gender, Status, and Ethnicity in early Christian Studies." In *Prejudice and Christian Beginnings: Investigating Race, Gender, and Ethnicity in Early Christianity*, ed. L. Nasrallah and E. Schüssler Fiorenza. Minneapolis: Fortress Press.

Slattery, M. 2003. *Key Ideas in Sociology.* Cheltenham, UK: Nelson Thornes.

STUDENT INTERMEZZI
What happens when students are abroad?

What it means to be human

CLARA YOON

You can't plan everything when you travel and volunteer abroad. As much as you do plan, some experiences and moments happen unexpectedly, as they so often do in life.

I didn't feel like I was in Africa for the first weeks in Kampala, Uganda. People from home would ask me if it was "undeveloped" or how bad the poverty was, and I didn't know how to respond. These questions became more real and complex to me as I walked through busy industrialized areas or dirt roads in the slums. Ever since high school I had wanted to go to Africa, specifically Uganda, because my heart was compelled by the war and conflict in the north of that country. For this trip I initially secured a placement at an orphanage and a crisis pregnancy centre. Little did I know that after two weeks I would meet a group of friends who introduced me to a place called the Uganda Jesus Village (UJV), a home for 62 Acholi children from Gulu, a northern district affected by the civil war. Some were ex-child soldiers and others had been affected by the war through the loss of family members and displacement. Meeting these children was not part of my original plan, but that was the beauty of how they were the highlight of my experience in Uganda.

Having spent a few weeks with the UJV, my motivations in wanting to go to Gulu changed when I knew the children more. I went to Gulu for a medical camp with a Korean doctor and nurse to help distribute medicine in a few villages. The first day we arrived, the doctor started seeing patients right away. I had no idea how I fit into the grand scheme of things here, but did as I was told. I filled up different bags of pills, handed out cough syrup and vitamins, and explained the instructions to the translator.

It all happened so fast. Then I took a second to stop and look around, and I saw many pairs of eyes staring back at me. These were the eyes of children, men, and women who seemed so distant and different than the people in Kampala. I felt vulnerable, and I asked myself, what am I doing here? What good will my presence or the medicine have when I leave and it all runs out? The last patient the doctor saw was a six-year-old girl named Florence. I'll never forget what she looked like. She had a severe eye problem – the doctor said that it was either eye cancer or a critical infection. The missionaries who stayed in that remote village had even taken her to Korea twice for surgery and treatment, but it never healed. I lay awake all night, having her image replay in my mind while I wrestled with questions of injustice and inequality, disturbed by the perennial question: why do such things happen to innocent people?

The next day we went to another village where almost three hundred people had gathered to see the doctor. We were working inside this time, and the distribution went much better. Towards the end of the day, I thought it would be harmless to give out candy to the children outside. As I was about to give the candy, the children grabbed and snatched it so quickly that I was shocked. This is life for them: surviving on a daily basis. They didn't line up and say thank you, like the children in Kampala. Why was I surprised by this? My expectations of Gulu were challenged and my perception of the people drastically changed by these and other actions. I felt unappreciated and helpless. I wanted to leave.

As we were leaving that day, the doctor told me that the translators and helpers were asking for payment because it was a public holiday. To me they seemed ungrateful, because we had volunteered our time and energy to help this village receive medicine, and in return they wanted money. My gut responses to those two occasions, upon reflection, taught me an utterly simple but precious lesson: the children, and the volunteers, were being human. They had helped, and thought they deserved something in return. Something clicked, and I no longer saw them as semi-exoticized Africans who needed my help; they were people, just like me.

Although the few days in Gulu were short, they were the most challenging. To some degree it was even painful at an emotional and spiritual level. I needed to experience the reality of injustice and inequality while seeing the humanness of the people. I also needed to see how real and deep these issues are in a real-world setting.

The expectations of these kinds of overseas experiences can be misleading, with the hope that you'll change the world and help people. Midway into my trip I felt the opposite, because I knew I could not resolve the problems in Uganda. Nevertheless, although I couldn't "save" Uganda, my time in Gulu marked a shift in the way I came to view volunteering and helping people. Those whom I encountered in Gulu are real people who have desires, needs, and dreams, just like me.

I end this story on a hopeful note, as I am now finding peace being back in Canada without feeling guilt. I'm sure that most people who travel abroad with the intention of changing the world discover that, in reality, it's not so easy. To me, Uganda was a catalyst. I certainly don't know Africa or even Uganda just because I've been there once. What I have now come to know, though, deeply in my spirit, is that I uncovered in myself a desire to see more of this world and be part of processes of change for the better.

A shared humanity

STEPHANY LAU

Bangladesh: "Bangla" is the name of the language spoken, and "desh" means "country." Considering its history, it is no surprise that the people would name their country after their mother tongue. After all, the war that was courageously fought, the blood and tears that were shed, and the trauma that resulted from the partition from Pakistan in 1971 was grounded in the people's desire to preserve their native language and culture. From that time forward, this independent state has endured famines, political turmoil, and many other hardships that have led to the investment of many foreign international development agencies. I thought, what a perfect country for a global studies student like me, someone in pursuit of international development exposure.

As I started my summer break after my third year of undergraduate studies at Wilfrid Laurier University, I had the opportunity to volunteer at a support centre for sex workers in Bangladesh's capital city, Dhaka. I embarked on this journey with a group of Canadian students with the hope of being inspired by a different culture, religion, and lifestyle. The idea of bursting my safe and comfortable "North American bubble" in a country largely removed from Westernization was endlessly exciting as I prepared to go. My primary contact with social injustices so far had been limited to the classroom setting, and I wanted to observe and learn first hand the realities of these injustices. Most important, I was intrigued by the potential of my education and status as a foreigner combining to benefit the development of this nation.

That's what I thought going in. It didn't take too long after landing to realize what this Bangladeshi experience would really encompass. For me at least, ridiculous traffic jams, masses of pollution and dust, and a city of more than seven million inhabitants can be described in one word: chaos. My impression of the children I encountered on the street was similar to those portrayed in the movie *Slumdog Millionaire*: filthy, aggressively begging by clinging onto my legs, willing to release their grip only at the sight of my money or the threats of onlookers. Contextually, as a woman, I was never to initiate a conversation with men nor would they ever speak to me in public. I quickly realized that I had been thrust into a situation deprived of the equality, respect, laws, and other Canadian societal norms that I had taken for granted.

Although some moments in Dhaka were harder to withstand than others, adjusting to this life was an attractive challenge. The most difficult challenge for me to overcome, however, was the recurring feeling of being utterly useless and powerless in this country's development process.

The volunteer placement unveiled the evils and injustices of the sex trade industry. I met women whose pimps were their own husbands, and girls who had been sold into the brothels by their families before their teenage years. At this centre, women were taught various skills with the goal of providing them an alternative livelihood. I visited the centre daily and listened to the stories and past experiences of these beautiful women. Despite my education and status as a foreigner, I found myself powerless and unable to make a significant difference in their difficult and painful circumstances. In retrospect, this should have come as no surprise, but at the time I found it debilitating.

A few days before my departure from Bangladesh, some friends and I decided to take a stroll on the streets of Dhaka. As we walked along that afternoon, we came across a child who was clearly homeless. On the advice of our host organization, which encouraged us to find alternative means of meeting the needs of the homeless besides distributing money, we had brought along several bananas. We handed one to the little boy, and within a matter of seconds we found ourselves surrounded by all of his friends asking us for food. My derisory first impression of these filthy, dirty children as beggars with the sole intention of asking for money dissipated as I saw the joy in their eyes as they bit into the fruit. They immediately grabbed the hands of my friends, grinning at us through missing teeth and calling us "bondhu," or friend in Bangla. They felt safe knowing we were not there to threaten or hurt them.

These were the same children I had passed every day on my way to my placement, but had failed to acknowledge in a different light. Their society sees them as valueless – as a burden and inconvenience to the higher social classes. What I saw that day was utterly different. They were priceless individuals, who begged only as a means of survival, but were also capable of experiencing joy, laughter, and happiness. How did I miss that? It was my privilege in that afternoon to share this beautiful experience of being equal, as human beings, with these children.

As they continued to play and talk with us, it didn't take long for a crowd of men to gather to observe and stare at us. Some appeared disgusted: these filthy children were not to be touched. Others appeared curious, perhaps wondering why foreigners would do such things. Without warning, a young man came up to one of the children who was walking beside me, kicked the child, spat on him, then walked away. My new little friend immediately burst into tears, and I followed my first instinct to hug and comfort him. At that moment, a male onlooker couldn't help but cross his own cultural and gender barriers to speak to me. He questioned me in English: "What are you doing? Don't you know that these children are dirty? Where are you from?" Caught by surprise, I quickly replied, "They are still human beings and they didn't choose to be poor."

Our conversation continued, and he asked me if all Canadians cared for the poor. I lowered my eyes and answered that, unfortunately, it was not the case – we, too, walk around, sometimes over, our street people. I then asked him if he cared about the poverty in his country. Without hesitation he commented on his love for Bangladesh, but he also quickly noted that poverty is overly difficult to combat. Clearly we both cared deeply, but were approaching this situation from different frames for reference.

My humbling encounter with these children and this man was brief, the result of the distribution of bananas rather than my volunteer work at the centre. In my naïveté, I had committed a cultural *faux pas* by interacting with children whose home was the streets. At the same time, however, as a result of my initiative to cross barriers between different social classes, a man had breached his cultural boundaries to talk to a woman such as myself. Although we were at best biased representatives of our cultures, countries, values, and beliefs, our paths crossed that day and we engaged in conversation. This interaction, to be sure, did not change our respective worldviews or solve deeply entrenched issues such as poverty. Nonetheless, the space for exchange and interaction was gripping, and for a couple minutes on the streets of Dhaka we listened to each other. Listening is hard.

PART III

The Good in Global Citizenship

5 Rethinking the "Good" in Good Global Citizenship: The Ethics of Cosmopolitan Pluralism

SARA MATTHEWS

5.1 Introduction

In an article entitled "American Students Abroad Can't Be 'Global Citizens'" (2008), Talya Zemach-Bersin, a graduate of Wesleyan University, describes her 2005 experience with a semester-long immersion program in India, Nepal, and Tibet. Hoping for a "life-changing" encounter with the world "beyond American borders," what she found instead was an experience of disillusionment: with her program providers, with the curriculum of cultural immersion, and above all with the premise of global citizenship itself. Enticed by the promise of refuge in what Martha Nussbaum calls a "worldwide community of human beings" (1996, 4), a cosmopolitan collectivity with the power to transcend what makes us strangers to one other, Zemach-Bersin experienced the failure of that fantasy as one of educational alienation and estrangement. Despite the lure of global citizenship, Zemach-Bersin concludes that she can only remain American.

One anecdote in particular provides a poignant expression of this estrangement. To facilitate her cultural immersion, she is billeted with a Tibetan family living in exile in Dharamsala. Encouraged to "live like the locals and be a resident," Zemach-Bersin calls her home-stay parents by the Tibetan "Amala" and "Pala" and they in turn refer to her as "daughter." Regardless of the contrived family dynamic she laments:

> they didn't treat me like family but as a guest of honor. Despite my protests, I always received five times more food than they served themselves, and I was never allowed to make my bed, step into the kitchen, or even turn on the bathroom light myself. During the last week of my stay,

my academic directors handed me a sealed envelope containing a cash payment for Jangchup and Sonam's hospitality, which I was expected to give to them. As a first-world student, I had literally purchased a third-world family for my own self-improvement as a global citizen. While I was more than willing to give Jangchup and Sonam the well-deserved payment, I began to question the relationship of global citizenship to power and privilege. (2008, 34)

Beyond Zemach-Bersin's critique of her immersion experience as one more form of cultural imperialism, other dilemmas are raised here. One involves how Otherness is positioned in learning abroad and how this dynamic plays out in post-colonial settings. Another is that global citizenship is not a neutral concept; rather, it is constructed in relation to particular ideas about national identity and humanity.

In this chapter I explore three broad themes with which to interrogate these issues. I begin by asking how we understand "good" global citizenship as both a concept and a practice inherent in programs of learning abroad. I extend this discussion by reflecting with others on cosmopolitanism and then on hospitality, with a view to exploring how university programs for learning abroad situate the concept of global citizenship, and how students in field settings encounter and make sense of these discourses through their lived experiences. To do this I draw on a program at Wilfrid Laurier University (WLU), in Waterloo, Ontario, that offers undergraduate students the opportunity to "connect academic inquiry with experiential activity by participating in volunteer placements around the globe."[1] Here I draw on data gathered in focus groups with undergraduate students at WLU who participated in that program, and give a Canadian perspective in relation to Zemach-Bersin's experience. My intent is not to prescribe particular practices of "good" global citizenship, but rather to explore the contradictions and possibilities of how these practices are lived by students learning abroad.

5.2   "Good" Global Citizenship?

Although the scholarly literature extolling the virtues of "good" global citizenship and its relationship to study abroad is vast, there is little agreement on what the concept of global citizenship entails, and there are few studies of how it is practised. Familiarity with one's rights and responsibilities as a citizen, whether it be the right to vote in national elections or the responsibility to uphold the Geneva Conventions, is often positioned as a prerequisite for democratic participation, and is therefore a common focus of liberal education. The trend towards internationalization in Canadian institutions of higher learning and the demand for citizenship education in K–12 schooling have produced a bevy of recent scholarship that explores global citizenship in contexts ranging from peace education to the promotion of international business competencies (see, for example, Abdi and Shultz 2008; Lewin 2009; Noddings 2005a; Nussbaum 1996, 1997; Peters, Britton, and Blee 2008; White and Openshaw 2005). A comprehensive overview of these perspectives is beyond the scope of this chapter, but I want to sketch some of the important debates in the field so as to orient the discussion that follows.

Pike (2008, 225) suggests that education has failed to explore fully one of the prevailing legends of global citizenship – namely, that "an individual's awareness, loyalty and allegiance can and should extend beyond the borders of a nation to encompass the whole of humankind, an idea variously termed 'post-national consciousness' ... or 'the cosmopolitan ideal'." As Appadurai (1996) points out, awareness of, or loyalty and allegiance to, those with whom one feels even a neighbourly relation might itself be a challenging demand, but global citizenship would have us extend this view to an entire world of imagined others. The problem, as Appiah (2006, 160) states it, is not that we have incredible obligations to others; rather, it is that the obligations themselves are incredible or extraordinarily difficult to fulfil. To think with this critique we need to understand more clearly the moral imperatives that are perceived to come with the tag of global citizenship.

In her volume bringing together research on educating citizens for global awareness in K–12 settings, Noddings (2005a) notes the difficulty of defining the concept of citizenship in terms of the global. A social relationship, citizenship is both institutional and ontological: it describes a contract of rights and responsibilities determined via national or regional affiliation, but it also delineates a mode of belonging or sociality (2). Is it possible, Noddings asks, to be simultaneously a national *and* a global citizen (7)? This question is important, because it points to the practical dilemmas of the term. What exactly does citizenship confer? Ladson-Billings (2005, 69) differentiates the political (the right to vote, to public assembly) from the social aspects of citizenship (the right to health care, education, employment, housing). She claims that global citizenship is at best a potentiality, given that people of many states remain disenfranchised from their rights as national citizens. Abdi and Shultz (2008) concur, suggesting that human rights are essential to any notion of global citizenship. This gap between the ideal and the lived experience of citizenship has led some scholars to ask, "are we all global citizens or are only some of us global citizens?" (Dower 2008, 39).

What the scholarly debates reveal is the tension between a view of global citizenship as, on the one hand, a set of humanistic ideals and attributes and, on the other, a set of juridical claims that brings with it both rights and responsibilities. We see this same tension reflected in Zemach-Bersin's anecdote, where her hopes for cosmopolitan collectivity meet the realities of economic, political, and cultural difference. Her declaration that "American students abroad can't be global citizens" renders this tension irreconcilable. From Zemach-Bersin's perspective, global citizenship is itself an economic transaction in which the cultural capital of "a third-world family" is purchased for her "own self-improvement as a global citizen." Here, global learning emerges as something that is done *by* the student from the West *to* the cultural Other. I suggest, however, that this transactional model of cultural encounter is not necessarily prescriptive of global citizenship as much as it is symptomatic of what Todd (2009, 23) recognizes as the "divided modernity" at the heart of the cosmopolitan endeavour. It is this notion of "divided modernity" to which I turn next.

5.3   On Cosmopolitanism

Todd's (2009) study of the cosmopolitan turn in education for human rights provides a cogent and much needed history of the debates in contemporary cosmopolitan thought. But, like the discourses of global citizenship that it informs, cosmopolitanism is a messy concept, and there is a vast literature on the topic. Waks (2008, 204) distinguishes the "moral-political" from the "aesthetic-cultural" qualities of cosmopolitanism: the first describes the personal obligations forged through one's relations with others, while the latter expresses the personal performance of a global sophistication or literacy. Todd (2009, 267) borrows a view of cosmopolitanism from Anderson (1998), who articulates it as that which entails "a reflective distance from one's cultural affiliations, a broad understanding of other cultures and customs, and a belief in universal humanity."

Differentiating classical from contemporary cosmopolitanism, Todd describes two parallel modes of thought, one derived from Stoic and Kantian philosophical systems that promote universality as the basis for just and humane relations, the other drawing on post-colonial and post-structural inquiries that attend to the specific ways in which "individuals and groups inhabit and create spaces of cross-cultural exchange" (2009, 25–6). Here we have the crux of what Todd and Anderson mark as the double commitment, or "divided modernity," at the core of the cosmopolitan project: the plea for universalism (human rights, global democracy) as negotiated against the desire for particularism (recognition of difference and diversity). We see this tension reflected in Zemach-Bersin's anecdote: she describes how the transfer of payment to her home-stay family revealed the dynamics of global power and privilege that structured the transaction. Although the idea of a human community united across cultural, ethnic, class, gender, and racialized differences is one desire of the cosmopolitan project, this desire does not preclude an accounting of the ways in which subjectivities are differently lived.

Benhabib (2006, 171) poses the problem of cosmopolitanism rather plainly when she queries the practicality of non-national modes of belonging. She asks, what of persons who are stateless? Are they global citizens or are they effectively non-persons, bodies "that can be moved around by armies and police, customs officers and refugee agencies" (175)? As we can see, the question of the universal is not so easily answered. Nussbaum, whose widely cited work champions the classical tenets of cosmopolitanism, writes: "The accident of where one is born is just that, an accident; any human being might have been born in any nation. Recognizing this, we should not allow differences of nationality or class or ethnic membership or even gender to erect barriers between us and our fellow human beings. We should recognize humanity – and its fundamental ingredients, reason and moral capacity – wherever it occurs, and give that community of humanity our first allegiance" (1997, 58–9).

Nussbaum ascribes particular value to humanity here: "reason and moral capacity" are to be given "our first allegiance." But what about differences of "nationality or class or ethnic membership or even gender" and how they complicate one's notion of allegiance? If we read Nussbaum's quote against Zemach-Bersin's anecdote, we quickly realize that experiences of political exile, poverty, and dispossession constitute tangible disparities that make one's primary fidelity to a "community of humanity" (59) at best a hope and at worst an illusion of how power creates relations of difference – see also Beck ([2004] 2006), who emphasizes openness to others and tolerance of difference as key components of the cosmopolitan vision. Perhaps the difficulty – and why Zemach-Bersin ultimately retreats into her American status – is not with the idea of "universal humanity" per se, but rather with the tenets that the ideal prescribes – or, more important, what they foreclose. Let us take a closer look at how humanity and the human are delineated in discourses of "good" global citizenship.

5.4   Delineating the "Human"

Noddings (2005b, 3–5) lays out several parameters that together constitute "good" global citizenship: a concern for economic and environmental justice, a commitment to end all wars, a respect for the diversity of human and non-human life, and a diligence to uphold the standards of human rights. In the Foreword to the Noddings collection, Ikeda takes these claims further, suggesting that "true education summons the innate goodness of humanity – our capacity for nonviolence, trust and benevolence. It enables individuals to reveal their unique qualities and, by encouraging empathy with others, opens the door to the peaceful coexistence of humanity. This kind of humanistic education is crucial if we are to foster global citizens" (2005, ix). I suggest, however, that these capacities are equally matched by their opposite: the potential for violence, deceit, and aggression. The idea that education will save us from the worst part of ourselves is a problem, argues Todd (2009), if it disavows the very imperfections that mark us as human.

How we struggle through these social dynamics given our very particular circumstances is to my mind the content of learning as opposed to its outcome. Todd describes this kind of dialogue around difference as the work of "facing humanity" (2009, 10), and argues for a view on learning that explores how human imperfection matters to our thinking about ourselves and others. She asks, for instance, how it is that individuals make particular emotional attachments to the world, and how universal rights count in relation to lived realities (4). We might add: how does citizenship as a juridical construct collide with differing moral and philosophical claims? Further, how might we reconcile our long history of human failings against the promise of peace and global fellowship?

To think about these tensions more concretely, it is useful to consider some perspectives on global citizenship offered by students at
WLU who participated in our Global Studies Experience (GSE). As an
option towards their undergraduate major in the Department of Global
Studies, the GSE typically is undertaken in the third and fourth years
and involves half-credit pre- and post-departure academic courses that
bookend a summer field experience abroad between the students' third
and fourth years of study. Students find their own volunteer placements and finance their trip through a combination of scholarships
and personal fundraising. Locations and activities are diverse: some
students join facilitated group programs that fall more readily under
the rubric of "volunteer tourism" (Simpson 2004), while others engage
more directly in humanitarian, ministerial, or education-related work,
with small development projects organized via personal networks. In
fall 2010 I invited students enrolled in the GSE to participate in focus
group interviews for the purpose of reflecting on the possibilities and
limitations of the program. Six students (representing approximately
35 per cent of the cohort that year) participated in these interviews at an
on-campus location. The focus group met several months after students
had finished their GSE academic program requirements. All the participants were female and in their third year of the Global Studies degree
program when they embarked on their volunteer placements abroad,
which ranged in length from four weeks to three months.

Students were familiar with the concept of global citizenship from
discussions and debates in their pre-departure academic preparation
course taken six to eight months before. In the following excerpts, we
learn how these students perceive "global citizenship" in relation to
their experiences of global learning.

Sandra[2] relates that, "ever since high school, [global citizenship had
seemed] like such an appealing role to play or fit into as you grow up.
It was kind of like a dream to go to Africa ... I had wanted to go for
some time. Being there, it's really hard because when you are interacting with volunteers from other places around the world ... they seem
to have another agenda or a different purpose – just for fun ... some
students were just there to party or to play with kids. Are they global
citizens? Who am I to be entitled to be a global citizen because I have
different reasons? I don't think we can ever fulfil that role. I am still trying to figure out what that means, in terms of global governance." In
Sandra's estimation, global citizenship is an ideal that she strives to "fit
into." On the ground she discovers that other student volunteers in her

project do not share the same agenda. This dislocation brings about her re-evaluation of the concept and her feeling that it is perhaps a role that she cannot fit. In Sandra's statement, we see a split between the idea of global citizenship and its practical significance, which she conceptualizes in terms of global governance.

Monika, another student in the program, echoes this latter view: "I don't think I went into this trip thinking that I would be a global citizen. It is something I am still struggling with as a concept; what does it mean? Is it a state of mind that we get into? Because practically it is not really attainable." Monika's query raises questions about how students relate to the concept in terms of lived experience.

The tension between global citizenship as an ideal and as a mode of social relating is reflected in the following excerpt from Julie: "I think it is very difficult ... to grasp what exactly being a global citizen means. You can know things about lots of other cultures and travel to lots of places but you are still rooted in your own community ... Does it mean growing beyond that and what else is out there and how people think differently? In that way, I am on a slow path towards that, but at the same time I wouldn't consider myself a global citizen. I think that would presume a lot and I would almost be thinking way too highly about myself to take that title. I don't feel that I have gained enough knowledge of everything to say that." The struggle for this student is an appreciation of how one's sense of self and one's community alliances are negotiated in relation to engagements with others, relations that provoke a sense of difference, rather than sameness. Global citizenship as a stable category of identity or as a developmental narrative of self-actualization is, in Julie's estimation, for the present at least, unattainable because she does not presume to have enough knowledge to settle into its "title."

Another way of framing this tension is to return to Todd's (2009) notion of "divided modernity," which registers the ways in which difference and diversity call into question the very notion of the universal. It may be that global citizenship is not an all-inclusive identity one can claim but a *process of becoming* a self in dialogue with others. What might be problematic about the concept of "good" global citizenship as a universal form of knowing or being is that this framework elides the temporal dimension of how relationships between people are built over time. As one student in the focus group remarked, global citizenship is "a very loaded concept; something that you just can't do in three months." From my conversations with students involved in the GSE, it seems that the concept of global citizenship was rather peripheral to more pressing concerns regarding the realities of adjusting to life "in the field." But if we think of global citizenship as a mode of relationality, as opposed to a stable category of the human, one might raise new ways of approaching issues of social difference and understanding that directly pertain to field experiences.

The interviews revealed how challenging it was for students to craft new understandings of self that were predicated on ethical relations with others. In contrast to their own experiences, which were fraught with breakdowns, misunderstandings, and missteps, although there were also times of genuine connection, accounts of global citizenship in the academic literature are replete with portrayals of intrinsic human "goodness" and "cosmopolitan harmony." These buzzwords seem particularly pleasant to the ears of senior university administrators who are looking for ways to increase institutional internationalization and attract the tangible benefits tied to these discourses. Left out of these discussions, however, are the ways in which the social realities of war, aggression, intolerance, apathy, and divisiveness are part of what it means to be human. Todd puts it this way: "the idea that education can ameliorate global conditions under the sign of humanity is a worrying proposition, not least because it fails to recognize that the very injustices and antagonisms which are the targets of such education are created and sustained precisely through our human talent for producing them" (2009, 8–9).

When the complexities of human encounter are sidestepped in talk about study abroad programming and global learning experiences, I too become worried, particularly when I see students heading off with enthusiasm for their volunteer experiences and returning with feelings of negation similar to those expressed by Zemach-Bersin. The problem for me is not that the "good" global citizenship program has become the "bad" educational experience, but how this split is encountered as a failure of learning as opposed to its content. We see this in Zemach-Bersin's negation of her immersion encounter, which did not deliver on its promise of cosmopolitan harmony. Encouraged by her university and program provider to "become a member of her host community" by speaking the local language, bargaining for prices in the market, and participating in everyday life as if she herself were Tibetan, Zemach-Bersin discovers a "vast discrepancy between the rhetoric of international education and the reality of her experience." Despite her familial performance, the reality on the ground tells a different story: of economic disparity, of social dislocation and loss, of cultural difference. Even her host family's efforts at hospitality mark the boundaries of her alienation. The curriculum of assimilation has become, for Zemach-Bersin, a curriculum of estrangement.

Estrangement is a term that brings with it a range of associations. It can mean disaffection, hostility, and antipathy, but it can also describe a separation, split, or breach. If we consider the second set of meanings, a curriculum of estrangement might describe the ways in which our attachments to others return to us a strange encounter in difference, not only with the Other "out there," but also within ourselves (see DiFruscio and Benham Rennick, Chapter 4, in this volume). A curriculum of estrangement lends itself to the work of facing humanity as a divided self. In the literature on the internationalization of curriculum, Aoki ([1978] 2005), Pinar (2006), and Wang (2004) discuss the educational potential of exile or estrangement, a third space of encounter where the self meets the self and others on unfamiliar terrain and that brings the possibility for new forms of knowledge and thinking. Estrangement is a problem only if one's view of cosmopolitan configures difference as something that must be overcome. When the fantasy of cosmopolitan harmony fails, as in Zemach-Bersin's narrative, then so too does her faith in the concept of global citizenship. "I was a foreigner," she reflects, "in all respects": "It was impossible for me to 'act like the locals' when everywhere I was viewed and treated as exactly what I am: a white, advantaged, American ... In no way did I feel like a universal or a political citizen of the world ... It is not possible for me to be a citizen of the world. But I am an American citizen" (2008, 34). But Zemach-Bersin's description of herself as a "white, advantaged, American" by no means captures the experience of all students who participate in global learning. Nor does it preclude global citizenship.

Do these differences matter for our understanding of what it means to be a "citizen of the world"? Thus far, I have argued yes. Zemach-Bersin's insistence on the impossibility of world citizenship might be true given the assimilative framework she takes on, but another configuration might be useful here, one that works from within and not against a curriculum of estrangement. In Appiah's terms, cosmopolitanism "begins with the simple idea that in the human community, as national communities, we need to develop habits of coexistence ... of living together in association" (2006, xix). At the outset this perspective, which attempts to bridge the tension between universalism and particularism, might not seem particularly radical. However, if we situate this notion in the context of Kant's political thought, which links cosmopolitanism to the "conditions of universal hospitality" ([1795] 2003, 15), then living together in association is not a feel-good philanthropy, but, rather, as Todd explains, a *right* with "moral obligations on the part of the state and its individual members to receive all others" (2009, 33). Hospitality has a particular meaning in Kant's work: the right of an alien not to be treated as an enemy upon arrival in another's country. In Todd's interpretation of hospitality, human difference is the very ground for political association (34); to be a cosmopolitan is to worry less about being a stranger in a strange land than to be concerned about "the possibilities and limits of hospitality in facing the other" (42).

5.5   On Hospitality

Kant's political notion of hospitality differs from the noun we use to describe, for example, how one makes a visitor feel welcome. If we think back to Zemach-Bersin's experience with her host family, however, it was just this kind of hospitality that brought her discomfort: "they didn't treat me like family but as a guest of honor. Despite my protests, I always received five times more food than they served themselves, and I was never allowed to make my bed, step into the kitchen, or even turn on the bathroom light myself" (2008, 34). In this instance, the hospitality offered to Zemach-Bersin by her Tibetan hosts marks a set of differences that become for her a barrier to relationality as opposed to the conditions for it. Lost in this description is the cultural Other's right to offer hospitality and honour a guest. In my view, this speaks not to some kind of failing on the part of the student, but to the failure of a particular version of the universal to describe ethical relations across differences. Under the expectations for cultural immersion dictated by her program provider, Zemach-Bersin's only ethical position to difference is one of retreat. In asserting her desire, she also refuses her hosts' right to care for her. If we are to think with Kant's understanding of difference as the grounds for political association, however, there might be another view. Here I turn to Derrida's work on hospitality, which reads the Kantian project of cosmopolitanism through an ethics of pluralism.

One of Derrida's major intellectual projects was the deconstruction of cosmopolitan thought through a reading of Enlightenment texts. His theory is that unconditional hospitality – in other words, hospitality without limits – is impossible because our relations with others are already circumscribed with conditions. For example, we might impose conditions that govern other people's movement in our domestic landscape – everything from the request to remove one's shoes at the threshold of an abode to the trials of national immigration.

Derrida's (2003) essay responding to the events of 11 September 2001, clarifies his theory. Tolerance, he suggests, is one way of relating to difference outside the self. The problem with tolerance is that it promises only a conditional acceptance of the Other, the condition being "that the other follow our rules, our way of life, even our language, our culture, our political system, and so on" (128). In distinction to this conditional relation, Derrida argues for a form of radical relationality that he calls unconditional hospitality, which has the qualities of a "visitation," rather than an "invitation" (129). A visitation brings surprise – the Other arrives without reservation – before we have had a chance to settle the rules of encounter, before we have set up our house, so to speak. Derrida explains it thus: "This visit might actually be very dangerous, and we must not ignore this fact, but would a hospitality without risk, a hospitality backed by certain assurances, a hospitality protected by an immune system against the wholly other, be true hospitality?" (129).

What makes hospitality without conditions dangerous, in Derrida's view, is that, without our "certain assurances," without our "immune system" that protects us against the "wholly other," we are made vulnerable (129). What we are made vulnerable to is the radical Otherness of the Other – the affective force of what the Other presents and represents to us. Take Zemach-Bersin's experience as an example. Rather than wishing for assimilation with her host family (imposing the rules stated by her program or her own personal expectations), what would it mean for her to encounter her hosts without immunity (immunity here might be ideology, reverence, revulsion, idealization, whatever condition we inscribe to mitigate the relation)? The risk of making an unconditional relation is the risk of feeling the force of affect before meaning is secured. The promise of the unconditional relation is the opportunity for thinking that this delay allows.

Having put forward the argument for an unconditional relation to the Other, in typical deconstructive fashion Derrida introduces a caveat: it is impossible, he argues, to "expose" oneself to the coming of the Other without giving something determinate in return. "This determination," he argues, "will thus have to re-inscribe the unconditional into certain conditions. Otherwise, it gives nothing" (2003, 130). I interpret this to mean that, in our relations with the Other, if the conditions are too rigid we risk missing the Other, because we protect ourselves against the possibility of being touched. Here we have Zemach-Bersin's insistence that one cannot be a global citizen because it can only mean cultural imperialism. By retreating into her national identity and hiding behind an intellectualization of the experience, Zemach-Bersin misses the radical instruction of being touched by difference.

If we approach encounters without conditions, as an empty receptacle, however, we have nothing of ourselves to give in return. The possibility for ethical relations lies in noticing the conditions we impose on our encounters with Otherness and opening ourselves to experiences, ideas, and perspectives that might surprise. Some of these conditions or limits are conscious and known, such as the juridical laws and institutions by which we abide, and others are unconscious, such as the ways in which we relate to the Other within ourselves. For Derrida, hospitality is an invitation to consider the ethics of our relations with others and with ourselves: "hospitality is culture itself and not simply one ethic amongst others" (2001, 16).

5.6   Conclusion: Global Citizenship as Hospitality

By way of some concluding thoughts, I want to consider several of the themes I have raised thus far as they pertain to student experiences in the field. The first idea comes from Todd, who suggests that, when we enter into dialogue with others, we have an opportunity to "face humanity" (2009, 10) by reflecting on the ways in which the imperfections of these dynamics are more than simply defeats; indeed, encounters with others that bring us close to differences within ourselves are valuable pedagogical experiences. As a process of becoming a "self" in relation to the wider world, I have argued that global citizenship involves the capacity to think about how encounters with others effect change, not only out there (whether one is building schools or community relationships), but also within one's internal or affective landscapes. To reflect on Todd's (2009, 4) question of how it is that we make particular emotional attachments to the world in the context of global learning, I turn again to several examples from the focus group interviews I conducted with students in the GSE.

In the following excerpt, Hannah discusses how she and her fellow volunteers were perceived by members of the community in which they were living and the challenges of understanding that this knowledge raised. She relates that the other leader who could speak Spanish was talking to our first local contact ... As soon as we got there, what [the local contact] had really wanted to say was pretty much how we benefit from their poverty. He just went on about how we just come here and we just leave and that's it and don't hear from them again. So we talked about it, and we tried to challenge that stereotype. It was really, really difficult to hear that, but at the same time it was good to hear how other people perceive you. You are going there invading ... their homes and doing work there. It was really helpful criticism ... being aware of that was really important. Our trip started off on that note ... to try and challenge that stereotype of coming here and doing whatever, our team made a greater effort to hang out with the host family more and get to know them.

When confronted with difficult knowledge concerning how the local community perceived her presence, Hannah is disturbed. But unlike Zemach-Bersin, whose home-stay experience was fraught with similar relations of power and privilege, Hannah chooses not to dismiss the value of her program. Instead, she attempts to assimilate the reality of what it means to work and live in relation to others. She uses the knowledge of her difference as a place to begin to construct what she sees as a more authentic relation with herself and with community members. Hannah is able to do this because leaders in her field experience encouraged conversation and reflection.

In contrast, the physical living arrangements described by another student seemed to preclude an engagement with this kind of emotional work. Shandelle describes the situation as follows: "We stayed in a gated compound ... We were in a rural area so we were far from everyone ... it was just me and my fellow volunteers and it became very hard to create personal relationships and have those conversations, and ask 'what do they think about us being here?' There was no point where it didn't feel that it was only 'us' and 'the other.' I was only there for a month and that doesn't allow the time to establish stronger relationships."

Shandelle's experience raises the locative dimensions of the learning encounter, suggesting that one's location in both time and space is relevant to the work of "facing humanity" (Todd 2009). Whether the immersive episode is a week, a month, or a year, it is difficult to gauge the threshold of what is adequate to establish the conditions for dialogue and mutual understanding. But what is made clear by the following student's example is that the time of learning is not limited to the time of the field experience. Indeed, what happens after the students return from their experience abroad might be just as important as what they do while they are there. Kate puts it this way: "I felt like I wanted someone to ask questions when I got back. Not just, how was it? What did you do? But questions that really made me think ... to help me sort things out and sort out what thoughts were going through my head that I couldn't figure out. That would have been very beneficial ... the sort of questions when you go into detail with what happened and how to think about it differently."

Another student reiterates this perspective, describing a two-day retreat her program had organized for group leaders immediately after their return: "It was really helpful. They actually had everyone that went away and they also had invited people who had worked in international development or had lived or volunteered somewhere – they were called the elders ... We went into a room and talked and vented ... The process of dealing with what I had seen was a lot easier. I didn't feel as alone. Having that debrief afterwards is extremely helpful."

What these students describe is the importance of having time to reflect on the meaning of experience. Meaning in this context is something that is made relationally – it is through dialogue with others that the student comes to new forms of self-understanding. The crucial question in my mind is not so much whether the framework of global citizenship can capture this process effectively, but how programs for global learning allow students to consider the conditions of dialogue they impose on the self and on others. It is within the rubric of hospitality, I argue, that we come closer to a global ethic under the name of humanity. This might be the orientation to which Derrida refers when he writes that "hospitality is culture itself and not simply one ethic amongst others" (2001, 16).

How does this insight relate to the concept of "good" global citizenship? At the beginning of this chapter, I stated my intent to explore global citizenship as a series of contradictions and possibilities, rather than a set of prescriptions or guidelines; to do so feels close to the universalist perspective that I have set out to critique. Rather, from my reading of philosophies of cultural encounter and from student experiences in the field, I have learned that what is at stake in global citizenship is a concept and practice of what it means to be human in relation to others. This kind of humanity, following Todd (2009), includes the vicissitudes of how cultural encounters can aggravate our vulnerabilities and the confusions of ethical relations. It is through opportunities for dialogue that we come closer to understanding these parts of ourselves and others.

"Good" global citizenship, therefore, might be concerned with producing opportunities for dialogue across difference and for learning about the limits of the self and the Other. Programs for learning abroad that include such possibilities as an essential element of the field experience might come closer to bridging the gap between the idea and the practice of global citizenship.

NOTES

1 Taken from the description of the Global Studies Experience in the Department of Global Studies, Wilfrid Laurier University; see the Web site at http://www.wlu.ca/page.php?grp_id=148&p=1769. The university's Research Ethics Board approved the research that supports this chapter, including these focus groups.
2 Pseudonyms are used throughout to protect anonymity.

REFERENCES

Abdi, A.A., and L. Shultz, eds. 2008. *Educating for Human Rights and Global Citizenship*. New York: State University of New York Press.
Anderson, A. 1998. "Cosmopolitanism, Universalism, and the Divided Legacies of Modernity." In *Cosmopolitics: Thinking and Feeling Beyond the Nation*, ed. P. Cheah and B. Robbins. Minneapolis: University of Minnesota Press.
Aoki, T.T. [1978] 2005. "Toward Curriculum Inquiry in a New Key." In *Curriculum in a New Key*, ed. W.F. Pinar and R.L. Irwin. Mahwah, NJ: Lawrence Erlbaum.
Appadurai, A. 1996. *Modernity at Large: Cultural Dimensions of Globalization*. Minneapolis: University of Minnesota Press.
Appiah, K.A. 2006. *Cosmopolitanism: Ethics in a World of Strangers*. New York: W.W. Norton.
Beck, U. [2004] 2006. *Cosmopolitan Vision*, trans. C. Cronin. Cambridge, MA: Polity.
Benhabib, S. 2006. *Another Cosmopolitanism*. New York: Oxford University Press.
Derrida, J. 2001. *On Cosmopolitanism and Forgiveness*, trans. M. Dooley and M. Hughes. New York: Routledge.

Derrida, J. 2003. "Dialogue with Jacques Derrida" and "Deconstructing Terrorism." In *Philosophy in a Time of Terror: Dialogues with Jürgen Habermas and Jacques Derrida*, ed. G. Borradori. Chicago: University of Chicago Press.

Dower, N. 2008. "Are We All Global Citizens or Are Only Some of Us Global Citizens?" In *Educating for Human Rights and Global Citizenship*, ed. A.A. Abdi and L. Shultz. New York: State University of New York Press.

Ikeda, D. 2005. "Foreword." In *Educating Citizens for Global Awareness*, ed. N. Noddings. New York: Teachers College Press.

Kant, I. [1795] 2003. *To Perpetual Peace: A Philosophical Sketch*, trans. T. Humphrey. Indianapolis: Hackett.

Ladson-Billings, G. 2005. "Differing Concepts of Citizenship: Schools and Communities as Sites of Civic Development." In *Educating Citizens for Global Awareness*, ed. N. Noddings. New York: Teachers College Press.

Lewin, R., ed. 2009. *The Handbook of Practice and Research in Study Abroad: Higher Education and the Quest for Global Citizenship*. New York: Routledge.

Noddings, N., ed. 2005a. *Educating Citizens for Global Awareness*. New York: Teachers College Press.

Noddings, N. 2005b. "Introduction." In *Educating Citizens for Global Awareness*, ed. N. Noddings. New York: Teachers College Press.

Nussbaum, M. 1996. "Patriotism and Cosmopolitanism." In *For Love of Country: Debating the Limits of Patriotism*, ed. J. Cohen. Boston: Beacon Press.

Nussbaum, M. 1997. *Cultivating Humanity: A Classical Defense of Reform in Liberal Education*. Cambridge, MA: Harvard University Press.

Peters, M.A., A. Britton, and H. Blee, eds. 2008. *Global Citizenship Education*. Rotterdam: Sense.

Pike, G. 2008. "Reconstructing the Legend: Educating For Global Citizenship." In *Educating for Human Rights and Global Citizenship*, ed. A.A. Abdi and L. Shultz. New York: State University of New York Press.

Pinar, W. 2006. "*Bildung* and the Internationalization of Curriculum Studies." Keynote address at the triennial meeting of the International Association for the Advancement of Curriculum Studies, Tampere, Finland, 26 May.

Simpson, K. 2004. "'Doing Development': The Gap Year, Volunteer-tourists and a Popular Practice of Development." *Journal of International Development* 16 (5): 681–92.

Todd, S. 2009. *Toward an Imperfect Education: Facing Humanity, Rethinking Cosmopolitanism*. Boulder, CO: Paradigm.

Waks, L.J. 2008. "Cosmopolitanism and Citizenship Education." In *Global Citizenship Education*, ed. M.A. Peters, A. Britton, and H. Blee. Rotterdam: Sense.

Wang, H. 2004. *The Call from the Stranger on a Journey Home: Curriculum in a Third Space*. New York: Peter Lang.

White, C., and R. Openshaw, eds. 2005. *Democracy at the Crossroads: International Perspectives on Critical Global Citizenship Education*. New York: Lexington Books.

Zemach-Bersin, T. 2008. "American Students Abroad Can't Be 'Global Citizens'." *Chronicle of Higher Education* 54 (26), 7 March. Available online at http://chronicle.com/article/American-Students-Abroad-Cant/25527/; accessed 20 September 2010.

6 Students as Culturally Intelligent Change Agents: Global Citizenship and the Workplace

NORAH MCRAE

6.1 Introduction

Increasingly, Canadian post-secondary institutions are emphasizing the importance of internationalization. Universities and colleges seek to recruit more international students onto their campuses and to send more students abroad to participate in international experiences. In the 2006–07 academic year approximately 18,000 Canadian post-secondary students participated in some form of international experience (Bond 2009). These experiences include such things as courses and term studies abroad, time spent at field schools, international cooperative education, and internships (see Johnston, Drysdale, and Chiupka, Chapter 3, in this volume, for a more detailed breakdown of international learning programs).

The motivation for internationalization on the part of universities ranges from financial to pedagogical – that is, from generating revenues from international student fees to developing students with the knowledge, skills, and abilities to function effectively in today's complex, internationally linked world. All things "global" matter to educational institutions, as is clear from other contributions to this book. Although the definition of "global citizen" is still developing and is not without its detractors (see Benham Rennick, Chapter 2, in this volume), the concept, Schattle (2008) notes, is linked to ideas of cosmopolitanism, multiculturalism, neo-liberalism, and environmentalism. As such, whatever definition or slant one adopts, "global citizenship" can be used in a multitude of environments, including the workplace, which is my focus in this chapter.[1]

First, a *caveat lector*: this chapter stands in creative tension to others in the book. Where others place emphasis on the humanist roots of international learning, I discuss the production of globally effective workers and entrepreneurs. Where others talk of social justice, and emphasize the complexities involved in setting up international learning programs and increased care for all on our planet, I argue that training and measuring outcomes are easier than we think. My goal is to empower students, university administrators, and employers by giving them readily accessible tools with which to assess the learning that takes place abroad and the benefits of hiring students who have had international experiences.

Canadian post-secondary institutions pursue internationalization agendas within the context of a society that needs to handle increased globalization that has made the world smaller – or flat, to use Friedman's (2005) term. According to a report by Statistics Canada (2010), by 2031 between 25 per cent and 28 per cent of Canada's population could be foreign born; nearly half (46 per cent) of those ages fifteen and over will be foreign born or have at least one foreign-born parent, up from 39 per cent in 2006. In addition, the percentage of the population professing a non-Christian religion will nearly double, from 8 per cent in 2006 to 14 per cent in 2031, while those with no religious affiliation could rise from 17 per cent to 35 per cent. As a result, Canadian organizations will face increased diversity within their workforces – and, to be sure, among their customers, suppliers, and markets, and they will need to hire employees who can function effectively in this culturally diverse landscape. Their existing employees will also need to find ways to train for and support cultural diversity.

How can the benefits of post-secondary internationalization support the needs of organizations and, ultimately, Canadian society as the cultural landscape becomes more diverse? With that question in mind, I examine the usefulness of the concept of cultural intelligence – which Ang and Van Dyne (2008, 3) define as "an individual's capability to function and manage effectively in culturally diverse settings" – as a frame through which to encourage internationalization at post-secondary institutions. More important, if students develop their cultural intelligence, how can they make a difference? How can they be agents of change for their employers and communities in both the short and long run? Identifying ways that this facilitation might occur could provide another compelling incentive for post-secondary institutions to continue providing international experiences for their students and to develop programming that supports students as culturally intelligent change agents. Finally, using a frame such as cultural intelligence could result in meaningful measures of international experiences that would be of interest to policy makers, researchers, and funders.

6.2   Cultural Intelligence as a Way to Measure the Effectiveness of International Experience

The idea of cultural intelligence is rooted in other types of theories of intelligence, but recognizes that to exist in culturally diverse settings requires additional competencies. Cultural intelligence is based on a multiple-foci model that identifies the meta-cognitive, cognitive, motivational, and behavioural factors influencing intelligence (Earley and Ang 2003; Sternberg and Detterman 1986). Other types of intelligence based on a multiple-foci model are emotional intelligence (Mayer and Salovey 1993), social intelligence (Thorndike and Stein 1937), and practical intelligence (Sternberg et al. 2000). What makes cultural intelligence a distinct construct is the way it can explain how people vary in their ability to cope with diversity and to function in cross-cultural settings (Ang and Inkpen 2008).

The cognitive dimension of cultural intelligence is rooted in knowing about norms and practices in different cultures; it includes an understanding of cultural particularities and systems, as well as cultural differences. This understanding enables an individual to better appreciate the underpinnings of a different culture (Van Dyne, Ang, and Koh 2008). Cultural intelligence's meta-cognitive dimension – sometimes called strategy – refers to an individual's awareness of difference during cross-cultural interactions, and involves capabilities such as planning, monitoring, and revising understandings of culture (Ang and Van Dyne 2008). This awareness promotes conscious self-reflection that challenges cultural assumptions and biases while developing new strategies to improve cross-cultural interactions (Van Dyne, Ang, and Koh 2008). The motivational dimension of cultural intelligence relates to an individual's ability to direct positive attention and energy towards culturally diverse situations (Ang et al. 2007). The idea is that individuals with high levels of motivation have high levels of extrinsic and intrinsic interest in culturally diverse situations and high levels of confidence in their ability and self-efficacy to be successful in these situations (Bandura 1977). The final dimension of cultural intelligence, as I am using it here, relates to individuals' ability to adapt their verbal and non-verbal behaviours appropriately for culturally diverse situations (Ang et al. 2007). Indeed, behaviour might be the most crucial of the four dimensions, as it is the one most apparent to others and, therefore, the one most likely to be used to interpret, or misinterpret, intent (Ang and Van Dyne 2008). Individuals who are capable of restraining and modifying their behaviour are better able to interact in diverse settings.

Cultural intelligence is an acquired capability (Ang et al. 2007); as such, it is for the most part distinct from personality, which tends to be a stable trait over time and situation (Costa and McCrae 1992). Research has shown discriminant validity between the four factors of cultural intelligence and the five key personality traits of openness, conscientiousness, extraversion, agreeableness, and neuroticism (Costa and McCrae 1992), implying a meaningful relationship, for example, between the personality trait of openness to experience and each of the four cultural intelligence factors (Ang, Van Dyne, and Koh 2006).

Proponents of the cultural intelligence model make several arguments favouring it over other intercultural competency constructs. For example, cultural intelligence is grounded in multiple intelligences theory and, as such, systematically measures four dimensions (meta-cognitive, cognitive, motivational, and behavioural); it is a construct that refers only to abilities and does not mix non-ability (or personality) and ability constructs; and, finally, it is not culture specific (Ang and Van Dyne 2008). These combined factors have shown cultural intelligence to have predictive validity over and above other measures such as demographic characteristics, personality, general mental ability, emotional intelligence, cross-cultural adaptability, rhetorical sensitivity, cross-cultural experience, and social desirability (Van Dyne, Ang, and Koh 2008). Furthermore, cultural intelligence can be used to predict adjustment, well-being, cultural judgment and decision making, and task performance in culturally diverse settings.

Using this four-factor framework of cognitive, meta-cognitive, motivational, and behavioural dimensions of cultural intelligence, the Cultural Intelligence Center[2] has developed a twenty-item Cultural Intelligence Scale (CQS; see Table 6.1, information used by permission of the Cultural Intelligence Center). Reliability and validity testing of the CQS has shown it to be a "clear, robust and meaningful four-factor structure" that is stable across samples, time, methods, and countries (Van Dyne, Ang, and Koh 2008, 34). The CQS can also be used for self-reporting, peer-reporting and supervisor-reporting, with self-rated scores showing positive correlation with observer-rated scores. I argue that CQS could give students a concrete frame with which to consider

Table 6.1. The Twenty-Item, Four-Factor Cultural Intelligence Scale

Knowledge	
COG1	I know the legal and economic systems of other cultures.
COG2	I know the rules (vocabulary, grammar) of other languages.
COG3	I know the cultural values and religious beliefs of other cultures.
COG4	I know the marriage systems of other cultures.
COG5	I know the arts and crafts of other cultures.
COG6	I know the rules for expressing non-verbal behaviours in other cultures.
Strategy	
MC1	I am conscious of the cultural knowledge I use when interacting with people with different cultural backgrounds.
MC2	I adjust my cultural knowledge as I interact with people from a culture that is unfamiliar to me.
MC3	I am conscious of the cultural knowledge I apply to cross-cultural interactions.
MC4	I check the accuracy of my cultural knowledge as I interact with people from different cultures.
Motivation	
MOT1	I enjoy interacting with people from different cultures.
MOT2	I am confident that I can socialize with locals in a culture that is unfamiliar to me.
MOT3	I am sure I can deal with the stresses of adjusting to a culture that is new to me.
MOT4	I enjoy living in cultures that are unfamiliar to me.
MOT5	I am confident that I can get used to the shopping conditions in a different culture.
Behaviour	
BEH1	I change my verbal behaviour (accent, tone) when a cross-cultural interaction requires it.
BEH2	I use pause and silence differently to suit different cross-cultural situations.
BEH3	I vary the rate of my speaking when a cross-cultural situation requires it.
BEH4	I change my non-verbal behaviour when a cross-cultural situation requires it.
BEH5	I alter my facial expressions when a cross-cultural interaction requires it.

their experiences, and the vocabulary to articulate their learning and cultural intelligence to others – particularly potential employers.

Moreover, the cultural intelligence framework could be a useful way for institutions to structure and establish pedagogy and to evaluate the learning outcomes of international experiences. By designing programs to develop meta-cognitive, cognitive, motivational, and behavioural attributes in students, and testing for these attributes, institutions could support their students' "capability to function and manage effectively in culturally diverse settings" (Ang and Van Dyne 2008, 3).

Articulating these outcomes would benefit institutions and individual students because the pedagogical objectives and achievement milestones are explicit and easy to monitor. Other benefits are linked to employability and competence in workplaces and organizations that require these abilities. The importance of workplace preparation for students merits particular attention, even in the context of post-secondary programs that emphasize more humanistic components of global citizenship. In the rest of this chapter, I make a case for how the cultural intelligence framework could benefit students, employers, and Canadian society.

6.3   The Student Worker: Cultural Intelligence in the Workplace

According to Statistics Canada (Usalcas and Bowlby 2006), employers increasingly look to students to find the workers they require for both part-time and full-time positions. In the 2004–05 school year, nearly half (45.9 per cent) of all students ages eighteen to twenty-four were employed; during the summer of 2005, 51.7 per cent of these students were employed. With a full-time student population of 2.4 million (of all ages), this is a significant portion of the temporary work force.

In the 2006–07 academic year, approximately 18,000 Canadian post-secondary students (2.2 per cent of the total) participated in some form of international experience (Bond 2009). Considering that nearly half are likely to return to work while studying full time, and that more than half will work in subsequent summers prior to graduation, these students have the potential to demonstrate their cultural intelligence in the workplace even before they graduate. Coupled with an understanding of employers' needs for culturally competent employees, students could demonstrate how their increased cultural intelligence might add value to the workplace, and thereby give themselves a competitive edge at a time when job competition is fierce.

We know that employers value students who have had international experiences. In a study commissioned by the Canadian Bureau of International Education, a small group of seventeen employers was asked if students should have an international experience during their studies. Sixteen employers responded in the affirmative, with 91 per cent identifying the importance of cultural and other such types of experiences, including learning other languages (Bond 2009). The report goes on to state that study abroad is no longer seen as a barrier to career advancement and that employers make positive links between international learning experiences and students' employment and career goals.

6.4   Understanding Organizational Change

There is more. Even if students are armed with the self-awareness of their newly acquired cross-cultural abilities or are welcomed into a workplace that values those abilities, the challenge remains for employers and employees to use those skills to benefit the entire workplace once they have been hired. How, then, can students become cultural intelligence change agents in their places of employment or communities of engagement?

To understand this potential, we need first to look at organizational change theory. A seminal thinker in this field, Kurt Lewin (1890–1947), was motivated to develop theories that help to resolve social conflict and support democratic values and the protection of minority rights (Burnes 2004). He developed his theories of change based on some key concepts: field theory, group dynamics, and action research (Lewin 1943, 1946). The basic premise of field theory is that individual behaviour is a function of the group environment, or "field," and as such any consideration for change must be considered in that context (Lewin 1943; Burnes 2004). Group dynamics refers to the importance of the group in shaping individual behaviour; accordingly, initiatives for change are best undertaken at the group level and need to factor in such issues as group norms, roles, interactions, and socialization processes.

In addition to considering the context and group dynamics, Lewin identified the need to develop a way for groups to initiate and participate in change. He called this "action research," which led to his model of change. First, change requires action; second, successful action requires appropriate research. The concept of action research brings together Lewin's previous two main ideas: for change to be effective, it needs to happen at the group level, and it must be in a context that is participative and collaborative, involving all those affected such that they are included in the building of evidence for change (Burnes 2004). Lewin's argument that change cannot be successful without considering the context, group, and evidence, and ensuring everyone's engaged participation is still relevant today.

In keeping with Lewin's first principle of change – understanding the context – we might ask how an organization embodies the complexities of modern society. According to Peter Senge (1992), a successful firm needs to become a "learning organization" and overcome learning disabilities. Senge identifies five disciplines to overcome such disabilities: personal mastery, mental models, the building of shared vision, team learning, and systems thinking. These disciplines address several features: the importance of personal learning as a foundation for organizational learning – that is, an organization is only as capable as its individual members; the continual challenging and revisiting of the tacit understandings, or mental models, held within an organization; the collaborative development of a genuine vision that resonates with all members of the organization; open communication and dialogue between and among groups; and thinking beyond an individual's or unit's needs to include the organization as a whole system (Pugh and Hickson 2007).

Bringing together the requirements for organizational change and the importance of organizational learning to this process, let me now turn to the role that more "culturally intelligent" students, in particular, might play as agents of organizational change.

6.5   Students as Change Agents

Senge's thinking about the five disciplines required of a learning organization can be augmented by James March's (1991) work on how learning happens within an organization. March notes that the process of organizational learning is complex, and involves a balance between exploiting existing knowledge and exploring new knowledge to remain competitive. With too much emphasis on exploitation, organizations run the risk of becoming complacent, or not adhering to what Senge (1992) refers to as the disciplines of personal mastery, challenging mental models, creating a shared vision, and team learning. March suggests that a way to mitigate this risk is through hiring what he terms "slow learners," or those new to or not completely familiar with an organization's way of doing things. Slow learners come into an organization through turnover and new hiring, and as long as turnover is not too high or disruptive, and as long as slow learners are not indoctrinated too quickly or aggressively, their contribution to the heterogeneity of the organization can be significant. When students are hired, even for short periods, as in the case of internships or summer jobs, they have the potential to act as "slow learners."

Students also increase an organization's heterogeneity, in the form of gender, age, race, ethnicity, and ability, which contributes to a more diverse workforce. Not only does heterogeneity lessen the risks of exploitation, as March outlines; it can also contribute to exploration. The new perspective that students contribute and the application of the theories and knowledge they have gained at their educational institutions and through their international experiences can add exploratory power to an organization and to the discipline of personal mastery and team learning.

How students can contribute to the learning organization and be change agents is determined by a range of variables that one can generally group into two categories: first, what the organization does to allow students to contribute and, second, the student's intrinsic ability to be a change agent. The former is a critical component of the student's ability to be an agent of change. How is the student socialized into the organization? March (1991) recommends, as I have noted, that this happen slowly and without indoctrination. Is the student made part of the group, and thus able to influence group dynamics and team learning? Is the vision of the organization shared with the student, and is the student fully engaged in that vision? While on the job, is the student's personal mastery supported, or is he or she considered a temporary worker whose own learning is of little consequence? How able are supervisors to make their tacit knowledge explicit for the student? Organizations that hire students without giving consideration to these questions are limiting the contribution students can make to enhance their exploitation and exploration of knowledge that would increase organizational learning.

Referring to Bandura's (2001) social cognitive theory, self-efficacy lies at the heart of the student's ability to be an agent of change. Self-efficacy is related to how one approaches tasks; it drives individual agency and affects motivation, models of decision making, causal attribution, thought patterns, and stress management. Students with high self-efficacy believe they can be successful in what they undertake. If they experience failure, they are more likely to blame it on lack of effort, situational circumstances beyond their control, or the use of inappropriate strategies. Students with high self-efficacy also look for opportunity, are resourceful, and can handle complexity better. When faced with stressful situations, Bandura argues, those with high self-efficacy are better able to control negative thoughts and manage their emotions; they are also better able to confront and deal with their stressors. In sum, students with high self-efficacy would likely be more effective as change agents within an organization because they are able to learn about and address tasks with high levels of motivation, persistence, and ingenuity.

Now to my key point: students with high levels of cultural intelligence have high levels of self-efficacy, which is one of the key components of the motivational dimension. If we accept that students can contribute to organizational change, their increased cultural intelligence could make a positive difference for employers and the work environment. By participating in team learning, challenging mental models, and helping to define shared vision, students – especially those with well-facilitated international learning experiences – could contribute to the development of cultural intelligence in their colleagues and managers. Organizations that allow for this contribution by students would enhance their ability to exploit and explore knowledge. Finally, organizations that support the development of students' individual self-efficacy could benefit from increased collective efficacy. In an increasingly globally competitive environment, tapping into the cultural intelligence of student workers would be an efficient and effective way for organizations to maintain competitive advantage.

Maximizing the potential of culturally intelligent students requires more, however, than hiring students with experience and knowledge of culturally diverse settings. It requires that their knowledge is valued, that they be allowed to contribute this knowledge verbally and non-verbally, that they be free to challenge assumptions and biases, and that they be allowed enough freedom to make mistakes from which all can learn without fear of reprisal. Although this approach might seem idealistic and time consuming, it should be considered an investment that will pay off in the form of organizational competitive advantage – and a better-adjusted, healthier workforce.

6.6 Conclusion

I began this chapter with a question about how post-secondary internationalization, and the development of students with more international learning experience, could play a role in supporting the needs of organizations and, ultimately, of Canadian society at large as the cultural landscape becomes more diverse. In response I proposed that the international experiences afforded students allow them to increase what Ang and others have called cultural intelligence. I further argued that student workers could use this cultural intelligence in their role as organizational agents of change in subsequent employment and community engagement. Canadian organizations that have employees with high levels of cultural intelligence might be able to put these assets to use to build their competitive advantage. Graduates who demonstrate high levels of cultural intelligence should be able to function more effectively in culturally diverse situations and to contribute to organizational learning, thereby contributing to a healthy, diverse society.

How might managers engage students more intentionally in their workplaces? How might they prepare co-workers for culturally diverse student employees? What human resource practices might be considered to recruit, retain, and maximize the contribution of culturally intelligent students? How could organizations benefit from the increased cultural intelligence of their student employees? My hope is that this chapter offers ways that support the internationalization agendas of educational institutions and helps shed new light on the untapped possibilities of hiring students with international learning experiences. Too often, students engage in such experiences without being provided a framework to help them articulate these experiences to others, thus diminishing their ability to understand and apply what they have learned. Too often, employers are reluctant to hire students who come from diverse backgrounds, or who have been trained in ways that do not follow the straight and narrow path. Supporting the development of cultural intelligence in students and promoting the role they can play as agents of change can strengthen Canadian organizations and, by extension, Canadian society at large.

My additional hope is that post-secondary institutions can strengthen their international learning programs in ways that authors of other chapters in this book suggest. Enhanced business and job successes are important, but if the agents of change in our businesses are students and graduates who also carry with them a clear vision of how to make the world more equitable and sustainable, then we will have the best of all possible outcomes.

NOTES

1 An earlier version of this chapter, co-written by Karima Ramji, was published in Coll and Zegwaard (2001). Research for this chapter was supported by Human Resources and Skills Development Canada in association with the Canadian-European Union Consortium for Strengthening
  Transatlantic Student Mobility in Co-operative Education. The research
  also received ethics approval from the University of Victoria.
2 The Cultural Intelligence Center is dedicated to improving the understanding of cultural intelligence. The Center offers the first academically
  validated instrument to measure cultural intelligence. The Center also
  sponsors research, conducts training, and presents workshops and information sessions on cultural intelligence to audiences around the world; see
  http://culturalq.com/index.html, accessed July 4, 2012.

REFERENCES

Ang, S., et al. 2007. "Cultural Intelligence: Its Measurement and Effects on
    Cultural Judgement and Decision Making, Cultural Adaptation and Task
    Performance." *Management and Organization Review* 3 (3): 335–71.
Ang, S., and A.C. Inkpen. 2008. "Cultural Intelligence and Offshore
    Outsourcing Success: A Framework of Firm-level Intercultural Capability."
    Decision Sciences 39 (3): 337–58.
Ang, S., and L. Van Dyne. 2008. "Conceptualization of Cultural Intelligence:
    Definition, Distinctiveness, and Nomological Network." In *Handbook of
    Cultural Intelligence: Theory, Measurement, and Applications*, ed. S. Ang and
    L.V. Dyne. Armonk, NY: M.E. Sharpe.
Ang, S., L. Van Dyne, and C. Koh. 2006. "Personality Correlates of the Four-
    factor Model of Cultural Intelligence." *Group & Organization Management*
    31 (1): 100–23.
Bandura, A. 1977. *Social Learning Theory.* Englewood Cliffs, NJ: Prentice-Hall.
Bandura, A. 2001. "Social Cognitive Theory: An Agentic Perspective." *Annual
    Review of Psychology* 52 (1): 1–26.
Bond, S. 2009. *World of Learning: Canadian Post-Secondary Students and the Study
    Abroad Experience.* Ottawa: Canadian Bureau for International Education.
Burnes, B. 2004. "Kurt Lewin and the Planned Approach to Change: A
    Re-appraisal." *Journal of Management Studies* 41 (6): 977–1002.
Coll, R.K., and K.E. Zegwaard, eds. 2011. *International Handbook for Cooperative
    and Work-Integrated Learning: International Perspectives of Theory, Research,
    and Practice*, 2nd ed. Hamilton, NZ: University of Waikato.

Costa, P.T.J., and R.R. McCrae. 1992. *Revised NEO Personality Inventory (NEO PI-R) and New Five Factor Inventory (NEO FFI) Professional Manual*. Odessa, FL: Psychological Assessment Resources.

Earley, P.C., and S. Ang. 2003. *Cultural Intelligence: Individual Interactions Across Cultures*. Stanford, CA: Stanford University Press.

Friedman, T.L. 2005. *The World Is Flat: A Brief History of the Twenty-first Century*. New York: Farrar, Straus and Giroux.

Lewin, K. 1943. "Defining the 'Field at a Given Time'." *Psychological Review* 50: 292–310.

Lewin, K. 1946. "Action Research and Minority Problems." *Journal of Social Issues* 2 (4): 34–46.

March, J.G. 1991. "Exploration and Exploitation in Organizational Learning." *Organization Science* 2 (1): 71–87.

Mayer, J.D., and P. Salovey. 1993. "The Intelligence of Emotional Intelligence." *Intelligence* 17 (4): 433–42.

Pugh, D.S., and D.J. Hickson. 2007. *Writers on Organizations*, 6th ed. London: Penguin.

Schattle, H. 2008. "Education for Global Citizenship: Illustrations of Ideological Pluralism and Adaptation." *Journal of Political Ideologies* 13 (1): 73–94.

Senge, P.N. 1992. *The Fifth Discipline: The Art and Practice of the Learning Organization*. New York, London: Century Business.

Statistics Canada. 2010. "Study: Projections of the Diversity of the Canadian population: 2006 to 2031." *The Daily*, 9 March. Available online at http://www.statcan.gc.ca/daily-quotidien/100309/dq100309a-eng.htm; accessed 13 March 2011.

Sternberg, R.J., et al. 2000. *Practical Intelligence in Everyday Life*. New York: Cambridge University Press.

Sternberg, R.J., and D.K. Detterman. 1986. *What Is Intelligence? Contemporary Viewpoints on Its Nature and Definition*. Norwood, NJ: Ablex.

Thorndike, R.L., and S. Stein. 1937. "An Evaluation of the Attempts to Measure Social Intelligence." *Psychological Bulletin* 34 (5): 275–85.

Usalcas, J., and G. Bowlby. 2006. "Students in the Labour Market." *Education Matters: Insight on Education, Learning and Training in Canada* 3 (1).

Van Dyne, L., S. Ang, and C. Koh. 2008. "Development and Validation of the CQS." In *Handbook of Cultural Intelligence: Theory, Measurement, and Applications*, ed. S. Ang and L.V. Dyne. Armonk, NY: M.E. Sharpe.

STUDENT INTERMEZZI
Repercussions for students when they come home

All in

CATHLEEN DIFRUSCIO

The adventurous and exotic stories of my time spent abroad roll off of my tongue so easily now. I have learned to tell them that way, mostly out of self-preservation, I think. Easier to skirt around the existential labyrinth that has become my mind post-Nairobi than try to navigate through it. I have learned to tell them that way because I really don't know how to talk about my time abroad. You see, my experience as an International Service Learning student seems to be different, although I choose to believe I am not the only one with these kinds of experiences. What I know for sure, though, is that when it comes to the frequently told stories of ISL students that circulate on blogs, that are recounted at fundraising events, and that appear as testimonials on recruitment websites, hardly an echo of my voice is there.

Instead, what surrounds me are fellow students talking about how much they learned about themselves and the world, the wonderful relationships they formed, and how much they transformed as individuals. Their eyes were opened. They had seen the hope that resonates from these communities and had discovered their own potential to create positive change. They just seem so confident ... so sure. And wasn't that what we were told would happen anyways? Truth be told, it always reminded me of an army recruitment advertisement: "*Be all you can be – non-violently, of course!*" Instead of guns and uniforms, we had notebooks, big hearts, and endless idealism. We were going to change ourselves, change the world, and come back stronger and better than ever. It was the most authentic kind of fieldwork we were ever going to have the opportunity to involve ourselves in.

Except that wasn't really my experience. I don't feel like I came out stronger on the other side. Oh, I changed, and changes happened when I went abroad, but were these for the better? I suppose it's not really up to me to decide. Life doesn't happen in vacuum – it is never truly just my experience. Even the tiniest movement in the water creates ripples all around it.

I did two stints abroad. Both placements were in Nairobi, Kenya. In Africa – the proverbial crown jewel of ISL-placement locations. I left the first time around with few expectations, but with the belief that I would find communities where I felt at peace, with people who were excited to learn and grow from one another, just like me. While there, my focus was on being present, soaking up every experience, every opportunity, good and bad. I hardly slowed down long enough to process the information that was coming in. It eventually caught up to me, though, as I said my goodbyes to the communities and people that had shared so much with me, whom I had given so much of myself to, and was now leaving behind.

After returning to Canada, the first time around, I had a difficult time reintegrating. I had trouble sleeping. I withdrew from a lot of people, buried a lot of troubling memories, and tried to keep so busy that I didn't have time to let my feelings catch up with me. I pretended that I was fine – just stressed with school and work. But nothing sent me into a dark place faster than an e-mail from Nairobi. I was overcome with shame and guilt over the impact of my presence there, which I now perceived as negative and selfish. I was disappointed in myself for participating in something I understood as being neo-colonial and oppressive to the communities I lived and volunteered in. I felt inadequate for not being able to make more substantial meaning from my experiences abroad. I was troubled by the harassment and violence that I faced and the dignity I felt I had lost because of it. And I felt helpless as I continued to receive news of friends and students of mine who had disappeared, were in jail, had lost their homes, fell ill, or who could barely make ends meet.

My memories of Nairobi were marked with the knowledge of people and resources I had used for the purposes of my own intellectual development – people I promptly abandoned for the comforts of Canada when it was all said and done, people who provided me with opportunities and experiences that had been reduced to lines on my résumé. Somehow I was supposed to just be ok with it all. It was a privilege to be able to participate in a program like that, to travel at all. And everyone else around me seemed to be moving along just fine, so I learned to do that too. At least, I tried to make people think I was doing that.

Whenever asked, I let everyone know how much I loved my time in Nairobi. Truth be told, I really did feel a strong connection there for some reason, despite the overwhelmingly negative feelings that I was having. I suppose it had to do with the sense of community I had felt there – a siblinghood of people committed to learning and changing the world around them. There was also an element of predictability behind the actions of people there that I came to find comfort in. Before I left the hot sun of Nairobi, I knew I wanted to return.

So I struggled through a year in Canada, packed my bags, and set off again to reunite with a beloved community, face some of my demons, and deconstruct the complex kyriarchal structures that played with my emotions and distorted my former understandings of reality.[1]

The second time around was different. I was there for longer, knew more people in the community, and felt more comfortable just diving right in to new and sometimes risky situations. As the months went by, I began to notice something different in myself, and something different about how I talked about my life there. The changes were subtle. It took me the better part of a year just to notice there was a difference. Nairobi had changed something inside of me. It took something from me – little pieces of me, actually: my sense of security, my faith in the good in people, my will to keep fighting, and my belief in the effectiveness of advocacy and activism. I had lost myself. I felt like Nairobi had taken all the things that made me, ME. I knew those things were buried deep inside of me somewhere still, but I didn't know how to get them back, and it seemed like they had been replaced by a healthy dose of cynicism. Still, I felt a deep need to be there. I wanted to stay, but I honestly didn't know how much of myself I had left to give. And I wasn't sure what I was learning anymore.

The thing is, though, now that I am back in Canada, I would give anything to be back there. I miss my community. I miss the work I did, the interesting people I would get to meet, the constant opportunities to learn, and the beaming faces and flurry of hands signing around me in the class of deaf students I taught. Not a day goes by where the sounds, sights, and smells don't come back to me. I feel overwhelming guilt for leaving people and unfinished projects. For choosing a certain amount of self-preservation over the work I was doing. For abandoning people, and coming out of it with a few more lines in my résumé. For not being a stronger and more effective ally. And I feel disappointed in myself

---

1 See Chapter 4, in this volume, for my complementary contribution, including details about the term *kyriarchy* in note 3.

because I have yet to translate these experiences into something mean-ingful, let alone understand what it is for something to be meaningful.

These emotions weigh on me most days, but what right do I really have to complain? Who am I to comment on what my presence meant abroad to the communities I was in? Perhaps this is just a vision of the world through the eyes of my ego. But for now this is my reality, and right or wrong these are the feelings that prevail as the months con-tinue to pass by.

Despite all of that, knowing what I do, feeling as I do, I would do it all again in an instant. My experience in Kenya was immeasurable. But if you are looking for a reason why, it escapes me. I just know it. I know it even in the face of such pain and uncertainty. I know it even as I recognize that I took more from these communities than I will ever be able to return to them in my lifetime. I know it even when the people I knew before my time in Nairobi now look at me as if they hardly rec-ognize the person before them. I don't blame them; most of the time, I don't either.

I want to move forward. I want to use these experiences abroad to shape my activism. I want to make sure that all of this was about some-thing, but I don't see how I can live here in Canada without turning my back on those communities in Nairobi. I don't understand how I can honour the experiences, the struggles, and the kindness of those I met there, while participating in a system that continues to silence their voices and contribute to their oppression. I feel as though I live in a world of shifting realities and partial truths that totally consume my thoughts. But perhaps it's time to enter the labyrinth, to move in any direction, because a world of shifting realities and partial truths can yield unlimited possibilities.

Staying involved

LYNN MATISZ

I am very fortunate to have had the opportunity to visit Peru on two separate occasions. In 2009 I travelled with a group of ten university student volunteers; then, a year later, I ventured back to the same three communities with a different group of students and as part of the lead-ership team. My experiences as a volunteer abroad have challenged my perspectives on the world while at the same time deeply inspiring me. They have also given me the opportunity to see first-hand what I study as a university Global Studies student. Moreover, I am grateful to have met amazing people who, despite facing extreme circumstances, dedicate their lives to helping others in their communities.

The district of San Juan De Lurigancho in Lima is a particular community that I will never forget. As Peru's capital, Lima is overcrowded and is by far the country's most populated area. The city is dry, with hardly any vegetation. The air is filled with smog and countless stray dogs roam the streets. The roads are noisy and packed with motor taxis and buses. And the contrast between rich and poor couldn't be clearer. I vividly remember riding a bus through San Juan and noticing many beautiful expensive houses, often guarded by a gate. On the edges of this district, however, the stark contrast in wealth is another story. There I saw poverty-stricken slums located on the dry dirt mountains that surround the city. Many of the houses there are built from cardboard or pieces of steel and sticks, and there is limited access to running water in these areas. San Juan is indeed unlike any other place I have ever been.

During my visits to the poorer areas of San Juan, I worked alongside volunteer nurses who dedicate themselves to eradicating dengue fever through a water-treatment campaign. Their aim: to visit each and every house in the district to treat their water, hoping to educate people on how to keep their water clean and free of disease. The nurses also operate an abused women's shelter. The Peruvian government does not provide funding for any of their efforts; it is their strong belief in social justice that motivates these individuals in the face of many obstacles.

I have come to understand how crucial the women's role is in their community. To put the situation in perspective, the district has only one registered doctor for its population of over one million people. The nurses understand that help is desperately needed and have relentlessly taken the initiative. More impressive still is the fact that these women have several other commitments such as jobs and families of their own.

Although witnessing the poverty that a large portion of San Juan faces helped rid me of some naïveté about the world, it was the perseverance and compassion shown by the nurses that truly moved me. During my second visit, I was able to see the amazing progress the nurses had made in just one year. They had reached an enormous amount of people in need of water treatment and had successfully helped a number of abused women get back on their feet. The nurses had accomplished so much since I had last seen them, yet it was clear that they continued to face the same difficulties and discouragement in finding support for their projects.

Despite the profound impact that the dedication of these nurses had on me when I was in Peru, returning to Canada I could not help but feel disconnected from them and from my experiences in San Juan. Within a few months of being home, a new school year had begun and life seemed to continue where it had left off before I went away. In my mind, the cultures and lifestyles of Canada and Peru were strikingly different. I realized that I was struggling to hold on to the memories and the lessons I had learned abroad.

I kept in touch with the nurses through e-mail, but I wanted to do something more to retain that connection and help those who had impacted me so greatly. Since being home, I had not forgotten about the nurses, but I was uncertain how to keep them in my life. The group of students I travelled with collectively decided to send money to the nurses. We organized two separate fundraising events and, to our surprise, were able to raise $2,000, which converts to almost 6,000 Peruvian soles. I was confident the money would be put to good use, expecting it, for example, to cover the high costs of rent for the abused women's shelter.

Although I did not return to Peru the following year, I was eager for stories from another group member who revisited San Juan. I was curious to hear about any progress the nurses may have made as another year passed by. Once again, the nurses exceeded my expectations. Through their continuous efforts and determination, not a single case of dengue fever had been reported that year in San Juan, demonstrating that the nurses' preventative measures were successful. In addition, the money my group sent was used to provide numerous training sessions for the women staying in the shelter. Two new sewing machines were purchased and handicraft and baking training sessions started, providing the women an opportunity to sell the products they made themselves. Lastly, the remaining money was spent on opening a small sandwich bar, providing employment to a lady who thought she had lost everything. After hearing this news, I was speechless. I thought to myself how my group's combined effort of raising money went a much longer way than expected in making a difference for both the victims at the shelter and the nurses. Despite the distance between us, the news impacted me by reminding me how outstanding these women are in making the world a better place.

Reflecting now on my experiences volunteering abroad, I have noticed a drastic change in my perspectives on the world. I have come to learn the importance of being aware of your surroundings: to take notice of the needs, issues, and concerns hiding beneath the surface of a community. Understanding the world is not easy; it requires effort. However, a desire to learn is what I believe makes long-term change possible.

Demonstrating by example, the volunteer nurses of San Juan did not ignore the pressing issues of their community. Instead, they took these problems into their own hands and showed immense strength by selflessly working to improve the lives of others in their community. This lesson of awareness, I believe, is applicable not only when travelling abroad, but also in local communities. I now recognize that the process of putting these lessons into action is a work in progress that requires me to make a daily decision to be a more conscious and active citizen in my community. My visits to Peru were just the beginning of this process.

PART IV

Case Studies

7 Educating Future Teachers through the Lens of an Equity and Diversity Course

JACKIE ELDRIDGE AND JOHN SMITH

7.1 Introduction

This chapter discusses the successes and challenges of a second-year university course called Equity and Diversity in Education (EDE) that is a required element of a Concurrent Teacher Education Program (CTEP) at the University of Toronto, Mississauga. The authors are both long-time educators with collective experience that spans elementary, secondary, undergraduate, and graduate education.

We strongly believe that all future teachers must have a global understanding regardless of where they find themselves in their careers. Our world is a global village, and understanding the impact of global issues on education and all its stakeholders is a crucial step in developing teachers who embrace issues of equity and diversity wherever they occur. One of our premises in developing the EDE course is based on Nieto's (2004, xxii) thesis:

> Our schools reflect the socio-cultural and sociopolitical context in which we live. This context is unfair to many young people and their families and the situations in which they live and go to school, but teachers and other educators do not simply have to go along with this reality ... [;] many school policies and practices are based on flawed ideas about intelligence and difference. If we want to change the situation, it means changing the curriculum and pedagogy in individual classrooms, as well as the school's practices. We need to create classrooms in which racism, sexism, social class discrimination, and other biases are no longer acceptable.

In our context at the University of Toronto, many of our graduates will be teaching in public, Catholic, and private schools in the Greater Toronto Area, one of the most culturally diverse areas in the world. In addition, according to its Web site, our university hosts "about 60,000 undergraduate students from over 150 countries. The University of Toronto boasts a culturally diverse student body, which is reflective of the multiculturalism that Canada is known for around the world." The issues that Toronto's schools face are not unlike those encountered in many other large urban centres. Moreover, there is also a need to address these concerns in areas where diversity is less obvious; in fact, the need for deeper appreciation of diversity is perhaps more acute in more culturally homogenous areas, so that people who do not "see" diversity in their immediate neighbourhoods can have a window into what is happening elsewhere.

This chapter is, in essence, a self-study that has enabled us to look at our own experience and share what we have learned about our program with other faculties, scholars, and administrators who are developing similar courses or programs. We are committed to helping teacher candidates become good global citizens who will in turn influence their future students to do the same.

7.2   The University of Toronto's Concurrent Teacher Education Program

In our Concurrent Teacher Education Program, equity and diversity do not stand alone. As a team of educators, we are devoted to ensuring that our content materials, teaching strategies, classroom management practices, and room displays all convey inclusivity and attention to multiple aspects of equity and diversity. To be sure, these ideals are not always reflected in practice, despite our best efforts. Equity and diversity are concepts that all of us understand incrementally, and invariably we develop more quickly with the help of others, including our students. In what follows, we examine CTEP's experiential learning component and instruction through the lens of the course's core values, the increasing need for stronger support and resources, and an ongoing need to understand how effective we actually are in reaching our students.

CTEP is one of the routes to becoming a teacher at the University of Toronto. The program began in 2006 as an option for graduating secondary school students and first-year university students interested in a career in education. The program allows future teachers to earn two undergraduate degrees simultaneously. One degree, either a Bachelor of Arts or a Bachelor of Science, provides the required content knowledge to teach in several subject areas, along with a number of introductory education-focused courses and field experiences. The other degree, a Bachelor of Education, helps candidates develop the practical skills to apply that knowledge effectively as teaching professionals. Graduates of the program qualify for certification as elementary or secondary school teachers in Ontario. In this program, University of Toronto candidates may choose from anchor subject areas such as mathematics, chemistry, French, or psychology. The first three anchors were developed for individuals wanting to become secondary school teachers, while the psychology anchor is geared towards those who would like to teach elementary school with a focus on learners with exceptionalities.

During the five-year program, teacher candidates study a number of education-focused courses that frame the vision of the entire program. Embedded in each of these courses are strong principles of inclusive education, communication, and conflict resolution, equity, diversity, and social justice, as partially demonstrated by the following course components: readings that include theoretical and practical understandings of equity issues; site visits to high-risk areas with follow-up to report findings and engage in discussions; tutoring students from marginalized groups such as students with exceptionalities or English-language learning challenges; and developing lesson plans specifically geared towards diverse learners. Instructors regularly infuse these courses with readings and discussion points that include the five principles listed above. As a teaching team, we are committed to helping students understand the importance of these core components, and with their help we seek to model new ways of learning in keeping with twenty-first-century Canadian global realities.

7.3   The Equity and Diversity in Education Course

The Equity and Diversity in Education course that we teach focuses on raising awareness and sensitivity to related issues facing teachers and students in schools and communities. The goals of both CTEP and this course are to assist teacher candidates in creating high-quality teaching and learning environments for all students, including students from socio-cultural groups that have not been well served by the educational system as well as students from mainstream white, middle-class communities. The objective of the course is to enable students to view the world of schooling from diverse perspectives and to develop an increased sensitivity to the needs of learners whose linguistic, cultural, gender, sexual orientation, social class, and racial backgrounds are different from their own. Marx and Moss (2011) demonstrate that teachers must strive to understand issues of equity and diversity so that classrooms are inclusive, and equity becomes the norm rather than the exception. The EDE course provides an opportunity for students to learn how educational responses to issues such as gender, sexual orientation, and disability affect educational outcomes. The course looks at issues affecting the entire world, and attempts to demonstrate how a global perspective can and must permeate all that we do and teach.

Our role is not limited to the classroom. As teacher educators we make frequent school visits where we see first-hand what is happening in primary and secondary classrooms as we supervise our candidates in their practica. We are often disappointed by what we witness. In our conversations with associate teachers and their teacher candidates, we see a continued lack of focus on the critical issues that are part of an equity and diversity mindset. Instead, practising classroom teachers tend to focus on literacy and accountability, and seem unable to make their lessons equitable – at least to the degree that we consider necessary. Although the halls and walls of schools display diversity, we do not see it embedded in curriculum, teaching, and learning.

We find ourselves wanting to advocate for positive changes. To truly embrace equity and diversity, teachers must have a range of resources that reflect the experiences of their diverse population, they should teach lessons in ways that meet the needs of everyone, not just a select few students, and their courses and texts should embrace more than a Eurocentric curriculum or the white middle-class experience. Although there continue to be many attempts to "fix" these concerns, we still have a long way to go. Students must see themselves in their schooling, and be able to construct their learning from their own experiences. So, too, must teachers; at times the problems seem to start from the fixed curriculum they are made to teach, the culture of a particular school, a teacher's overly cautious response to a contentious issue – or, dare we say, to an education program like ours in which they were trained. The problems are easier to perceive than their roots, or their solutions.

The EDE course requires an experiential learning component that is intended to educate students about the need for cultural awareness at various levels, from their local milieu to the international stage. We operate from a social constructivist framework – that is, we emphasize the importance of understanding that culture and context play a central role in how knowledge is constructed within our society (Derry 1999; McMahon 1997). This perspective is closely aligned with that of many contemporary theorists such as Vygotsky, Bruner, and Bandura.

One of our greatest challenges in helping our students to understand the issues of equity and diversity lies in providing them enough opportunities to see how these issues relate to their undergraduate studies in math, chemistry, French, and psychology. As teacher educators we believe that teachers of every subject area must be able to teach with equity and diversity in mind; however, our students are not seeing it modelled for them in their Bachelor of Arts and, especially, Bachelor of Science classrooms. In fact, there is often a strong disconnect between the strict adherence to the content focus of such courses, the teaching methodologies employed, and the social constructivist teaching and learning that we ask them to consider in their own classrooms. In their extensive research on teacher education programs, Beck and Kosnik (2006) suggest that teacher educators must use a social constructivist framework in their work with teacher candidates to demonstrate the critical importance of culture and social context for informing knowledge (see also Vygotsky 1978). But suggestions like these, while helpful in theory, do not always have their intended effect.

Through our personal interactions with students and the reflections they write for course work, we have noted that it is much easier to bring awareness to our French and psychology students because natural cultural components, links, and theories are embedded in these undergraduate courses; math and chemistry students, however, need more convincing that culture and context matter to teaching their disciplines. We frequently hear our science students saying that they cannot make a connection in their classroom to what we teach them in ours because their subjects are so "formulaic" or content focused. In their minds there is no room in their disciplines for equity and diversity teaching. They believe they must "add" equity and diversity instead of embedding such principles, and they do not have a sense of how that might happen. It is with these challenges in mind that we see an even greater importance for this course in teacher education programs. The question is how to teach these principles effectively, especially to students who resist their applicability.

In addition to content knowledge and class discussions, EDE students engage in a mandatory twenty-hour field experience to help expand their understanding of social diversity and marginalization. They observe and participate in schools or community organizations serving various marginalized groups including immigrants, the LGBTQ population, people with disabilities, the aged, cultural and racial minorities, and economically disadvantaged communities in the Greater Toronto Area. Students are expected to participate actively in a field placement that challenges them to move outside their comfort zone by working where they can be the exception to the norm and by extending their participation in this placement over a minimum of six weeks. Much of what other chapters in this book discuss concerning international learning abroad applies to the types of placements we try to get our students to take on locally.

This field experience is an essential step for teachers to help students identify and engage with diversity issues while also recognizing that this knowledge is critical to their students and themselves as professionals in the field of education. Indeed, the Ontario College of Teachers requires their members to abide by Standards of Practice for the Teaching Profession and Ethical Standards for the Teaching Profession (Ontario College of Teachers 2006a, 2006b). Standards of practice include commitment to students and student learning, leadership in learning communities, on-going professional learning, professional knowledge, and professional practice; the ethical standards are care, trust, respect, and integrity. Embedded within all of these standards are references to the demonstration of such practices as "facilitating the development of students as contributing citizens to society," "honouring human dignity," and "modeling respect for spiritual and cultural values, social justice, confidentiality, freedom, democracy and the environment." For us the global is embedded in the local. We have seen that students in our CTEP who do not have opportunities for interacting with diverse populations are more likely to struggle with these goals when they are introduced to them because they are not as familiar with dealing consciously and practically with diversity. Instead, they seem to develop a mindset that frames those who are different from the majority as the Other, a mindset that can dehumanize people.

In her reflective journal one CTEP student commented that her visit to a "high-risk" area was "too depressing," so she left. Another student told her instructor that she did not see the point of diversity placement since she would "be going back to her hometown where there is no diversity." Reaching students with such a mindset presents a challenge for those working towards a greater appreciation of equity and diversity. It tells us that we need to redouble our efforts and that we should find ways to provide more field experiences with far deeper connections for our candidates.

7.4   The Key Literature

The EDE program vision, mission, courses, and field experiences are grounded on the conceptual framework of equity, diversity, and social justice formulated by researchers such as Banks (1994) and Lindsey, Robins, and Terrell (1999).

Banks (1994) includes a conceptual model for progression that teaches students (and their teachers) about building inclusivity and taking action to make the world a more equitable place. There are four stages involved, starting from the most basic and moving to the most developed, which Banks calls contributions, additive, transformation, and social action. In stage one (contributions), teachers simply increase the diversity of heroes and heroines in the already-established curriculum; the point is to show that it is not only dead, white, heterosexual, Euro-descended, Christian males who are worthy of attention and admiration. In stage two (additive), teachers add a variety of content, concepts, themes, and perspectives to the curriculum without changing its basic structure. They might celebrate Black History Month or Chinese New Year with their students, or talk about the religious significance of Ramadan or Holi. These types of themes are added from time to time, and are not introduced on a regular basis. In stage three (transformation), teachers change the actual structure of the curriculum to help students view concepts, issues, events, and themes from the perspective of diverse groups. In this stage, teachers embed their students' experiences into all that happens in the classroom, including the curriculum and content materials; the classroom is transformed when students see themselves implicated in all that happens. Finally, stage four (social action) is where teachers allow students to make decisions on important social issues and take actions to help solve them. In this stage, teachers transform their classrooms by providing students the intellectual and emotional space to make a difference in addressing issues they will face throughout their lives and throughout the world.

For their part, Lindsey, Robins, and Terrell (1999) discuss the need for schools and other organizations to become "culturally proficient" to build inclusive environments for all. In a similar vein to McRae's contribution (Chapter 6, in this volume) on cultural intelligence in the workplace, cultural proficiency is promoted as a means of developing in students and educators the confidence to embed issues of equity, diversity, and social justice in all their classroom experiences. For some, it is a paradigm shift, because their teacher education experience might not have placed much emphasis on these issues and because their home and social environments might have been far more culturally limited. In addition, if teachers do not see ways of embedding the issues, they are likely to see them as add-ons and claim that they do not have time to introduce anything else to their already-packed curriculum.

Lindsey, Robins, and Terrell also recommend the use of specific tools for effectively describing, responding to, and planning for issues that emerge in diverse environments. If teachers are not prepared to meet the issues head-on, students will almost certainly get the wrong messages and fail to see the importance of diversity work. It is therefore incumbent upon teachers to seek professional development and to learn the tools necessary for working with all students. Teachers who do not have the appropriate skills tend to see all students in the same light, and do not understand that difference should be embraced rather than ignored or feared. Teachers often seek their own forms of professional development, but school boards, school districts, and legislative bodies must also be willing to provide further education as well as clear policies and practices at the organizational level. From the minister of education all the way to support staff in schools, all must model and implement the values and behaviours that enable effective cross-cultural interactions among students, teachers, administrators, and the learning community at large.

Finally, Lindsey, Robins, and Terrell insist that, to achieve this last aspect of cultural proficiency, teachers must know what the global community looks like, sounds like, and feels like. They must investigate issues of equity, diversity, and social justice as they are manifested throughout the world, they must be prepared to face such issues when they arise in their classrooms, and they must understand how to teach in ways that embrace these issues. When diversity is woven into the curriculum and educational landscape, teachers can create powerful learning environments for all.

7.5   Applying the Literature

The models we have presented implicitly form the framework of all CTEP teaching, and they are taught explicitly to our second-year students. In the EDE course, teacher candidates are challenged to look beyond the surface level of the curriculum and to reflect more deeply on the culture of the classrooms they will create and serve. These learning communities should be spaces where students can move beyond awareness to action that will lead to transformation, inviting them to think about global issues and deconstruct the many stereotypes and inequities that exist in North America and around the world.

Reflecting on Lindsey, Robins, and Terrell (1999), students in our program are encouraged to engage in conversations about the relationship of diversity to the teaching and learning communities in which they will teach. In addition, as program developers and instructors, we hold ourselves accountable for modelling inclusive and globally conscious behaviours. In doing so, we ensure that the cultural proficiency model of Lindsey, Robins, and Terrell is embedded in our teaching and learning environment as well as in the course content. For example, when students return from their field experiences, they are asked to report their findings. In the debriefing sessions, they are challenged to think about the cultural proficiency model and to discuss what they have witnessed in terms of the school's place along the continuum and how students and faculty treat each other in terms of developing relationships. We also make a point of discussing the impact of diversity in terms of our Child and Adolescent Development and Communication and Conflict Resolution courses, which are also required program components. We want our students to see that difference does not make individuals the Other or "lesser than." Philosopher Martin Buber (1965) put it this way: "The life of dialogue reaches its height when we are able to 'make present' the other as just that other that he is. We are able to think, imagine, and feel how the other is thinking, imagining, and feeling. We do this neither by projecting our own feelings onto the other nor by remaining detached but by being open to that which is taking place in the person before us" (quoted in Witherell and Noddings 1991, 149).

Lindsey, Robins, and Terrell add to this ideal by insisting that effective schools and classrooms must move along the model's continuum so as to become increasingly proficient. Their model begins with what the authors deem "cultural destructiveness," and moves to the ideal that we should all strive for in schools: cultural proficiency. The first three points along the continuum are, in fact, dangerous places to be if we have any hope of overcoming stereotyping and barriers to cultural proficiency. "Cultural destructiveness" is thus the attempt to eliminate other peoples' cultures – the Holocaust and other genocides are clear examples of such acts of destruction. The second point is "cultural incapacity," where there exists a strong belief that one's own culture is superior to others; consequently, behaviours manifest themselves that disempower the cultures of others. For example, the view that "Third World" countries are "lesser than" other countries denigrates the lives of the people who live in those cultures, while the belief that certain cultures are superior in intelligence because they have reached a world level of power assumes that might is right. "Cultural blindness" occurs when people act as if the cultural differences they see do not matter – or when they fail to recognize differences. People who propose that they do not see colour are, in essence, "culturally blind" because they choose not to acknowledge that difference exists and that diversity should be embraced.

In all of these areas on the continuum, people are reduced to the Other, and there is a danger of perpetuating the marginalization of certain groups. Lindsey, Robins, and Terrell explain that institutions, if they are to make a greater, positive difference, need to become aware of where they are on the continuum so that they can consciously move past those three points to others along the continuum.

In addition to building on Banks (1994) and Lindsey, Robins, and Terrell (1999), our students also learn about global values through the Tribes Learning Process (Gibbs 2006). This process is widely used in schools around the world in an effort to build community and inclusion for all students. Tribes provides teachers a framework for teaching and learning that is grounded in theories of child and adolescent development, multiple intelligences, brain-compatible learning, cooperative learning, resiliency, equity and diversity, and communication and conflict resolution. Through this process, teachers are given a variety of tactics, skills, and strategies that enable them to build classrooms and schools that will meet the needs of all students. Gibbs, a highly respected American educator, explains: "If we are to succeed as a nation ..., we need to use the diverse cultural laboratory of our own country as a training ground for producing citizens who value differences, respect the validity of our own perspectives, understand the independence of people, and who have the interpersonal skills to effectively communicate across all spectra of ethnicity, language, culture, gender, values, and even political ideology" (2006, 22). To be sure, this is an American ideology that attempts to be universal in scope, but the view is still helpful to us. Gibbs goes on to state: "from all sides of the globe people recognize that survival now depends upon our capacity for cooperation, interdependence, conservation, and respect for a diversity of people and nations" (24). The Tribes Process can also be taken out of its US framework, and partly also out of this nationalist context, and applied in our classrooms. It emphasizes a more wide-ranging synthesis of concepts, agreements, and strategies woven into a new pattern of interaction to create caring environments for human growth and learning (3).

Our program and courses are grounded in the inclusive process of Tribes as students learn about global issues of equity and diversity. We begin by teaching CTEP students about understanding and practising four community agreements that Gibbs outlines: mutual respect, attentive listening, appreciation/no putdowns, and the right to participate/right to pass (2006, 9). There is nothing new in these concepts, but we have found that, together, they form an effective teaching philosophy. The agreements reinforce the learning environment as a safe place where all students are appreciated and their thoughts, ideas, and opinions are welcomed and heard. In their first year of study in CTEP, students are continually reminded of these agreements, which are posted in our classrooms and discussed throughout the year; the agreements are then reinforced throughout all the years of the program by every education instructor. As they progress in the program, students become adept at using the agreements during class time, and at using them with their own students in turn when they go to their field placements.

7.6   Distinctive Components of the Course

As CTEP educators we choose to be very transparent about our methods as we model the use of strategies such as cooperative learning and give students the "how and why" of the process. We are keenly aware from our experience that this transparency is critical to enable our students to learn to use these tools with their own diverse populations once they are teaching in schools (see Bennett and Rolheiser 1999).

There are also frequent class discussions about the ways in which future teachers can embed the elements of equity and diversity in their own content teaching. For example, cooperative learning strategies give students opportunities to work in small groups to talk with one other and to rehearse their ideas and opinions before presenting them to the larger group. Graphic organizers help students who are English-language or visual learners to have the same advantage as others. Small-group-inclusion activities allow students to get to know one other on a more intimate level, rather than being just a single person in a sea of strangers. From the perspective of teacher educators, the focus on inclusion for our students is an important way to help them understand how to break down barriers in the classroom. This strategy of inclusiveness has demonstrated that classes can be safe places where students feel free to share their thoughts, opinions, and ideas without fear of being put down.

In the first few weeks of our EDE course, we often see students struggle with the issues that are addressed and the content that is taught – especially since the vast majority are in their late teens or very early twenties. We present them with scenarios that many have not witnessed or might have avoided in their young lives. Stories of homophobia, racism, and poverty in schools are shared to enable these future teachers to recognize that these experiences exist and that they will have to address them in their careers. Some students actually have confided that they believed these situations happen only on television or in movies.

Other students make a point of sharing that their religion or culture has strong beliefs about certain issues, such as the role of women or homosexuality. These students are very clear about their strict adherence to such beliefs, and adamant that they cannot change their way of thinking. We nonetheless push their boundaries by discussing subject matter that disputes their belief systems. Let there be no misunderstanding, though: this can get messy. Educators love to talk about ideals and to quote from the literature that nicely compartmentalizes learning stages, but in honouring other people's views we face challenges to our own and to those embedded in our course design. Life never fits into boxes, and core beliefs take years to change, if at all. What do we do in class, for example, with a young Catholic student who, in good faith, insists that gay sex and abortion are evil? Or a young Hindu who considers himself superior to others because of his caste? Longstanding religious beliefs, in particular, by their very nature invariably stand in tension with twenty-first-century Canadian realities. When these sorts of worldviews emerge in the classroom, and when the teachers themselves are unsure about their own beliefs and ethical principles, what happens is often unpredictable – as it is for international internships, which typically generate learning that rarely fits tidily into the boxes prescribed by the literature and the course plan.

Stereotyping is another discussion topic that helps students become aware of self and the Other. In our first class we ask students to list the stereotypes they have used or heard. They find it very easy to recount things such as "all Asians are good at math but they cannot drive"; "poor people will never amount to much"; "Pakistani people smell of curry"; and "Muslims are the reason for terrorism." After a brief discussion we explain that we are about to embark on an educational journey that requires them to question, critically engage, and, we hope, eliminate these sorts of stereotypes so that their minds can become more culturally proficient.

We reinforce the four community agreements, and we hold a "funeral for stereotypes" so that students can participate fully without the discrimination associated with the closed-mindedness of such terms. The "funeral for stereotypes" is a group brainstorming activity in which students list all the stereotypes they know, then share their lists with the class. The number of stereotypes is often astounding, both to us and to the students. Many of them also say they truly believed people were "just joking" when they said such things. But as their student colleagues give first-hand accounts of how these words have affected them, there is a palpable change of tone in the classroom: stillness when people share their stories, and the beginning of self-reflection. After this class discussion, participants sign a contract promising they will "bury" the stereotypes, then bring their lists up to the front to be shredded.

Through readings, guest speakers, and simulations, students are presented with a wide range of information, thoughts, opinions, and ideas about topics from around the world. Our work with these teacher candidates over the years has made us appreciate that our equity and diversity work with them is only just beginning, and that our own ideas and presuppositions are also constantly in need of refinement.

Perhaps our greatest challenge in delivering this course is the field experience. We know from research and practice that a field experience is highly beneficial and warranted. We ask our students to seek out placements that challenge their belief systems and to work with marginalized persons – to step outside their comfort zone and look into places they have never been or of which they have little or no experience. We give them ideas and community connections with partners that include shelters for the homeless or abused women, food banks, mental health and new immigrant agencies, HIV/AIDS clinics, and cultural and religious centres. Many take up these challenges, but some remain reluctant to take on the risks and challenges inherent in these types of placement, preferring to go to safe, familiar places such as community centres and schools.

As part of the assignment for this course, students are asked to reflect on their experiences, from which we know that more work needs to be done with our candidates. Some students write such comments as: "I don't think I need to see how poor people live"; "I can't go to that place because I am scared"; "I don't understand why we have to learn about 'white privilege' because blacks have a lot of privilege now, too." Seeing, hearing, and participating do not necessarily lead to understanding. We know that we need to encourage our students to spend a lot more time in a wider range of contexts to understand varying global perspectives. We want them to go abroad and learn in challenging situations. And we want them to participate in activities that allow them to understand the importance of social action and the need for global transformation.

As instructors we are also concerned that our teacher candidates eventually be placed fully prepared to appreciate the diversity of the students they will teach. Moreover, we agree with Noam Chomsky, who urges us to become "agents of history so as to make this world less discriminatory, more democratic, less dehumanizing, and more just" (2000, 12). Yet we are not always sure how to do this as educators, despite all our planning and experience. Yes, we read our Freire, but it nevertheless continues to be difficult to trust that our graduates will have the wisdom, and know how to gain more, to become even more active participants in changing their societies.

Our field experience is designed to help our students move away from levels of blindness and pre-competence by respectfully easing them into "cultural competence" and "cultural proficiency," so that they can see and understand the diverse perspectives that exist in our schools. Unfortunately, twenty hours in a placement in their own communities is not nearly enough time to develop a deep understanding of the global village and all the issues inherent in equity and diversity. Many students find it a chore to get to the placement. They see it merely as a course requirement, and do not want to vest their time and energy in the proposed learning outcomes, preferring to do "it" to get "it" done. Although we understand the nature of this attitude, much of which is based on the stress and tight schedules that university students face, it is disappointing to us as teacher educators. Given the importance we attach to the course, we need to find ways to help students become more aware and competent in making their classrooms equitable. Currently, because of time restrictions, academic scheduling, and the framework of the program, we cannot increase the number of hours allotted to the course. We are also severely restricted by a lack of resources to go above and beyond the bare bones of running the program. At the same time, we see both the need and the desire on the part of some students to extend their learning and understanding in this area; we thus have to be creative in providing as many opportunities as we can.

One way we are attempting to meet this need is by scheduling courses to enable students to plan their field experience better and, possibly, to spend a term or the summer abroad; at one time, the challenges of our program all but prevented students from taking on a longer placement. We also encourage students to complete their internships abroad so that they have some international experience – although the purpose of such internships does not cohere fully with our course, since students are required to gain experience primarily in their anchor subject area. Moreover, the opportunities for exploring issues of equity and diversity are somewhat limited in internships where the focus is on math, chemistry, French, and psychology. We agree with Marx and Moss (2011), who argue that study abroad programs are an innovative way to promote teachers' intercultural development by providing them opportunities to confront their ethnocentric worldviews and begin to consider cultural influences and differences in ways that enable them to grow and to increase their appreciation of others, but we continue to question how best to do that in the context of concurrent education programming.

7.7   Conclusion

If students in CTEP had opportunities for international teaching internships, they could enhance their understanding and perspective of global issues that would serve them well in the increasingly diverse classrooms in which they will teach. To get to that point, however, a number of challenges would have to be addressed, including institutional will, human and financial resources to support the teacher education program, and student financial assistance. Nonetheless, we believe such opportunities would make a significant contribution to the student learning experience. We agree with Beck and Kosnik when they say that, "apart from resources, hiring, reward structures, and the like, less tangible factors are also important such as moral support and the valuing of teaching and teacher education" (2006, 115). In this case, Beck and Kosnik are referring to the need for strong administrative understanding of such a program and its needs, and for support that allows the program to grow so that it reflects more fully its mission and values.

In short, challenges continue to exist in teaching the Concurrent Teacher Education Program, but we are more convinced than ever of its importance, and we are heartened by the tremendous growth we have seen in so many of our students, who regularly share stories of their own experiences and help to bring a human face to the discussions. In the process of sharing, it becomes clear that the issues we discuss in the course are real for them and are happening in the here and now. As instructors we undertake ongoing assessment of our students' understanding of global issues, of our organization's culture, and of our own individual understanding of how best to meet students' needs. In addition, we pay attention to the dynamics of difference within CTEP.

At times we have had to rethink our plan when we became aware of biases that previously were not apparent to us. For example, we initially required students to travel to the Ontario Institute for Studies in Education in downtown Toronto for a program orientation. When we noticed that a lot of the young Muslim women were absent, we probed to find out why and realized that their parents would not allow them to make such a trek unaccompanied by a family member or an appropriate adult. There we were, teaching others about cultural sensitivity while overlooking a basic cultural assumption of our own. Thus, we are constantly adapting our own values and behaviours by reflecting on CTEP policies and practices. Taking an "inside-out approach" (Hunt 1987) to these reflections requires us to look at all aspects of the program, including the effects of the course on ourselves and our students. At the core is a greater sensitivity to others. Lisa Delpit (1995) says that listening requires not only open eyes and ears, but open hearts and minds. We see primarily through our beliefs, so for dialogue to work effectively it must start with an openness to other people's beliefs.

For us the Equity and Diversity in Education course extends far beyond the walls of the university and our teaching requirements. We view our role as agents of change, and we believe that offering this course to teacher candidates begins to foster the change necessary to make a difference in the world.

REFERENCES

Banks, J.A. 1994. *Multiethnic Education: Theory and Practice*. Boston: Allyn & Bacon.

Beck, C., and C. Kosnik. 2006. *Innovations in Teacher Education: A Social Constructivist Approach*. Albany: State University of New York Press.

Bennett, B., and C. Rolheiser. 1999. *Beyond Monet: The Artful Science of Instructional Integration*. Toronto: Bookation.

Buber, M. 1965. *The Knowledge of Man*. New York: Harper & Row.

Chomsky, N. 2000. *Chomsky on MisEducation*, ed. by D. Macedo. New York: Rowman and Littlefield.

Delpit, L. 1995. *Other People's Children: Cultural Conflict in the Classroom*. New York: New Press.

Derry, S.J. 1999. "A Fish Called Peer Learning: Searching for Common Themes." In *Cognitive Perspectives on Peer Learning*, ed. A.M. O'Donnell and A. King. Mahwah, NJ: Lawrence Erlbaum.

Gibbs, J. 2006. *Reaching All by Creating Tribes Learning Communities*. Windsor, CA: CenterSource Systems.

Hunt, D. 1987. "Beginning with Ourselves." In *Practice, Theory and Human Affairs*. Cambridge, MA: Brookline.

Lindsey, R.B., K.N. Robins, and R.D. Terrell. 1999. *Cultural Proficiency: A Manual for School Leaders*. Thousand Oaks, CA: Corwin.

McMahon, M. 1997. "Social Constructivism and the World Wide Web – A Paradigm for Learning." Paper presented at the ASCILITE conference, Perth, Australia, December.

Marx, H., and D.M. Moss. 2011. "Please Mind the Culture Gap: Intercultural Development during a Teacher Education Study Abroad Program." *Journal of Teacher Education* 62 (1): 35–47.

Nieto, S. 2004. *Affirming Diversity: The Sociopolitical Context of Multicultural Education*. New York: Longman.

Ontario College of Teachers. 2006a. *Ethical Standards of Practice for the Teaching Profession*. Toronto: Queen's Printer, Ontario Ministry of Education.

Ontario College of Teachers. 2006b. *Standards of Practice for the Teaching Profession*. Toronto: Queen's Printer, Ontario Ministry of Education.

Vygotsky, L. 1978. *Mind in Society: The Development of Higher Psychological Processes*. Cambridge, MA: Harvard University Press.

Witherell, C., and N. Noddings. 1991. *Stories Lives Tell: Narrative and Dialogue in Education*. New York: Teachers College Press.

8 More than the Money: Creating Opportunities for Students to Consider Their Responsibility for Global Citizenship in Their Local Internship Experiences

TRACEY BOWEN

8.1 Introduction

It has always been my assumption that one of my primary duties as an educator is to create opportunities for my students to question what they see, read, hear, and do in the world, and to experiment within different contexts. I assume that these opportunities help students grow emotionally and intellectually, engage with others in a respectful manner, and see themselves as responsible and contributing citizens. I also expect that, to the degree I am successful, students will consider more possibilities as they embark on their life journey beyond the university. Such reflection, as Maxine Greene (1995) suggests, can lead students to approach the stories of others with respect, empathy, and a will to make the world a better place for all.

Students, however, can have different priorities. Many of the fourth-year students I teach, who are nearing the completion of their undergraduate degrees, are focused intently on the next real-life step of getting a challenging, full-time, well-paying job. Students in professional programs and in the communications and technology disciplines are anxious to enter the market and apply their recently developed skills, test their worth in dollars and cents, and join like-minded professionals. Before graduating, some of these students try on professional persona through work-based learning programs and internships, often hoping thereby to gain a competitive advantage in the large pool of their graduating peers.

In this context, which includes a climate of intense competition and economic fluctuation, how do we as educators ensure that our students are graduating with the characteristics we profess to be teaching – in my case with the kinds of "creative, ethical, and intellectual" capacities to which my university is explicitly committed – and that we are facilitating a sense of social responsibility and accountability to "the broader community," along with quantifiable academic skills and marketable attributes? How do we help students understand their role as members of a variety of communities, some of whose goals might be contradictory but in all cases implicate them in issues and concerns much larger than their individual goals? Hands-on learning experiences can provide students the kinds of intercultural, team-based collaborative interactions and opportunities that help them develop as active global citizens. That said, their ever-present, overriding goal is to secure a well-paying job in what they increasingly see as a global workforce.

This chapter emerges out of the tension between the more holistic, longer-term goals of educators like me and the (equally valid) more practical, individually focused goals of the students I encounter. I explore the ways in which situated learning environments such as internships can foster in students broader concerns, and help them develop as responsible participants in the many diverse communities they will encounter.

After situating the discussion, I focus on data that have emerged out of a self-study, or classroom assessment technique, that I have prepared on a course I teach: the fourth-year Communications, Culture and Information Technology (CCIT) internship at the University of Toronto, Mississauga.[1] This course creates opportunities for students to debate, define, and rewrite their understanding of global citizenship and "community" in relation to the contexts they negotiate locally. I examine how students recognize the implications of their contributions to their local internship organizations, and the dynamics and tensions involved in how the various communities to which they belong coexist and, in some cases, compete. My objective in opening up this dialogue in my teaching is to help students explore their responsibility and accountability to others, and to identify actions that have a local dimension, whether in conjunction with their profession, their industry, their work culture, or their various communities. My challenge is to generate this sort of learning in the context of preparing students for for-profit, industry-based internships.

One prominent question that frames the study is how defining the terms "community," "responsibility," "accountability," and "reciprocity" becomes part of the process of understanding how we position ourselves in relation to others and what it means to be a global citizen. The theoretical framework for the exploration consists of a set of lenses that include situated learning (Gee, Hull, and Lankshear 1996; Lave

1996; Wenger 1998), social capital building within professional sectors (Brown, Flick, and Williamson 2005), Gee's (2000) perspective on communities of practice, and Karlberg's (2008) position on global citizenship, discourse, and identity construction.

I am particularly struck by the usefulness of Karlberg's emphasis on social justice – by which is meant respecting the rights and responsibilities of oneself and others – including his definition of global citizenship as "a way of thinking and talking about our global relationship to others, about our place in the world, about our perceived interests and, most fundamentally, about our identities" (2008, 311). It is through the students' connection between professionalism and identity construction that I see a place for this discussion within a local context. Karlberg suggests that "identity constructs lie at the core of human perception, motivation, and action" (311). Although the CCIT students do not travel abroad for this internship course, they are working within an international community of students, many of whom (possibly including themselves) are first-generation Canadians, immigrants, or international students who will return to their home countries after they graduate. Developing a responsible, imaginative professional persona is a priority for many internship students. It is also an opportunity for educators like me to nurture in them a sense of global citizenship.

In this chapter, I present one model for explicitly connecting awareness of the global village – with all its moral, social, cultural, political, and economic diversity and complexity – with the local contexts that students negotiate. Eldridge and Smith (Chapter 7, in this volume) also address the need to develop students' global awareness within local contexts as an important aspect of professionalism in teacher education. As with the CCIT internship self-study, their work with students at the same institution where I teach also serves the objective of better understanding how to help students achieve their personal and professional goals, develop autonomy, and become "effective agents of change; and creative, ethical, and intellectual forces in the broader community," as outlined by the goals of the university in its Undergraduate Degree Level Expectations policy (University of Toronto 2008, 4).

8.2   Situating the Discussion and Defining a Position

What does becoming a global citizen mean to the near-graduate who dreams of innovative projects and becoming a successful professional? Is such a "citizen" a transnational business professional who is environmentally aware and sensitive (and sometimes responsive) to the effects of global commerce, or someone who thinks globally and acts locally, or someone who understands the social, economic, and affective implications of participating as a member of various communities, knowing their responsibility to act for the "greater good," or perhaps someone who is electronically connected with "friends" around the world via e-mail, cell phone, and Twitter? I rely on Oxfam's description of a global citizen "as someone who: is aware of the wider world and has a sense of their own role as a world citizen; respects and values diversity; has an understanding of how the world works economically, politically, socially, culturally, technologically and environmentally; is outraged by social injustice; participates in and contributes to the community at a range of levels from local to global; is willing to act to make the world a more sustainable place; takes responsibility for their actions."[2]

My thinking on this issue also relates to Norah McRae's study of the connections between cultural intelligence and employability (Chapter 6, in this volume). She, too, acknowledges the importance students place on acquiring the right combination of skills to secure a "good" job. McRae uses the work of Earley and Ang (2003) to define cultural intelligence as the capacity "to work effectively within culturally diverse environments," a competency that students can develop through local experiences in diverse centres. I use the connection between cultural intelligence, diverse settings, and marketable skill sets as a way to explore global citizenship through awareness, practice, and reflection as crucial components for developing a professional identity in an era of best practices and cultural interconnectivity.

The model I propose for developing the concept of global citizenship in the internship course curriculum focuses on the identification by students of the possible global implications of how they live, work, and interact with others. I ask them to engage in a "critical re-appraisal" (Karlberg 2008, 311) of their negotiating, problem-solving, and decision-making strategies, and to explore their responsibilities and accountability to their workplace organizations, the communities in which they live, and the broader global village of which they are part.

Wrestling with definitions in a way that does not universalize values and beliefs or exclude voices – marginal, "developing," or otherwise – is not an easy task for students who are looking for the "right" answers or a simple frame in which they can position themselves. Wrestling with words and concepts that affect our relationships to bodies and lives, I have found, is one way to become comfortable with ambiguity and uncomfortable situations. CCIT internship students use local experiences in diverse workplaces – a form of situated learning – to test their cultural intelligence and develop global awareness and, in doing so, continue to construct their professional identity, a part of which, I hope, is a sense of global citizenship. Before saying more about the course with which I have been involved, let me turn to some of the supporting literature and with broad brushstrokes suggest how it is relevant to my teaching responsibilities and intentions.

8.3   Using a Social Learning Lens

Gee, Hull, and Lankshear use the relationship between situated learning concepts and the "new work order" to explore a socio-cultural approach to learning, literacy, and the mostly capitalist-based work world into which students will graduate and with which they must learn to negotiate. The authors contend that it is not enough to prepare students to understand their particular social and cultural settings; they must also understand the work world in which they will participate (1996, 4). If some form of global citizenry is part of the students' future focus, that is all the more reason for them to learn what impact these work worlds have on other social and cultural communities, both locally and globally, and how their participation as workers has consequences and effects beyond profitability and industry sector development (6–7). Students, the authors argue, need to develop a global awareness of their responsibilities and how they are accountable to others, known and unknown, including how their work affects what others do.

Brown, Flick, and Williamson (2005), for their part, suggest that, in many cases, disciplinary knowledge construction and skills building are unfortunately addressed as entities separate from social responsibility and accountability in the teaching-learning equation. Their research with engineering students links collaborative learning and collective problem solving with the building of social capital, which can lead individuals to think about the collective whole in their society and to consider the contribution of their work to the greater good.

Social capital is generally understood as community resources that can support an individual, or the people and communities on which one can count for help in, for example, getting a job or getting out of trouble. Social capital is not money in the bank, but at times it can be more valuable than that sort of capital.[3] Terry Hyland has much to say about this in his 1996 article, "Professionalism, Ethics and Work-Based Learning." He notes that students build different degrees and types of social capital in their various learning communities, whether disciplinary based or self-selected peer groups. Learning communities are social networks students often experience through group projects, team-building assignments, and active peer-to-peer discussions.

Focusing on the ways in which social networks function in communities to achieve communal goals is the foundation for developing an awareness of civic responsibility and collective engagement beyond the academy. Students need to recognize, Hyland argues, that they are part of a "learning society" where everyone participates and contributes towards a "collective intelligence" that serves a broader social network (1996, 177). At the University of Toronto, Mississauga, many of the learning communities that students encounter are already multicultural and diverse, providing cultural challenges and opportunities. There are, however, few opportunities for students to articulate these challenges, including their own personal stories, as part of their learning about the world and becoming global citizens. Students, I feel, need to recognize the "cultural intelligence" (see McRae, Chapter 6, in this volume) they are acquiring and how that knowledge can help them further develop as global citizens.

A practical way to reinforce Hyland's suggestion to develop a socially situated sense of responsibility and accountability and to understand the effect of knowledge application is through an internship that positions the student in a context that offers "the challenge of discovering and aligning the goals of multiple players," who might include academic advisors, placement supervisors, co-workers, community advocates, industry lobbyists, and upper management (Reeders 2000, 210).

What happens when these goals do not align? Aligning the goals of all the parties with respect to a given issue or problem is a complex exercise that might not have a clear resolution. Ambiguity is one way to challenge students' thinking and provoke a critical reappraisal of their view of the world, particularly in terms of their ethical and moral positions. Research certainly indicates that students need the time and space to reflect on these questions as part of their process of defining who they are as global citizens while they explore what it means to exercise agency and their will to act.

8.4   The Accountability Inherent in Collaborative Learning and Community Participation

Inculcating a sense of global responsibility and socially situated attitudes and ethics in a private sector internship requires an understanding of how collaborative learning creates a culture of knowledge sharing and common goal formation that results in particular kinds of communities of practice. These communities rely on the acquisition of social capital that, as David Coleman suggests, is "embodied in the relationships among people who trust one another" (quoted in Brown, Flick, and Williamson 2005, S3D-10). Students typically learn about work cultures through participation in particular contexts where they experience a variety of rituals, processes, and negotiations that affect how and where the learning takes place. Learning in this way is not just about the application of theory and skills in a practical setting, but also about how the setting affects the learning process through the ways in which skills and knowledge are applied and understood as assimilating positively in the given context (Lave 1996, 150). Learning through "enculturation" to various communities of practice – a term coined by Etienne Wenger to describe learning as "social participation ... a more encompassing process of being active participants in the practices of social communities and constructing identities in relation to those communities" (1998, 4) – also requires the individual's ability and agency to translate knowledge sharing effectively from one community to another, and to develop trust in the community members who are collaborators in this process.

Contrary to the individualistic, competitive model perpetuated by academic institutions and to subject-specific mastery, a model that privileges collectivism emphasizes socially situated communities of practice in organizations.[4] Many tenets of academic learning, such as competitive scores, sole authorship of coursework, and individual competition for grades, reinforce the culture of individual success over group recognition. Although such a culture is necessary for building disciplinary knowledge and developing academic integrity, it does not easily privilege collective knowledge sharing, unrestricted collaboration, or responsibility to the group before the individual. The consequences of student coursework fall to the individual student. As Howard contends, "the dilemma here is that the nature of the traditional classroom encourages individual responsibility rather than social responsibility" (1998, 24).

Interaction and participation across different communities of practice enable students not only to understand their accountability to others, but also to experience the effect of what it means to be a member of a larger, diverse group. New understanding of the nature of collaborative problem solving and first-hand experience of the challenges that arise helps students prepare for and commit to the diverse communities they encounter (both local and global). Understanding in this context is developed through working with groups that comprise the communities of practice.

8.5   Knowledge Sharing, Communal Responsibility, and the Potential for Reciprocity in the New Work Order

Not surprisingly, given what I have been saying, learning about reciprocity and ethics through industry-based work experiences requires a connected way of knowing that is grounded in a philosophy of moral education. Saltmarsh contends that students need to experience "meeting the other in a moral relationship, forming the foundations of a connected and engaged citizenry" (1997, 82). Decision making in a moral context presents more challenges than simply finding the best technical answer to a problem. Students must consider the consequences of the various solutions they propose, and understand the values and assumptions inherent in those solutions.

The by-product of increased global connectivity is a growing sense of being implicated in these connecting issues – knowing that we are all involved in much larger projects than ourselves. This is why the adjective "global" is increasingly added to words such as "world" and "citizen." Gee uses the term "distributed systems" to describe networks of connections and relationships (2000, 44), and maintains that "knowledge is not first and foremost either in heads, discrete individuals or books but in networks and relationships" (54). Relationships that develop from new connections require reciprocal activity or participation of some kind.

Gee uses Lave's theories on communities of practice, which are premised on the perspective that "learning is not best judged by a change in minds, which is the traditional school measure, but by 'changing participation in changing practices'" (Lave 1996, 161). Learning "must be reconsidered as a social, collective, rather than an individual psychological, phenomenon" (149). Students, according to this way of thinking, must learn to experience reciprocity by participating in and contributing to their social situations in ways that facilitate change for added value.

These experiences come, as Gee and others contend, through collaborations and team-based work activity.[5] Knowledge is constructed through connecting with others, and reciprocity becomes possible through publicly sharing knowledge that leads to common goals and endeavours that benefit the community. Individual investment in the group is part of the responsibility and is certainly required for any reciprocal activity. If today's students are to meet the global challenges, not only in terms of the new work order but also as humans who share this planet, they must think collectively, not individually (see also Homer-Dixon 2000). As Karlberg laments, "as long as we continue to understand the world in terms of 'us' and 'them,' whatever the categories are, we will be unable to overcome our narrowly perceived self-interests and work together to create a peaceful, just and sustainable future together" (2008, 313).

The problem is that traditional university learning tends to focus on the individual, which is contrary to the type of progressive pedagogy I have just described. Let me turn now to my own course, and to what I have tried to do to marry the individual to the collective.

8.6   One Course Can Make a Difference

Learning in the academic context engages students in a process of seeking, receiving, and interpreting information with the intention of constructing knowledge, testing, and retesting the knowledge gained through critical analysis of subjects in distinct disciplinary categories, then appropriating the knowledge in ways that affect the individual's worldview – or, as Gee suggests, "changes minds" (2000, 51). The focus of this academic learning process, as I have argued, typically does not privilege the form of connected knowing and cultural intelligence required for participation in communities of practice, where knowledge construction develops through connections and interactions with diverse others, mutual accountability, and understanding the role of reciprocity for adding value to the community and the larger social world.

I have tried to make this difference in the university course I teach. As the first step to introducing the concept of global citizenship, my CCIT internship students were asked to read Karlberg's work on discourse, global citizenship, and identity construction as a point of departure for class discussion. The class activity that is part of the process of having students reflect critically on their own learning was developed using a social learning lens based on the creation and exchange of social capital in communities of practice in regards to specific work worlds.

Figure 8.1. Personal Positioning Diagram

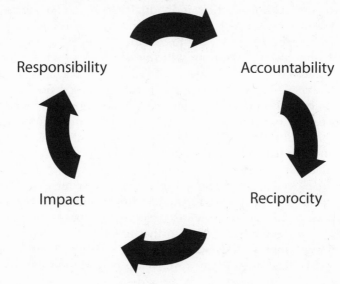

The Personal Positioning Diagram illustrated in Figure 8.1 reflects the competencies and expectations for graduates of my course. The composition of the diagram is informed by the ideology of social justice in relation to global thinking and the discourse of identity construction that Karlberg outlines, as well as the need for cultural awareness in terms of McRae's concept of cultural intelligence (Chapter 6, in this volume). The diagram provides a tangible format that students can use to define global citizenship through a process of articulating their beliefs and positioning themselves in relation to their practical internship context. It highlights students' capacity for social responsibility and accountability, their understanding of reciprocity, and their ability to recognize and predict the impact of workplace contributions both inside and outside the organization. Further, the diagram has helped me to reframe the pedagogical assumptions and strategies that I use to challenge students throughout their internship experiences, partly by asking students: "what is it like to have a certain experience?" and "how do those experiences affect others both known and unknown?" (Van Manen 1982, 296).

Although the CCIT internship courses typically use reflective writing (learning journals) as a way for students to process and deconstruct their experiences, this type of activity still privileges students' inward reflection and reinforces their individualistic identity construction. Many students focus on developing a professional identity in their organization or industry, but fail to consider their role as community members and citizens. Working with the diagram presents students with a different way of reflecting on the values and beliefs that underline their experiences and our class discussion based on Karlberg's work. Using the Personal Positioning Diagram as a vehicle for reflection and review of prior journal writing provides impetus for further discussion about global citizenship. It also offers a site where students can conduct a critical reappraisal of their decision making and problem solving in local industry-based internships.

Introducing global citizenship into the internship course curriculum, I have found, creates openings for students to question their beliefs and their actions as they analyse their experiences. Karlberg's reading provides the impetus for debate and further reflection and action, while raising the question of how we can become global citizens at home. The diagram illustrates a way to develop new responsibilities that become evident from practising a "wide-awakeness" to the world (Greene 1995), and for predicting and understanding the effect of actions and decisions developed through knowledge sharing, group responsibility, and reciprocity.

Through the exercise of positioning (reflecting and recording) their beliefs, values, actions, and goals around the various quadrants of the diagram, students begin to recognize that the *impact* is not always immediate, although it is sometimes predictable, and that it potentially carries further implications for the community and its members in the long term. Students also discuss the difference between making a contribution or impact and becoming an imposition to others in the short term.

Further to issues of imposition that are often a concern when students enter a community in which they expect to gain experience, the Personal Positioning Diagram is predicated on a philosophy of connected knowing, rather than a separate, disciplinary expertise form of knowing. Connected knowing requires students to understand how knowledge is constructed with others, and how it is affected by as well as how it affects others, both inside and outside the community where it is situated. I constantly nudge students to consider to whom they are accountable, what they must bring to the "community table," and what accountability involves, not just today but also in the future.

Reciprocity relies on an individual's ability to listen to the stories of others, reflect on those stories, and act in collaboration with others to make a situation better for those affected. Students must "be able to think 'critiquely' about issues of power and justice," not just critique systems for gaps or inefficiencies. Thinking "critiquely," Gee contends, means that students understand and critique systems of power where they might be implicated in any imbalance (2000, 63). Thinking "critiquely" requires participation, empathy, and investment to do something about the imbalance.

8.7   The Personal Positioning Diagram as a Site Where Students Reappraise Their Beliefs and Actions

The Personal Positioning Diagram, simple as it is, provides an effective site where students can question their position in their various communities and develop the values, attitudes, and active participation that could foster a sense of global citizenship in their everyday actions. Not all students use it to full advantage – nor do I. How do we as educators practically facilitate the components labelled on the diagram through an internship course curriculum? How do we assess students' progress in terms of community responsibility, their level of accountability, their capacity for reciprocity, and, possibly the most difficult of all, the impact of their work, when that impact is not evident in the framework of an academic term?

These are the challenges inherent in "counternormative pedagogies" that do not fit neatly in traditional academic schema (Howard 1998, 24). I propose, however, that reappraising the internship curriculum is a place to start by engaging students in discussion, asking them to reflect using multiple modes of communication and to speak about their opportunities to engage as citizens. What I have observed, in the internship course I teach, the reflective writing I have analysed through a recent study on students' capacity for professionalism and autonomy (Bowen 2011), and how I have used these data along with the research cited in this chapter, is that industry best practices and the professional, active citizen relationship in the CCIT internship course support the need to continue these discussions and to consider global citizenship as a component of professional, social, and intellectual development.

Reflection in action through the course's required use of journal writing gives students a process for understanding problems and situations, a way to understand responsibility and accountability, and a means to consider their role in the new community of practice they have entered through their internship. I firmly believe that students need to learn how to ask questions to understand the situation, and to listen to all the responses, instead of looking for a single "right" answer. The reflective journal-writing practice helps prepare students to participate in class discussion and to chart their beliefs and proposed actions on the Personal Positioning Diagram. Reflective writing prompts students to ask questions about how to engage in dialogue with others, how to participate ethically as a member of the community, and how to identify the impact of what they intend to leave behind, thereby facilitating their "ability to reflect on the endeavor as a whole system, not just their part in it" (Gee 2000, 53).[6]

Accountability is also evidenced in the supervisor evaluations of the students' ability to work within a team and to contribute positively, responsibly, and professionally in their internship placement communities. As previously stated, the communities in which students participate as interns have multiple partners with a diversity of interests, which implicates students in terms of how they are accountable and to whom. Students are continually encouraged to think about the audience or target groups that will be the benefactors of their work when they are making decisions, in contrast to thinking about the usual audience of the one who grades their academic assignments.

Reflecting on this process raises challenging questions when the student sees a misalignment of values between themselves, the placement organization, and the identified benefactors. The learning journals are a site where students can work through this tension and sometimes wrestle with the discomfort of ambiguity or unresolved problems. The inability to resolve tensions runs counter to the "find the right answer" mindset with which students are accustomed to achieve success in their courses. My view is that students need to *become comfortable with the uncomfortable* in terms of ideas and values that clash and collide, when working in diverse contexts that incorporate multiple cultures and ideologies.

The Personal Positioning Diagram further challenges students first to define their understanding of *accountability, responsibility,* and *reciprocity,* and then to reflect on how they position themselves in relation to those definitions and the class discussion regarding those terms. Their recorded reflections and positions become a declaration of their commitment to these aspects of professionalism. My students typically use declarations such as "I must be accurate" in how I complete my work and represent others, "I must provide quality work," and "I must make sure my actions and my work reflect the values" of the organization – and in some cases, other co-workers, placement supervisors, and even "the public" to position themselves on the diagram.

Although the course goal is to inspire students to think and act as good global citizens, actual outcomes depend on numerous factors, including the student's aspirations of attaining that objective. Similarly, as the person preparing and leading this course, I continually need to reflect on my own approach in the programming. One area at least that needs much more attention, to reframe the pedagogical assumptions of what the for-profit, industry-based internship can teach students, is reciprocity between my students and me. Brown and Campione (1994, 232) look at reciprocal activities within the classroom, beginning with the teacher-student power relationship. In a reciprocal teaching context, the role of teacher and learner shifts so knowledge is both shared and distributed. This again is counter-normative in that expertise does not lie within any one person or authority; rather, it is distributed across a variety of "teachers" who include, for example, community members, co-workers, clients, and the students themselves.

The learning dynamic in the community is based on giving and sharing: "students and teachers each have 'ownership' of certain forms of expertise, but no one has it all. Responsible members of the community share the expertise they have or take responsibility for finding out about needed knowledge" (Brown and Campione 1994, 234). I am still working on deconstructing the usual classroom learning and power dynamics between teacher and student, especially when I encounter students who are strongly oriented towards getting a high-paying job and find broad discussions about "good global citizenship" distracting at best and puerile at worst.

How do students transfer this distributed way of knowledge sharing from classroom context to other communities of practice and to the larger social world? What are some practical applications to facilitate collaborative and distributed ways of constructing knowledge in the classroom that give students the tools to share and reciprocate the knowledge they are receiving at their placement? Let me offer some examples from my 2009–10 cohort.

Some students claimed that listening is a reciprocal gesture that helped them gain respect from their colleagues; without respect, reciprocity has less impact. Some students admitted during the class discussion that they are often not very good listeners and want to impart their knowledge before they understand what is needed in the situation. In the end they were convinced by others that being a good listener would help them gain respect, and only after gaining respect could they create an impact through reciprocity or other actions.

Students eagerly discussed how to identify, propose, and carry out new initiatives in a sustainable fashion that reduces the imposition of their ideas upon the organization or community. They reflected on how to contribute ideas supported by action in ways that have potential benefits for continued growth and strengthening of that community, while providing them with strategies for action. Students came to realize that not only must they listen to identify needs in the community, but they also must explore possible solutions collaboratively from an ethical and "wide-awake" position. They began to confirm that they needed to overcome the urge to find the "right" answer and always look for recognition as an individual. Through interaction and collective problem solving (including seeking out information from all partners involved), students realized that they could learn through experience that "diverse individual skills and cultures are recruited as resources for the community, not as identities that transcend the community of practice itself" (Gee 2000, 54). As Gee contends, "people are made to display and share their knowledge publicly for the benefit of the group and, in fact, the system as a whole" (52).

The effects of students' contributions in the internship organization or community can be perceived as both potential and actual. Leaving something behind that is sustainable and has the potential to grow may be their initial goal, yet students recognized that this *impact* is not necessarily immediate – it might have multiple effects whose implications and consequences might not be evident in the organization but remain important to the broader community. Students at first do not recognize the impact stemming from individual contributions; rather, they tend to consider that it arises from collective activity. The *impact* stage of the Personal Positioning Diagram refers to students' capacity for what Biggs and Collis call the Extended Abstract Stage[7] of cognitive development. As I note elsewhere, this means their ability to "[transfer] knowledge from their lived experiences to possible future contexts across industry sectors," thereby also learning to predict future challenges for their community and beyond. "[I]nternship experiences become a rehearsal for future encounters and the reflective journal writing is a site for reviewing and rethinking decisions with consistency and accountability in mind. It is at this level of learning that students begin to understand best practices within an industry context and how they are accountable to those standards" (Bowen 2011, 474).

The onus is on instructors. We need to confirm whether we are teaching students a particular set of values or teaching them to be conscious of the values they hold and how those values affect their thinking, actions, and decision making. Students and educators also need to interrogate their assumptions about what it means to be a professional, a citizen, and a global citizen, how we all act on those assumptions, and whom those actions affect. The classroom discussions, I have found, only begin to address these issues. My students still have difficulty thinking about communities beyond their familiar local organizations, and I continue to struggle with who is teaching whom, and how, in the classroom.

8.8   Moving Forward: Developing Global Responsibility at Home

According to Gee, my role as instructor or leader of the CCIT internship course is to "help [students] turn their tacit knowledge into explicit knowledge to be used to further develop that community of practice, while realizing ... only knowledge that can be extracted from situated socio-technical practices can be spread and used outside the original community of practice" (2000, 54). I am convinced that instructors can open up possibilities for the development of good global citizens through dialogue about ethical issues and community impact, and by understanding the organizational values students help to perpetuate through their industry-based work. Students looking to climb corporate ladders need to recognize that life-long learning, service, and reciprocity will help them build communities locally that could affect the world globally – that is, they can be as financially successful as they had hoped while still taking into account broader global concerns.

One broad question I wanted to explore through the process of writing this chapter was, what are we doing for students who do not travel to far-off places to help them become global citizens at home? I am increasingly convinced of the value of basing pedagogical assumptions and strategies on a model that highlights responsibility, accountability, and reciprocity as necessary competencies for learning. Students need to understand who they are in relation to others; they also need to reflect on their position of privilege and to recognize the implications of how they take up the responsibilities of this position. They must have the capacity, confidence, and commitment to take risks, and to ask what they can do to make this world a better place for all.

The results of developing a global backdrop to the Communications, Culture and Information Technologies internship course and of providing a different model for reflecting on responsibility, accountability, and reciprocity have been encouraging. But they are only a small start. *Declaring* our responsibilities and accountabilities to others is not enough. As educators we must continue to teach students across disciplines how to trust, how to cooperate, how to listen, how to question their own motives, and how to leave an imprint through collaboration and reciprocity, rather than through imposition. And we must continue to study and interrogate effective ways of meeting and measuring these goals.

NOTES

1 This curriculum development exercise did not require an ethics review from my institution, and no personal details or student work are included in this chapter.
2 The quote is from the Oxfam Web site at http://www.oxfam.org.uk/ education/global-citizenship/what-is-global-citizenship.
3 There is much literature that deals with social capital, including some that is critical of the loose use of this notion; see, for example, Fine (2010).
4 Gee (2000) believes that the new work order, including the people within it, is based on the formation of communities of practice.
5 Among those who support Gee's claims regarding the relationship between reciprocity and team-based work are Lave (1996); Pratt and Pratt (2010); Saltmarsh (1997); and Wenger (1998).
6 Some types of questions (based on Ash, Clayton, and Moses 2009) used as prompts for structured reflective writing include: What did I do? What did others do? What actions did I or they take? What were the consequences of these actions? What assumptions or expectations did I bring to the situation and to what extent did they prove true? What assumptions did others bring to the situation – how do I know that? How did I handle my emotional reactions – would I react differently next time? How did I judge the situation and what evidence did I use? How did this situation challenge or reinforce my values, beliefs, convictions, my sense of right and wrong, my priorities, and my judgments?
7 Biggs and Collis's SOLO (Structure of the Observed Learning Outcome) taxonomy is informed by Piagetian stages of development, but extends the various theories developed by Piaget, Bloom, and others to focus on

structured learning outcomes and the quality of learning through an evaluation of the organization and structure of thought; see Biggs and Collis (1982, xi).

REFERENCES

Ash, S.L., P.H. Clayton, and M.G. Moses. 2009. "Teaching and Learning through Critical Reflection." Under development and presented at a Faculty Summer Institute, University of Toronto, May.

Biggs, J.B., and K.F. Collis. 1982. *Evaluating the Quality of Learning: The SOLO Taxonomy (Structure of the Observed Learning Outcome)*. New York: Academic Press.

Bowen, T. 2011. "Examining Undergraduate Student Learning Journals for Indicators of Developing Autonomy and Professional Capacity in an Internship Course." *Higher Education Research & Development* 30 (4): 463–75.

Brown, A.L., and J.C. Campione. 1994. "Guided Discovery in a Community of Learners." In *Classroom Lessons: Integrating Cognitive Theory and Classroom Practice*, ed. K. McGilly. Cambridge. MA: MIT Press.

Brown, S., L. Flick, and K. Williamson. 2005. "Social Capital in Engineering Education." Paper presented at the 35th ASEE/IEEE Frontiers in Education conference, Indianapolis 19–22 October.

Earley, P.C., and S. Ang. 2003. *Cultural Intelligence: Individual Interactions Across Cultures*. Stanford, CA: Stanford University Press.

Fine, B. 2010. *Theories of Social Capital: Researchers Behaving Badly*. London; New York: Pluto.

Gee, J.P. 2000. "New People in New Worlds, Networks, the New Capitalism and Schools." In *Multiliteracies, Literacy Learning and the Design of Social Futures*, ed. B. Cope and M. Kalantzis. New York: Routledge.

Gee, J.P., G. Hull, and C. Lankshear. 1996. *The New Work Order: Behind the Language of the New Capitalism*. Boulder, CO: Westview Press.

Greene, M. 1995. *Releasing the Imagination*. San Francisco: Jossey-Bass.

Homer-Dixon, T. 2000. *The Ingenuity Gap*. New York: Alfred A. Knopf.

Howard, J.P.F. 1998. "Academic Service Learning: A Counter-normative Pedagogy." *New Directions for Teaching and Learning* 73: 21–9.

Hyland, T. 1996. "Professionalism, Ethics and Work-Based Learning." *British Journal of Educational Studies* 44 (2): 168–80.

Karlberg, M. 2008. "Discourse, Identity and Global Citizenship." *Peace Review: A Journal of Social Justice* 20 (3): 310–20.

Lave, J. 1996. "Teaching, as Learning, in Practice." *Mind, Culture, and Activity* 3 (3): 149–64.

Pratt, C., and J.C. Pratt. 2010. "New Generations of Global Entrepreneurs: Global Citizenship through Work Integrated Learning in the New Economy." *Journal of Cooperative Education and Internships* 42: 1–8.

Reeders, E. 2000. "Scholarly Practice in Work-based Learning: Fitting the Glass Slipper." *Higher Education Research & Development* 19 (2): 205–20.

Saltmarsh, J. 1997. "Ethics, Reflection, Purpose, and Compassion: Community Service Learning." *New Directions for Student Services* 77: 81–93.

University of Toronto. 2008. "Undergraduate Degree Expectations." Available online at http://www.utm.utoronto.ca/dean/sites/files/dean/public/shared/pdfs/dle.oct08.pdf; accessed 1 June 2011.

Van Manen, M. 1982. "Phenomenological Pedagogy." *Curriculum Inquiry* 12 (3): 283–99.

Wenger, E. 1998. *Communities of Practice*. Cambridge: Cambridge University Press.

9 Relating across Difference: A Case Study in Transformative Learning

DAVID PEACOCK

9.1 Introduction

This chapter examines the process of "transformative learning" for the 2008 cohort of the St Thomas More College–Intercordia Canada (STM/IC) international community service learning (ICSL) program. My primary data come from the eight students who were part of that cohort when I was their program coordinator. The data later became the heart of my Master's thesis (Peacock 2009), which was approved by the Research Ethics Office of the University of Saskatchewan. Here, I focus on three of the eight participants, and outline the critical elements of their experiences that were conducive to their transformative learning. To be sure, my sample size is too small from which to draw generalized conclusions, but the quality of information I received from these students and their colleagues, coupled with the accompanying literature and follow-up conversations I had with other educators, supports the value of reflecting at length here about these students' comments. I chose to highlight the experiences of these three participants because together they provide a range of experiences that best enables an analysis of the conditions that both did and did not lead to transformative learning. This case study suggests that transformative learning occurs through the dynamics of vulnerability, a discovery of persisting differences in interpersonal relationships, and an experience of welcome and hospitality in the host environment.

In contrast to other studies that focus on the enhanced capacities, skills, and subsequent employability of participants through international education, transformative learning for these students required a relinquishing of securities, a disorientation and critical interrogation of the self, and enhanced receptivity to the newly recognized Other. Moreover, consistent with the critical-humanistic educational philosophy shared in different ways by the participants of the STM/IC program, this study suggests that ICSL can contribute most responsibly to good global citizenship through the construction of relationships of solidarity across difference.

9.2   Background

The STM/IC is a partnership between a Catholic liberal arts college – St Thomas More College, at the University of Saskatchewan – and Intercordia Canada, a small, Toronto-based non-profit organization that partners with Canadian colleges and universities to enable undergraduate students to live and work with, and learn from, marginalized peoples throughout the world. Established by Jean Vanier, the founder of L'Arche, an international network of "people with developmental disabilities and those who come to share life and daytime activities in family-like settings" (L'Arche 2013), Intercordia Canada can be seen as an extension of L'Arche's model of interpersonal encounter with the Other. Intercordia Canada also partners with small, non-governmental organizations or placement agencies throughout the world. The eight STM students in my research study who used the services of Intercordia Canada lived with host families and worked in communities in Ecuador, Ukraine, Bosnia and Herzegovina, Ghana, and Nicaragua from May through August 2008. Although this chapter most closely deals with the experiences of the three students I will call Steve, Haley, and Sarah, several other students were involved. The responsibilities of all eight students included assisting at medical clinics and in agricultural work, teaching in primary and high schools, working with children in orphanages and with persons with disabilities, and teaching English at a summer camp.

As participants in the STM/IC program, students complete two, one-term sociology classes, the first prior to their departure abroad and the second remotely while the students are abroad. Taught by a sociology professor whose research interests include food security, the nature and effects of globalization, global solidarity, and social justice, participants study "the impact of globalization on human development (education, health, income), human rights and democracy, and issues of social equity (inequality and poverty)"; participants are also educated in "the processes by which the Global South has been constructed as 'Other' by the Global North" (McLaughlin 2007, 2). The participants complete academic work (journals and academic reflections) in the field and a major essay upon their arrival back home. In my capacity as STM/IC program coordinator in 2008, I facilitated this process and accompanied some of the students to Ecuador.

9.3   Transformative Learning and a Global Consciousness

Jack Mezirow, an adult educational theorist, defines "transformative learning" and its synonym for him, perspective transformation, as "the process of becoming critically aware of how and why our presuppositions have come to constrain the way we perceive, understand and feel about our world; of reformulating these assumptions to permit a more inclusive, discriminating, permeable and integrative perspective; and of making decisions or otherwise acting on these new understandings. *More inclusive, discriminating, permeable and integrative perspectives are superior perspectives* that adults choose if they can because they are motivated to understand the meaning of their experience" (2000, 14; emphasis in original). I interpret Mezirow's definition as tracing the movement from unreflexive assumptions and practices to a more critical consciousness in which perspectives and practices are seen as historically and culturally contingent – and also, I would add, more open to encounters with difference.

Transformative learning requires a critical analysis of how our assumptions shape what we know and experience. The transformative learning process is more likely to occur when these assumptions are challenged, such as in the presence of the Other, whose differences provoke in us new interpretive and ethical horizons and draw us to consider new interpretive frameworks for understanding. Furthermore, the presence of a mentoring community of support and the opportunity for various forms of committed social action facilitate the transformation (Parks Daloz 2000, 113).

Richard Kiely's (2002, 2004, 2005)[1] longitudinal study builds on Mezirow's theory by conceptualizing both the forms and processes of transformative learning within an ICSL context. In his case study of a three-week ICSL program in Nicaragua, Kiely found that, after they returned home, his students spoke of their "emerging global consciousness" (2002, 152). Kiely identifies three stages in their development: a heightened concern for social justice, a "dynamic shift" in how they saw themselves as agents in the world, and a "chameleon complex," or the longer-term challenges they face in making their lifestyle accord with their new sense of self (2004, 9–10).

To describe how his students experienced transformative learning Kiely effectively recasts Mezirow's ten-phase, transformative learning process through five movements: contextual border crossing, dissonance, personalizing the experience, processing it, and connecting with others (2005, 8). I will say more about these later, but let me note here that contextual border crossing involves the students' "repositioning" that Kiely describes as "a cognitive, affective, and behavioral shift – across physical, personal, social, cultural, political, economic, and historically constructed borders" (2002, 57). Mezirow's "disorienting dilemma" (2000, 22), the crucial and often unsettling trigger for perspective transformation, becomes for Kiely an encounter with "high-intensity dissonance" (2005, 11). Individuals who respond to this high-intensity dissonance through critical reflection and acts of care and solidarity, he argues, can experience transformative learning in ICSL education.

In this chapter I ask, did these STM/IC participants experience transformative learning according to Kiely's model, and did the particularities of the STM/IC program have any impact upon their transformative learning?[2] My study followed the students over a six-month period and identified signs of transformative learning from May 2008 through November 2008 by employing a qualitative, interpretivist-hermeneutical research methodology (see Gadamer 1989; Ödman 2007; Schwandt 2000). Of course, transformative learning is not simply an outcome; it is a process that unfolds over time, even years after the participants' re-entry to their country of origin. As such, I identify the early stages of transformative learning processes and forms.

I conducted semi-structured interviews with participants at three points in time: pre-departure, in the field (with the Ecuadorian participants), and in final interviews in November 2008, two months after the participants' return to Canada. Pre-departure interviews were conducted to assess basic demographic data and to gain insight into the "contextual baggage" (Kiely 2005) participants brought to ICSL, as well as basic opinions, feelings, beliefs, motivation, knowledge, and behaviours within the six "transforming forms" Kiely (2004) identifies as the political, moral, intellectual, cultural, personal, and spiritual. In the post-experience interview, I focused the interpretive lens upon changes in participants' opinions, feelings, beliefs, motivations, knowledge, behaviours, and intentions. I also collected data through participant observation and document analysis of program materials, course outlines, and student academic writings and reflections. I did not inform the participants directly about Kiely's theory of transformative learning, but instead asked more general questions stemming from Kiely's categories that were designed to elicit their interpretations of their experiences abroad.

The case study offers a new approach to evaluating and refining Kiely's theory. Recognizing the pronounced power imbalances between Canadian undergraduate students, their host universities and colleges, and the communities with which they typically engage if they are learning or volunteering in regions of the developing world, the study also suggests that global citizenship is most responsibly developed through the construction of relationships of solidarity across difference.

9.4   Data Analysis

I have already touched on some of Kiely's reflections about the transformative learning process. He has more to say on the topic. Kiely establishes six forms within his participants' transformative learning that emerged as a result of their international service experiences. He defines these as: 1) *the political* – an expanded sense of social responsibility and citizenship that is both global and local; 2) *the moral* – developing a relationship of mutual respect and care, and sense of solidarity; 3) *the intellectual* – a questioning of the origins and nature of, and solutions to, social problems; 4) *the cultural* – a rethinking of dominant US cultural and social values, norms, and rituals and a questioning of US global hegemony; 5) *the personal* – rethinking their previous self-concept, lifestyle, relationships, and career; and 6) *the spiritual* – a movement towards a deeper (un)conscious understanding of self, society, and the greater good (Kiely 2004, 11).

I employed Kiely's transforming forms to code my data.[3] Furthermore, I employed Kiely's (2005) processes of transformative learning (contextual border crossing, dissonance, personalizing, processing, and connecting – noted above and elaborated below) within an ICSL context to code and group texts from each participant. Finally, I inductively developed codes of the particularities of STM/IC program experiences, such as witnessing suffering and impoverishment, the socio-economic status of the host family, welcome and acceptance by the host community, and participants' experiences of vulnerability and insecurity.[4]

9.5   Three Student Experiences: Hayley, Sarah, and Steve

Hayley's international experience took place at the Faith and Light community of persons with intellectual disabilities in Lviv, Ukraine.

When she entered the STM/IC program, Hayley was a twenty-year-old sociology student aiming towards a social work degree and career. Her motivations for entering the program were to "get out of [her] comfort zone" and "for probably the first time in [her] life do something on [her] own," away from her family. Hayley has Ukrainian heritage from her father, grew up in a mid-sized urban Saskatchewan community, and has a history of volunteering in that community. She looked forward to working as a counsellor with at-risk teenagers.

After her experience abroad, Hayley noted in her journal that Ukraine and its people taught her about "World War II, communism, poverty, corruption, Russian exchange rates, the language, gardening, cooking, and the Ukrainian traditions." Her experiences at the Faith and Light community left her with the sense that the greatest way to foster solidarity with the people of Ukraine was to help fund education programs dedicated to the rights of persons with disabilities.

The transformative learning Hayley experienced is apparent when it comes to the moral and personal domains. Although Kiely distinguishes the moral and personal forms of transformative learning – the former being related to new modes of solidarity with marginalized peoples and the latter encompassing self-identity shifts, increasing self-confidence, and more socially oriented academic and career trajectories – for Hayley these two forms of transformation are intertwined. What brings them together is the profound experience of "friendship." She writes:

> I did not know that eight intellectually disabled adults working in a small workshop in Lviv, Ukraine, would be able to have such an impact upon me and change my perspective of myself ... I met caring, intelligent, and talented people in Ukraine who soon became my friends, teachers and role models. I entered Ukraine assuming I was going to be the teacher and the helper to intellectually disabled adults. As foolish as it may sound, I never thought I would learn much from them. I could not have been more wrong. These intellectually disabled adults, my friends, taught me more than I could ever imagine. Unknowingly, my friends taught me life-long lessons that I hope never to forget. They taught me about compassion, patience, and friendship. My friends taught me to love others as well as myself, with all my flaws and talents. Finally, they taught me to simply live for right now, in this moment, and enjoy it.

Hayley's perspectives shifted as a result of a newly discovered mutuality and a questioning of her prior assumptions. Through being invited into mutual relationships of care in the Faith and Light community, her self-identity and sense of purpose moved from "teacher and helper" to "friend and learner." Looking ahead, she does not know exactly what job she will take as a social worker or with whom she will work, but she has found through her experience in Ukraine that she is "happy working with marginalized people," and is convinced "that's what I need to do with my life." Since her return to Canada, Hayley has also sought part-time work at a sexual assault centre and as a counsellor at a summer camp. For Hayley the transformative learning is apparent not so much in a shift to a different career, but in a renewed solidarity with others based upon the recognition and practice of mutual learning, instead of what might be called an authoritarian approach that served to preserve the distance between her and those she wanted to help.

Sarah entered the program as a nineteen-year-old student completing a three-year biochemistry degree with the hope of entering a medical program. She describes her family as "upper-middle class," Catholic, and professional. She had previously travelled to Mexico, Japan, and the United States. She describes her political views before her experience in Ecuador as "to the left" of those of her family. Sarah had experience as a volunteer in the pediatrics wing of a Saskatoon hospital, and saw the STM/IC program as a way to experience something "a little less sheltered" than her day-to-day life.

In Ecuador, Intercordia Canada partners with the Fundación Reto Internacional, which works with local communities to "facilitate sociocultural processes in which the participants learn (a) to develop a critical conscience, as well as an understanding and respect for other cultures, and (b) that respect unites us all and makes us responsible for the realities of and solutions to the currently existing problems in the world" (FRI 2006). Sarah lived with a host family in the town of Cayambe in the central highlands, and she worked at a medical clinic serving the town and surrounding areas.

For Sarah, transformative learning in the intellectual domain began even before she left Canada, during the sociology class she completed before departure. This course emphasizes the structural determinants of global poverty and the participants' own privileged social location, and helped Sarah develop a critical awareness of how her own privilege in some way contributed to the marginalization of the poor. Kiely notes that the intellectual form of transformation is epistemological, causing participants in ICSL contexts to re-evaluate the origin and construction of knowledge, the value of service as charity, and the cause of and solution to social problems (2002, 255). Sarah described this realization to

me in her pre-departure interview: "I just felt ... how much my decisions affect those people, [it] was quite disturbing ... I said the roses
thing, and how roses and chocolate and coffee and everything, dia-
monds, everything that's romantic and luxurious for us comes at the
expense sometimes of the life of people down there – people in the
global South."[5] As with other participants, Sarah's original desire to
"help" or "serve" was problematized through a critical examination of
her own assumptions about people in less developed regions of the
world, her own privilege, and the often exploitative economic relations
linking her life with theirs.

Once in Ecuador, Sarah's intimacy with her host mother formed
another context for a critique of her own assumptions about who exer-
cises public leadership. In an academic reflection completed while
abroad, Sarah writes:

> The one aspect of the social situation of my host family that surprised me
> the most is how much of a leader my host mother is within the commu-
> nity ... My host mother holds weekly community meetings, where about
> 30 people gather and discuss community agricultural issues and initia-
> tives, and arrange trading. She sets up numerous plastic chairs all around
> the main room of the house and holds these meetings which she said are
> "about half business and half fun conversation." She can barely read or
> write. Anytime she needs to write something she dictates to the daughter,
> who writes the letter for her. When she receives a letter or something writ-
> ten she also asks the daughter to read it to her.
>
> My host mother's leadership role surprised and impressed me. It shook
> my naïve impression of leaders as typically well-dressed, well-educated,
> often financially well-off, and often male. She has none of the above traits
> and yet provides a tremendous leadership role within her agricultural
> community. I am pleasantly surprised by the independence, work ethic,
> and leadership role of my host mother, and I feel very encouraged by her
> progress in the community.

Although Sarah had studied women's movements among the
Indigenous peoples of Ecuador before she arrived in her sociology
class, it was the personal relationship with her host family that enabled
her to understand how indigenous peoples can be authors and leaders
of their own development.

Yet participation in ICSL per se does not guarantee transformative learning. Of our eight participants that year, Steve stands out as

someone whose experience abroad was "enjoyable" and "affirming," but not transformative – at least as I might imagine it. Steve joined the program as a twenty-year-old English major with interests in drama and history. He had travelled before, to France and the Dominican Republic, and had experience as a tree planter in northern Canada. Steve was attracted to the STM/IC program because he had always wanted to do humanitarian work, but up to then had "never had a good feel for it" or "really made a connection with it."

Steve travelled to Estelí, in Nicaragua, a city of around 120,000 people in the northern highlands surrounded by forested mountains. Estelí was the site of the famous Frente Sandinista de Liberación Nacional resistance against the US-backed Contras. One of Intercordia's partners here is the Unión de Cooperativas Agropecuarias Miraflor, a union of small agricultural cooperatives whose members farm sustainably on the Miraflor Nature Reserve and run an eco-tourism program. Steve had two host families, one in Estelí, where he stayed on weekends connected with other participants, and the other on a farm in the Miraflor Reserve, where he lived during the week without electricity or vehicles. There Steve planted cabbages and tomatoes, helped build three houses, milked cows, and cared for the cattle that tilled the land. Steve's host family on the farm consisted of a mother and father, five children, and numerous grandchildren.

Steve writes that the experience at the Miraflor agricultural cooperative "exceeded all of my expectations. How welcoming the host families were, that was excellent too." Steve worked hard to acculturate himself to a self-sufficient, agricultural way of life in keeping with his host family and community, and because of this effort was accepted and respected by the local community as a real co-participant in their work. In my interview with him after his return to Canada, I asked if he felt that by living and working alongside the labourers he had earned their respect. He replied:

> I think it definitely did ... like there was just nothing I wouldn't try ... Also they asked me "do you play any sports" and I would be like "yeah I wrestled in university." Of course the first thing that comes to their minds is what they see on TV and I'm like, "No it's not quite that, but I do know how to throw a guy," and eventually it's like "well can you demonstrate on my little brother" and I'm like, "yeah why not, bring him over, he's not doing any work" (laughs). I remember he would be like a few times "we are gonna go to my grandma's." "Ok, what for?" "Oh just to say hi kinda

thing," and then we'd go and he would be like, "oh and he's a wrestler, so don't mess with him" (laughs).

From the community's perspective, Steve's ability to live simply and work hard distinguished him from some of the other international volunteers. Yet despite these positive encounters with the community, Steve's narrating of his experiences in journals, interviews, and academic writing do not suggest any transformative learning across the intellectual, moral, political, cultural, personal, or spiritual domains, at least as defined by Kiely (2004).

When Steve was asked explicitly in my final interview with him whether he felt he had changed through his Nicaraguan experience, he tells the following story:

> I remember there was a really funny conversation that came up at Thanksgiving dinner where [someone from his host family commented], "you have told me so many stories about how much you've seen and how much people have. Can you just do this without feeling guilt?" [by eating as much as Steve did at their Thanksgiving meal] and I'm like "Oh I really can." And they're just like "you can do that guilt free?" and I'm like "I sure can" (laughs). And yeah they [family] are just like "that [Intercordia program] hasn't changed you at all." And I'm like "no not at all." I mean it sounds bad but I just I haven't noticed that much change. Like I know a lot more facts, dates, information, I mean I know a lot more first-hand experience.

To learn more "facts, dates, and information" and to gain more "first-hand experience" of a phenomenon is a worthwhile goal, but it is not indicative per se of a transformational learning process. Of course, some people are transformed in ways that are not outwardly evident, or that take longer to appear, and Steve could be one of those. One thing is certain: his comments about change differ from those of the other two participants. Both Hayley and Sarah commented on transformative learning, particularly in the intellectual, moral, and personal domains. As "transforming forms," these experiences can act as ongoing stimuli for change across these domains of perspective transformation. What was different about Steve's experiences? A further analysis of the *processes* of transformative learning suggests some possibilities, and also partially explains why Hayley's and Sarah's experiences seem to have had more profound effects on them.

9.6   Transformative Learning Conditions for STM/IC Participants

The STM/IC program spans multiple geographic and socio-cultural contexts across the globe. Even when participants experienced life and work in the same vicinity, their host family experiences and work placements were sufficiently distinct to provoke diverse types of learning. The most significant programmatic differences between the STM/IC program and Kiely's original case study concern the role of critical reflection, followed by the length of the sojourn abroad, and the length of time the student participants spend with their hosts. These differences, which are part of the "contextual border-crossing" (Kiely 2002, 161–4; 2005, 9–10), seem to have affected the conditions for transformative learning by STM/IC participants.

The STM/IC program differs from Kiely's in that his had more scheduled group reflection activities through which participants could discuss and articulate their experiences in light of academic content, community presentations, and lectures. In the STM/IC program, in contrast, the theoretical learning was completed prior to departure. Critical reflection, bringing together prior academic learning with immediate experience, was conducted mostly in a solitary manner via journals and academic papers e-mailed to a professor in Saskatchewan. Local community leaders typically did not assist participants by speaking to their own understanding of the challenges of their regions. The effect on these programmatic differences seems to be less articulation of transformative learning from STM/IC participants in the political and cultural domains, or forms identified by Kiely. Although a couple of the eight STM/IC participants clearly framed their learning by acknowledging the wider socio-economic and political forces operating in their experiences abroad, most did not. Other research on community service learning and transformative learning suggests that more group reflection activities, dialogue, and public discussions generate more transformation for participants (Eyler and Giles 1999).

However, if STM/IC participants had fewer opportunities for critical reflection than those in Kiely's program, they also had more opportunities to construct relationships with their host families and the community. Kiely's participants spent three weeks abroad, but STM/IC participants lived and worked for three months in intimate quarters with a host family, immersed in community activity, and remained relatively independent of other program participants. This intensive immersion proved crucial to the perspective transformation of STM/

IC participants, who frequently articulated how their interpersonal relationships were the foundation of their subsequent questioning of assumptions and learning. In short, the programmatic features of the STM/IC can be seen to both inhibit (by providing fewer critical reflection opportunities) and enhance (by providing greater opportunities for interpersonal relationships) the conditions for transformative learning.

STM/IC and dissonance. The intensive immersion of participants' in their host culture also created conditions likely to evoke experiences of high-intensity dissonance, which, Kiely argues, is necessary for transformative learning to begin. Kiely also suggests that such dissonance needs to persist in duration and be able to leave a "permanent marker" in a participant's "frame of reference" (2005, 12). For STM/IC participants, dissonance most often happens when they encounter extreme poverty and suffering. In these instances, participants cannot rationalize the dissonance away through further reflection or service in the community. Instead, the experience provokes participants to re-examine their existing knowledge and assumptions regarding solutions to these "ill-structured" and "ambiguous problems" (11).

In my final interview with participants, I asked whether they were disturbed or shocked by anything they witnessed or experienced abroad, including persons living in poverty. Despite having experienced the dissonances of crossing linguistic, geographic, socio-economic, and other environmental boundaries, Steve (Nicaragua) did not experience the effects of poverty and suffering in an intimate and personal way, nor was he disturbed or shaken through his experiences abroad as other participants were. There was poverty, of course, in Estelí and environs, but Steve was not engaged in close relationships with persons living in these conditions. His host families' work did not involve them in interpersonal relationships with persons who were suffering deeply through poverty.[6] The other STM/IC participants, in contrast, experienced extreme forms of poverty and were left disturbed in some way by what they had encountered. Hayley experienced the poverty and stigmatization of many persons with intellectual disabilities; she also described being particularly affected by witnessing the hopelessness of the elderly lining up hoping to withdraw money from a Ukrainian bank long left empty by the Russian government.

STM/IC and personalizing. Highly intense, dissonant experiences in Kiely's model are expressed personally through feelings of "anger, shame, guilt, sadness, confusion, denial, and moral outrage" (2005, 12), and often lead to greater compassion and empathy. Sarah felt guilt, shame, anger, and confusion through her encounters at the medical clinic. She here describes a particularly difficult episode:

> In one instance, a 15 year old girl was brought into the ER by paramedics, unconscious and unresponsive to any stimuli due to extreme intoxication. She was three months pregnant with a baby she felt she could not care for, and consequently drank over 50 ounces of hard alcohol in an attempt to abort the pregnancy. I stood there waiting as the obstetrician performed an ultrasound to determine if the baby had survived this terrible binge. After a few minutes the heartbeat of the baby was found; it had survived. Unfortunately Hermana said that the damage to the baby would likely be quite substantial due to the severity of the mother's intoxication. The saddest part for me was realizing that this girl is only a child herself, her tiny pregnant belly peeking out of her "Blue's Clues" children's flannel pajamas.

After she returned to Canada, I asked Sarah how she felt about this incident with the young mother: "Ah sick ... I just felt sick when the baby was born. Like just I don't know if it's guilt or ... you just feel like almost pain for them so ... yeah physically I felt sick. And I think it's partially guilt although I never thought in my head ... oh my God this wouldn't happen in Canada, I was thinking oh my goodness this is happening here ... So I don't know if it was guilt already but just an awareness that was just hard to stomach, like I don't really know how to explain it."

STM/IC and processing and connecting. Sarah's description of "an awareness that was just hard to stomach" signals the start of the transformative learning that is possible through ICSL. In crossing contextual borders, experiencing intense dissonance, and encountering poverty and suffering, STM/IC participants are able to process analytically their experiences through written reflections and connecting with their host communities.

In her essay, prepared at the end of her time abroad, Sarah situates the following tragic story within its wider social context, and critically analyses the assumptions she had brought to the question of abortion:

> The majority of the poor population in Cayambe work in large greenhouses where the employers make the women take routine pregnancy tests and often fire women from work if they are pregnant, cutting the women off from the minimal financial income they rely on ... I just thought to

myself, "who am I to judge?!!" These were the situations that really made me open my eyes to see black and white issues as so much more complex than they are made to be. It was easy for me to judge abortion as morally wrong when I assumed that every girl has the same opportunities and support that are offered to me, but wow, are those women walking a very different mile than I ever have or ever will (or any priest ever will for that matter). Now I would not say that I disagree with my previous Pro-life stance as I believe that children and life are a blessing, but I believe that in issues such as this, tolerance and empathy are needed where too often we place blame and judgment.

This entry suggests that Sarah is now able to approach complicated social problems from a broadened social perspective that rejects simple solutions. Her moral reasoning shifts from abstract, *a priori* judgments to more contextual, nuanced distinctions sensitive to the life conditions of marginalized people.

Because STM/IC students live with host families and work in disadvantaged settings for a three-month period, developing relationships across difference while abroad becomes paramount not simply for their academic study but also for their general well-being. As a consequence, affective learning through relationships (Kiely's "connecting") becomes necessarily pronounced, and it is to those relationships that I now turn.

9.7   STM/IC: Constructing Relationships across Difference

Although the STM/IC participants' experience of transformative learning in their diverse ICSL contexts supports Kiely's model of transforming processes, distinct themes arise from their experiences. These include vulnerability, the discovery of persisting differences in interpersonal relationships, and the experience of radical acceptance. As well as contributing to Kiely's theory of the process of "connecting," these themes are particularly relevant to the "good global citizen" discourse, and suggest an alternative educational approach to a more functionalist emphasis upon skills development.

Vulnerabilty. I have already described how the STM/IC program requires participants to be thoroughly immersed in a web of new relationships. Through the Intercordia seminars and their pre-departure sociology class, participants prepare to encounter the radically Other, separated by language, socio-economic status, cultural differences, and geographical distance. Sarah describes how she prepared for such an encounter: "I knew before I left that I was making a choice to make myself vulnerable in a way. I was knowingly allowing myself to be exposed to things that I will not be able to forget, things that will change who I am and my views, and that was frightening!"

To encounter and learn from the Other, I argue, one must become vulnerable. One must allow oneself to be affected by what one senses and feels and thinks, and open oneself to difference. STM/IC participants approach their host families and communities without linguistic competence or in-depth knowledge about their hosts. They approach the Other humbly and openly, and effectively place themselves in the care of the "stranger" who houses, feeds, teaches, and protects them.

STM/IC participants have been influenced in these reflections by Jean Vanier's philosophy that genuine interpersonal encounter across difference begins from a position of weakness, not strength. In his book *Becoming Human* (2003), Vanier elaborates a humanistic anthropology infused with thirty years of experience working with persons with intellectual disabilities. He writes: "to be human is to be bonded together, each with our weaknesses and strengths, because we need each other. Weakness recognized, accepted and offered, is at the heart of belonging, and so is at the heart of communion with another" (40).

For STM/IC participants, not surprisingly perhaps, cross-cultural encounter is as much about a discovery of their own weakness and need for "belonging" and "community" as it is about service to the poor. By living and working in contexts in which the Other's "weakness" is apparent, participants are challenged to see the strengths of their hosts in the face of adversity. Furthermore, participants come to recognize not only their own weakness, psychologically or spiritually, but also the part they play within social systems that exacerbate marginalization.

Similarly, Canadian educational philosopher Sharon Todd (2003) argues that, to learn from the Other, one must assume a posture of nonviolent passivity and, through attentive listening, become vulnerable and susceptible to suffering. Learning, for Todd (following Levinas 1987),[7] arises not through knowledge about the Other, but through a relationship with the Other, who ultimately remains ontologically unknowable.

When STM/IC participants relinquish the securities of place, identity, status, and role, and are immersed in the strangeness of a new family and community and language, they more closely approximate Todd's attentive listening, and open themselves to the unpredictable that occurs in the presence of others. This personal vulnerability is at once both an expectation of the STM/IC program and a personal choice of the participants. It begins with extensive personal sharing in pre-departure seminars, and continues with prolonged immersion in a family and community where participants might not be able to anticipate or control the outcomes. It is a voluntary vulnerability, entered into freely by the participants' desire to encounter the unknown Other face-to-face.

The discovery of persisting difference. It would be naïve to think that STM/IC participants do not carry with them into their new relationships vestiges of their power and privilege. Their social location,[8] as they are informed through sociological theory before their departure, continues to structure their interpersonal relationships in their host communities. This is a necessary, and sometimes painful, realization for participants, who too easily and dishonestly might fall into identification with their new friends. The reminder of participants' own Otherness to the local community is a necessary step to reconfigure relationships across difference in social solidarity.

Sarah narrates how difficult this reminder can be.

Yeah that was a frustrating night ... My fourteen year old host sister invited me to go for pizza with her and her friend and I said "oh sure thank you." ... I went to my room and got ready and she popped her head back in and said, "Oh you'll pay ten dollars and we'll pay five." And it was five dollars difference – it wasn't a big deal, but I said "Why?" And she said, "Oh because you're rich." Like straight up, and I was insulted and I said, "Oh no thank-you, I would rather not go." And she said "Oh sorry, sorry, sorry" and I said "That's ok, I don't want to go." ... We hugged at the end of it and it was fine but it was just ... yeah it really rubbed me the wrong way. And then when I was writing my journal I was thinking, "But I am rich compared to them. I really, really am." That's not even a point for discussion. And like things they'd ask me, like "Do you have a car?" and I would say "Yeah." And then they would ask me "Well what kind of car does your dad drive?" and I would say "Oh a black one" [laughs] ... like try to avoid the issue. But the reality is we have four nice cars for four people, you know? And so time and time again it was like I'll try and pretend that I'm not rich but I am and they knew that – I knew that. It caused a barrier to becoming fully ... in their situation, fully like them. That's something you can't change but, yeah I would feel so much like I was a part of their family and a part of their culture and their reality because I did live quite humbly while I was there. Like I had one pair of pants and, you know, I made an effort because I was trying to live like them. And it was just like, "Oh geez I am so not." So that was good too.

When describing her life back home with her family in Canada, Sarah uses the words "accountability" and "responsibility" as ways of describing her new awareness: "My family is sort of seeing things differently and making changes just because they feel, through me, a bit of a connectedness and a bit of a responsibility so yeah ... accountability I guess. Like a sort of ... we could go through our lives living with our heads down or you could lift them up. But, I don't know, I think it is just that effort to make a connectedness and an awareness as best as we can."

The discovery of persisting difference, through an honest acknowledgement of the participant's more privileged social location, is a necessary step to forging a new solidarity. Moreover, as Sarah notes, this new solidarity is accompanied by a commitment to live responsibly back in Canada, which, for her and her family, begins with aligning consumption habits with fairer trade practices.

Once back in Canada, some of Sarah's first actions were to educate others, including some Saskatoon florists, about the exploitation of Ecuadorian floriculture workers and the alternative fair trade flower movement. The success of these political actions will depend upon collective consciousness-raising efforts, but Sarah's experience in Ecuador has resulted in an expanded global political consciousness for her.

Radical acceptance. A related dynamic in the transformative learning process is that, when participants become vulnerable in the face of the Other, an offer of acceptance becomes the gift of the Other in return. This experience of acceptance by host communities – the welcoming into homes, communities, and workplaces – can trigger transformative learning for STM/IC participants and new patterns of solidarity across difference.

Hayley articulates this process most succinctly through her experience of acceptance by the Faith and Light community members in Ukraine: "I found it strange how openly loving, affectionate, and accepting my friends were to me, a stranger ... I was able to discover how wonderful it feels to be on the receiving end of compassion and acceptance." This radical acceptance of Hayley, who did not possess the same skills or abilities as people in the Faith and Light community, began a process of personal liberation for her and a transformation within the personal domain: "From their acceptance I have come to understand that I should not be ashamed of my flaws. My flaws are a part of me just like my talents and my flaws and weaknesses have helped shape who I am today."

Acceptance, like vulnerability, is an experience that is both structurally designed at a programmatic level and personally felt by STM/IC participants. Host communities, through Intercordia Canada's international partner agencies, are involved in the construction of family stay experiences – finding appropriate families, resourcing them with money for the costs of providing food and general care, and finding suitable work placements where participants can make meaningful contributions to community-identified needs. This gift of acceptance arises from a community that hopes to share its wisdom and culture, while also teaching and challenging participants to understand both the joys and struggles of its members' lives.

Host communities and families understand when they are being respected, listened to, and approached sincerely. When that happens they respond with openness. STM/IC participants experienced this acceptance in intimate ways into the lives of their hosts as both an act of affirmation and a challenge. In a welcoming embrace, participants recognized their privilege vis-à-vis (literally, face-to-face) the Other in a new way, and were empowered to reconfigure their relationships in light of a new solidarity with and responsibility for others.

Steve's experience, however, demonstrates that acceptance by community partners alone does not guarantee transformative learning – participants' vulnerability and susceptibility to epistemological change are critical. Perhaps Steve failed to find a mentoring community soon after his experience that might have helped him to imagine local projects for social action and solidarity.[9] Alternatively, Steve might have quietly resisted the Intercordia narratives on vulnerability and transformation or the sociological theories used pedagogically to frame his experiences in Nicaragua.[10] Ultimately, there could be any number of reasons, both personal and programmatic, that individual participants do not interpret their experiences as transformational. Educators, however, have a responsibility to establish conditions most conducive to transformative learning, and to provide the balance of challenge and support most likely to encourage these learning processes.

9.8   Conclusion

During the period of this case study (May–November 2008), the experiences of STM/IC participants Sarah and Hayley, especially, were consistent with Kiely's model of the processes of transformative learning in an ICSL context. For them, perspective transformation occurred at least in part because of their experience of high-intensity dissonance, as a result of their personal encounters with poverty and suffering.

Although limited in scope, the case study supports research indicating that programmatic conditions in ICSL programs can affect the transformative learning experiences of participants. The unique characteristics of the STM/IC program have both facilitated and hindered transformative learning. Extended immersion in communities (both host families and workplaces) provided crucial opportunities for the construction of meaningful interpersonal relationships, and so expanded the potential for the affective and connected learning for STM/IC participants intrinsic to their transformative learning. The lack of opportunity for group reflection processes among participants while they were away might have made transformative learning more difficult for some participants, such as Steve. The dynamics of vulnerability, the discovery of persistent difference, and acceptance in the STM/IC program experience help to further elucidate how Kiely's process of connecting, or affective learning, can lead to transformative learning. As STM/IC participants discovered strengths in their host communities and shared in local struggles, they also became aware of their participation in systems that marginalize people, and were inspired to lead more responsible and accountable lives on returning home.[11]

Further empirical research of ICSL programs at the programmatic level might yield insights into how the transformative learning of participants is either helped or hindered by specific program features. For instance, research into the programmatic conditions that prove most conducive to supporting experiences of participants' vulnerability and receptivity to the hospitality of their hosts would help improve the experience for both groups.

This case study of an ICSL experience also has implications for pedagogies designed to develop "good global citizens." From a critical-humanistic perspective, the enormous differences of power and capital between Canadian ICSL programs and the communities that receive our students require our pedagogies to problematize our naïve desire to help. The process of ICSL must see our critical gaze turn away from those "people down there," to use Sarah's language, and back onto ourselves, including our own complicity in economic and cultural systems of exploitation. If ICSL experiences aim for this outcome, and inspire in participants a more critically informed sense of social justice alongside further opportunities for mentoring and engaged social action, then we will have gone some way to forming global citizens who can be said to be "good." If, however, our pedagogical aims are more aligned with the abstract development of capacities such as cross-cultural competency to enhance employability, then we run the serious risk of reproducing the economic and cultural exploitation of our international partners. In that case, we would be well advised to take Ivan Illich's (1968) advice and simply stay home! This case study suggests that pedagogies that focus instead on critical analysis of social location, and vulnerability and humility in the face of the Other, offer more life-affirming possibilities for participants and host communities alike.

NOTES

1 Kiely was the coordinator and instructor of a New York-based community college ICSL program from 1994 through 2001. Each January intersession (three weeks), the college offered a six-credit CSL program in Puerto Cabezas, Nicaragua. Kiely's original case study (2002) of the transformative learning of its participants was subsequently published in the *Michigan Journal of Community Service Learning* in 2004 (the transforming forms that changed) and 2005 (the transforming processes involved). Kiely's participants were mostly white, female, middle-class graduates of a nursing program and between eighteen and twenty years of age (2002, 96).

2 This case study is more limited in its scope than Kiely's original (2002) case study, which searched for transformative learning by its participants anywhere from a few months to seven years after they completed their international community service learning. Following Patton (2001) and Stake (2005), I devised a case study design and developed a "bound" case (Creswell 2007) based on the 2008 STM/IC program, during which eight students lived, worked, and learned in an ICSL context. The opportunity I had as program cocoordinator of the STM/IC to travel to Ecuador during the 2008 program for both quality assurance purposes and research enabled a profitable further purposive "within-case sampling" (Punch 2005) of the three Ecuadorian-placed students.

3 Although there might well be some cultural differences between students from New York (Kiely's program) and Saskatoon (the Intercordia program), the form of cultural hegemony to which Kiely's model refers remains relevant for Canadians. The unreflective assumptions and globally dominant values that often structure international service learning encounters between American students and peoples of the developing world are

not, it seems to me, qualitatively different than those of many Canadian students, given the imbrication of Canadians in the economic, political, and military structures of the United States. The cultural form and its transformation as articulated by Kiely remain relevant for Intercordia participants, even if they retain "Canadian values" articulated in opposition to US hegemony.

4 To ensure the credibility of my research and the "fit" between my interpretations and participants' own interpretations of the data, I followed the strategies of Guba and Lincoln (1989), including prolonged engagement, persistent observation, peer debriefing, negative case analysis, and member checks. For a more detailed account of my methodology and methods, see Peacock (2009).

5 The term global South is a contested term in development circles for a number of reasons, including the idea (evident in Sarah's remarks) that it perpetuates geographic, racial, and economic hegemony and infers cultural inferiority.

6 In part this was because of the agricultural nature of Steve's work, which saw him spend most of his time with family and relatives on the land or in their humble but self-sufficient accommodations. By Steve's standards, his host families were poor, but they were not regarded as such by the wider Estelí community or by themselves.

7 Todd, like Levinas, emphasizes the primacy of ethics over epistemology, and so seeks to unchain the Other in an educational setting from the controlling gaze of the knowing subject.

8 The term "social location" arises in the participants' preparatory sociology class. It originates in feminist intersectionality theory, which seeks to "locate" the social, cultural, economic, and political contexts of an individual through axes of social organization (Stasiulis 2005, 36–61). Collins (2000) also uses the term "matrix of domination" to refer to a system wherein race, class, and gender intersect at the level of personal experience, community, and social institution.

9 Parks Daloz (2000, 113) names both a mentoring community and opportunities for local social actions as key dimensions of the transformative learning experience.

10 Locklin (2010, 10–11) questions whether the normative commitments of Intercordia to personal transformation through Vanier's categories of "vulnerability" and "belonging" adequately describe the complexity and open-endedness of transformative learning.

11 I do not analyse here Kiely's "chameleon complex" (2005), describing the difficulty in living differently back home again.

REFERENCES

Collins, P. 2000. *Black Feminist Thought: Knowledge, Consciousness, and the Politics of Empowerment*, 2nd ed. New York: Routledge.

Creswell, J. 2007. *Qualitative Inquiry and Research Design: Choosing among Five Approaches*, 2nd ed. Thousand Oaks, CA: Sage.

Eyler, J., and D. Giles. 1999. *Where's the Learning in Service-learning?* San Francisco: Jossey Bass.

FRI (Fundación Reto Internacional). 2006. "Who Are We?" Available online at http://www.fundacionretointernacional.org.ec/who_EN.html; accessed 7 March 2011.

Gadamer, H.-G. 1989. *Truth and Method*, 2nd ed., trans. J. Weinsheimer and D.G. Marshall. New York: Crossroad.

Guba, E., and Y. Lincoln. 1989. *Fourth Generation Evaluation*. Newbury Park, CA: Sage.

Illich, I. 1968. "To Hell with Good Intentions." Available online at http://www.swaraj.org/illich_hell.htm; accessed 7 March 2010.

Kiely, R. 2002. "Toward an Expanded Conceptualization of Transformative Learning: A Case Study of International Service-learning in Nicaragua." PhD diss, Cornell University.

Kiely, R. 2004. "A Chameleon with a Complex: Searching for Transformation in International Service-Learning." *Michigan Journal of Community Service Learning* 10 (2): 5–20.

Kiely, R. 2005. "A Transformative Learning Model for Service-Learning: A Longitudinal Case Study." *Michigan Journal of Community Service Learning* 12 (1): 5–22.

L'Arche. 2013. "What Is L'Arche?" Available online at http://www.larche.ca/en/larche; accessed 11 March 2013.

Levinas, E. 1987. *Time and Other Additional Essays*, trans. R.A. Cohen. Pittsburgh: Duquesne University Press.

Locklin, R.B. 2010. "Weakness, Belonging, and the Intercordia Experience: The Logic and Limits of Dissonance as a Transformative Learning Tool." *Teaching Theology & Religion* 13 (1): 3–14.

McLaughlin, D. 2007. "Course Outline: Social Change and Global Solidarity." Saskatoon: University of Saskatchewan, St Thomas More College.

Mezirow, J. 2000. "Learning to Think Like an Adult: Core Concepts of Transformation Theory." In *Learning as Transformation*, ed. J. Mezirow and Associates. San Francisco: Jossey-Bass.

Ödman, P.-J. 2007. "Hermeneutics in Research Practice." In *The Principles of Knowledge Creation: Research Methods in Social Sciences*, ed. B. Gustavsson. Northampton, MA: Edward Elgar.

Parks Daloz, L.A. 2000. "Transformative Learning for the Common Good."
    In *Learning as Transformation*, ed. J. Mezirow and Associates. San Francisco:
    Jossey-Bass.
Patton, M.Q. 2001. *Qualitative Research and Evaluation Methods*. 3rd ed.
    Thousand Oaks, CA: Sage.
Peacock, D. 2009. "Transformative Learning via the Construction of
    Relationships across Difference: A Case Study of an International
    Community Service-Learning Experience." MEd thesis, University
    of Saskatchewan. Available online at http://hdl.handle.net/10388/
    etd-08312009-110030.
Punch, K. 2005. *Introduction to Social Research*. Thousand Oaks, CA: Sage.
Schwandt, T.A. 2000. "Three Epistemological Stances for Qualitative
    Inquiry: Interpretivism, Hermeneutics, and Social Constructionism." In
    The Handbook of Qualitative Research, ed. N.K. Denzin and Y.S. Lincoln.
    Thousand Oaks, CA: Sage.
Stake, R.E. 2005. "Qualitative Case Studies." In *The Handbook of Qualitative
    Research*, ed. N.K. Denzin and Y.S. Lincoln. Thousand Oaks, CA: Sage.
Stasiulis, D. 2005. "Feminist Intersectional Theorizing." In *Inequality in
    Canada: A Reader on the Intersections of Gender, Race and Class*, ed. V. Zawliski
    and C. Levine-Rasky. Don Mills, ON: Oxford University Press.
Todd, S. 2003. *Learning from the Other: Levinas, Psychoanalysis, and Ethical
    Possibilities in Education*. Albany: State University of New York Press.
Vanier, J. 2003. *Becoming Human*. Toronto: House of Anansi Press.

10 International Internships: Creating Conditions for Critical Dialogue

NADYA LADOUCEUR

10.1 Introduction

Growing numbers of educators in colleges and universities around the world share the conviction that establishing international internships can enrich students' learning experience and foster the development of good citizenship (Ramaley 2000). As such programs gain momentum and the number of interns increases, many voices raise concerns about the risks associated with internship programs, and argue for further consideration of the ethical implications and pedagogies associated with them (see, for example, Crabtree 2008; Epprecht 2004; Grusky 2000; Heron 2006; Kiely 2004; Sichel 2006; and Tiessen 2007).

As an internship program coordinator at a university college in Canada and former intern myself in Costa Rica and Nicaragua, I have witnessed first-hand how international internships can create both benefits and problems for students and the communities they join overseas. I have seen students become more culturally aware and civically responsible, but I have also seen some develop patronizing attitudes. In my view, however, the benefits outweigh the problems. Although I share Crabtree's feeling of being "intellectually and ideologically conflicted" about international service learning (2008, 19), I believe, like Tiessen, that "the risks of no cross-cultural communication," which she sees as "increased stereotyping, racism, lack of understanding, lack of respect for other cultures, etc." (quoted in Sichel 2006), are potentially more harmful.

Like many critical educators, I believe it is important for our students to shift focus from themselves to those with whom they come into contact, and to the relationships of power that produce social injustice. This awareness can give them a better understanding of the complex realities shaping their lives and the lives of others, and can help them perceive themselves as agents of progressive change once they come back from their internship. The internship experience can also help students develop a more inclusive practice based on a deeper appreciation of the assets and resources of the people and the communities with whom they work during their internship. The challenge they face during their time abroad is to appreciate the complexity of social issues such as poverty and discrimination that affect the communities they join, to recognize the strength of those communities, and to learn from and with them. The challenge I face is to prepare these students adequately for this demanding experience. Somehow, they need to develop a strong bond with their host communities in a short space of time. They need to see themselves not as charitable donors, but as partners and allies whose attitude and actions are guided by the belief that change is a collective effort that starts by recognizing everyone's humanity and agency.

The critical pedagogy of Paulo Freire has helped me meet these challenges. His theory concerning critical dialogue is especially relevant to our international internship program. This chapter discusses how critical pedagogy – specifically, Freire's work – is guiding my efforts to develop and teach the international internship course at the University of New Brunswick's Renaissance College.[1] I first present Freire's theory; I then introduce the institutional context in which it is applied. In the final section, I explore the challenges associated with establishing the conditions for dialogue, using data from informal discussions with students and alumni, students' exit surveys, and students' assignments. The first two challenges are related to the differences in power and privilege that exist between the interns and the communities they join, and also between Renaissance College and its partners abroad. A third challenge is associated with the nature of internship projects that too often fail to address the needs of host communities. A fourth challenge is linked to providing students the opportunity to share people's lives. Finally, I explore the emotional challenge of such intense experiences. I hope my analysis will encourage others in this field to examine their practice with reference to Freire's critical pedagogy.

10.2   The Theoretical Framework

What cannot be questioned (it can of course be ignored, suppressed, or misunderstood) is that [service learning] is fundamentally a question of pedagogical strategy.

– D.W. Butin

Paulo Freire, a prominent and influential twentieth-century educator, is considered one of the founders of critical pedagogy (Giroux 2010). His work has influenced generations of progressive educators around the world. His acclaimed book, *Pedagogy of the Oppressed*, published in English in 1970, has sold more than a million copies. Born in 1921 in Recife, Brazil, Freire worked to help people learn "to perceive social, political, and economic contradictions, and to take action against the oppressive elements of reality" (Freire 1972, 19). He encouraged people to reflect critically on the social and political sources of inequality and privilege that shape and rule their lives so as to act upon and transform them.

Central to Freire's critical pedagogy is the strong conviction that learning is relational and that knowledge is produced through interaction with others. Critical awareness, therefore, is a "dialogical" process where everyone contributes knowledge and learns from one another. Knowledge cannot be imparted from above; it needs to be created collectively using people's experience as a starting point. This collective endeavour calls for people living in situations of injustice and those who are in solidarity with them to establish dialogue. Dialogue, Freire advocated, cannot exist without humility and mutual respect, without faith in people's agency, and without a profound love for the world and for humanity. Only then can dialogue, based on trust, bring people together in an equal relationship to learn from one another and transform an oppressive reality (Lloyd 1972, 8).

This approach to learning suggests that critical education is as much an emotional endeavour as an intellectual one. Freire's critical pedagogy is, in summary, "a project of individual and social transformation" (Giroux 2010, B15) that calls on everyone involved in the learning process to engage intellectually and emotionally through relationships to reflect critically and act on his or her reality to create a more socially, politically, and economically just world. Freire's work, however, as Giroux reminds us, "can never be reduced to a method" because "pedagogy is defined by its context" (B15).

10.3   The Institutional Context

Renaissance College's primary purpose is "to nurture and develop leadership potential and engaged citizenship through the liberal education of [its] students."[2] Learning is interdisciplinary, experiential, and outcome based. Classes are small and typically seminar-style. Community plays an essential role in the programming, and over the years the college has formed rich and diverse connections with community partners who have been involved in courses and extracurricular activities. Located in a historical house in downtown Fredericton, the college bustles with students and with community organizations that use the space for meetings and workshops.

The international internship program is an integral component of Renaissance College's Bachelor of Philosophy degree in Interdisciplinary Leadership Studies. Information collected through informal discussions with students and alumni, students' exit surveys, and students' assignments indicate that students generally regard it as the most rewarding part of their education. After their second year of study, students travel in pairs or small groups of three or four to countries where the cultural and economic reality differs significantly from their own. For a period of ten weeks, they immerse themselves in a community, living with host families in some cases, and engage in volunteer work with local organizations. Their work is related to education, health, the environment, human rights, community development, or a combination of these. Students have been asked by our partners to teach, develop leadership programs for youth, help at local community clinics and orphanages, support community planning and development initiatives, provide computer support, attend community workshops, and help in reforestation efforts. As the main goal of the internship is for students to learn with and from their hosts, rather than imparting Western-based standards and values, we do not expect them to lead projects but to contribute to a community effort led by our partners. Placements are created by Renaissance College, although students can submit proposals for independent sites. In summer 2011, for example, twenty-one students travelled to seven different countries (Bhutan, Vietnam, Sri Lanka, Ecuador, Malawi, South Africa, and Ukraine).

The academic component of the internship helps students refine their understanding of self, others, and the world. Students also reflect on the concepts of leadership and citizenship in different social and political contexts. Pre-departure training includes intercultural, linguistic, and logistical preparation, as well as training in group dynamics. Upon their return, students take part in post-internship debriefing sessions. Other courses they take, such as world views, citizenship, public policy, cross-cultural leadership, and community problem solving, also contribute to preparing them for their experience abroad, and give them opportunities to push their critical reflection and engagement further upon their return. In their final portfolio submission and during discussions, students often describe their international internship as a key learning experience that allowed them to connect knowledge and practice. They also find on returning home that they can summon examples from their internship to make sense of what they are learning or have learned in other classes.

Students at Renaissance College are predominantly female and come from middle- and upper-class Caucasian families from across Canada. They are mainly recent high school graduates who are academically proficient and involved in a number of community and school organizations as volunteers. As part of their degree, they complete a Minor in another discipline of their choice. Popular disciplines among our students include environmental studies, international development studies, science, business administration, and anthropology.

10.4   The Renaissance College Internship in Light of Freire's Critical Pedagogy

Looking at the internship in light of Freire's critical pedagogy, I believe its main purpose is to help students nurture dialogical relations and develop an inclusive practice as future leaders. Such practice, as Freire (1972, 77) emphasizes, is an "existential necessity" for change to be truly liberating. For meaningful dialogue to happen in a Freirean sense, students must comprehend the dynamics of power and privilege at play between them and the people with whom they will interact during their internship. For the college, it means acknowledging and addressing the same dynamic at play between us and our partners abroad. It also requires us to establish the conditions for more genuine dialogue to take place by developing internship projects that benefit both our students and our partners. Furthermore, a Freirean base implies creating opportunities for students to share the lives of the people in the communities they will join. Finally, because entering into dialogue is as much an endeavour of relationship as an intellectual one, we need to make sure we prepare students to deal with the emotions associated with this often intense experience.

10.5   Exploring the Dynamic of Power and Privilege with Our Students

Critical dialogue can take place only when the contribution of everyone involved is recognized not only as important, but as vitally necessary, and is actively sought. Most of our internships at Renaissance College take place in economically developing countries. In this context, the balance of power is frequently already tilted in favour of the interns. For example, by and large, our interns are wealthier than their hosts, in both absolute and relative terms. They are frequently perceived as being better educated and better able to find solutions to issues affecting their host community simply because they come from a more "advanced" country. In contrast, the interns often carry a number of deeply entrenched and even unperceived assumptions about their hosts, including that they are uneducated, backward, and lack moral judgment. Furthermore, gender has a significant influence on the dynamic between interns and members of their host communities. The power and privilege enjoyed by male interns are often significantly greater than those they have in Canada, whereas female interns experience a loss of status and might become victims of discrimination (more on this below). These disparities can problematize relations between intern and partner. Miller and Hafner contend that the "uneven balance of power" between university students and community participants is "an obstacle to collaboration" (2008, 70). To address this problem, Freire reminds us of the importance of continually re-examining our attitude towards the people with whom we engage to avoid objectifying and patronizing them.

A strength of the international internship at Renaissance College is its integration into a broader educational experience. Throughout the degree program, assignments include a self-reflective component that helps students examine their thoughts and actions and uncover underlying assumptions, values, and personal worldviews. Second-year courses are designed to allow students to learn about the social, political, and economic realities of their countries of internship and to explore cultural differences.

The internship preparation process itself, taking place over a period of six months, explores notions of power and privilege through discussions on the ethical implications of volunteer work abroad. Although this exploration helps raise students' awareness, participants still struggle to address ethical issues while on their internship. For many, the internship is the first time they experience the contrasting dynamics of power and privilege. The change in their status makes this concept real, and they must face the challenges associated with their new situation. I realized how unsettling it can be for students when I received an e-mail from one of my students, who addressed this very issue while on his placement in Vietnam: "Nadya, something I struggle with is that I really love living here. It is amazing, and the people are amazing. I just wonder how much of that is because I am relatively rich and I am white and speak English ... I wonder how much my skin holds me back from truly immersing myself into the culture."

Later on in his e-mail, the student expressed concern about whether or not he was being immoral because he admitted enjoying some of the advantages associated with his new status. While reading his message, I realized that the emphasis we place on getting our students to be self-reflective before they embark on their internship helps them to assess their new standing in their host communities critically; the intern might never have questioned his skin colour before or seen it as a barrier to intimacy, and he would certainly never have wrestled with the moral challenges it presents.

Most of our students confront their position of power during their internship, women more so than men as the change for them often involves a loss of status. The fact that students travel in small groups affects their awareness of the change in the dynamics of power, especially when the groups are composed of both males and females. One male student reflected on how he found his newly elevated status unsettling mainly because it also meant a loss of status for the three female classmates travelling with him. As they are in a leadership program, students are asked to pay specific attention to leadership practices in their country of internship and within their own group. What prompted his reaction was that he had been appointed leader of his group and was expected to make all decisions for the group without consulting its other members, which was in direct contradiction to their established practice of shared leadership.

These two examples show that the internship experience can push students to recognize the existing imbalance of power and address it.

This recognition is eased when students are aware of other, more egalitarian models of interaction, and are willing, as Freire says, to re-examine their position and attitude.

For some students, though, this change in status gives them a "bloated sense of self-importance" (Tiessen 2007) that feeds their need to "make a difference" and become the recognized leaders they aspire to be. Students in a leadership program can feel the pressure to show themselves to be confident leaders, to succeed in solving problems, and to provide evidence of their competency. Thus, during their internships, they might be inclined to take action that shifts the focus from learning with and from the local people to trying to solve their problems in a condescending fashion. These students often experience strong feelings of hopelessness as they realize how complex are issues such as poverty, violence, and inequality. At the same time, they feel guilty about their own privileged status. It is little surprise, then, that some interns adopt the role of rescuer, taking it on themselves to make decisions without collaborating properly with their hosts. This is in sharp contrast to Freire's critical pedagogy, where humility is central and dialogue essential for individual and social transformation.

Although students at Renaissance College might adopt superior attitudes, in my experience few actually do. Nevertheless, this illustrates a challenge inherent in our program. I stress to students that the purpose of their immersion abroad is educational. Any action they take with the partner organization is an opportunity for them to learn through discussion; it is not a particular expected outcome of their internship. The fact that the internship is integrated into a broader educational strategy most likely helps drive home the message that actions are encouraged only upon their return and should take place in their home environment. Scheduling a community problem-solving course after the students return reinforces this message.

As I was finalizing this chapter, political instability in one of our internship countries forced us to cancel four internship positions. Working with the students to find them an alternative placement, I found it rewarding to hear them express concern about some of the options put forward, which they perceived as reinforcing power differences instead of creating the conditions to work with and learn from the partner organization. Some organizations, for instance, tend to treat the interns as experts in governance, communication, finance, technology, and so forth, a model that does not suit our college's ethos.

My experience as internship coordinator over the past five years has shown me that, if students are to come to grips with the complex dynamic of power and privilege, we need to do more to guide their experience. We must get them not only to report on what they have seen and experienced, but also to explore the root causes and effects of this power imbalance. We also need to help them relate this knowledge to their life in Canada. The year-long community problem-solving course students take upon their return offers such an opportunity, as they engage with community organizations in which power imbalance is an essential factor.

10.6   Exploring the Dynamic of Power and Privilege with Our Partners Abroad

Exploring the dynamic of power and privilege with our students is one step towards creating internships where our students and partners can build relationships of respect and trust. A complementary step involves exploring this dynamic with our partners abroad, especially the relationship between our college and the partner organizations. I realized the importance of this step when I started collaborating with our partners in Bhutan five years ago. Over the past twenty years, this tiny Himalayan country has received support from Canada to develop its educational system. Thanks to the Canadian International Development Agency, many Bhutanese have come to Canada to pursue post-graduate degrees before entering the teaching profession, and several Canadian professors have travelled to Bhutan to help design curricula. The discourse around this partnership in both Canada and Bhutan often casts Bhutan and the Bhutanese as the fortunate beneficiaries of Canada's largesse. When I started working more closely on this internship placement, I realized that some people had adopted a similar attitude of deference towards us and our interns. After discussion, we realized that the distance it created between the interns and the Bhutanese students with whom we hoped our students would interact was preventing them from developing meaningful relationships.

Acknowledging this problem was the easiest part; finding a way to address it proved more difficult. During a scholarly visit to Canada by two of our Bhutanese partners, we realized that, to modify the terms of the internship substantially, we needed to look at what we could contribute to and gain from this partnership. This has led to a change of focus, from an internship for Canadian students to a cultural exchange that takes place in Bhutan, where both Canadian interns and Bhutanese students are involved as participants. In this process, Bhutanese students no longer play the role of hosts who look after Canadian interns' every need; instead, they are now an integral part of the exchange. In the first year, we assumed that simply pairing Bhutanese students with Canadian interns would set the stage for the emergence of more equitable relations. It certainly helped them develop strong bonds of friendship, but their collective involvement in a community project remained affected by the perceived difference in status between them. Comments by one intern illustrate this situation and the difficulty she faced trying to address it: "At Sherubtse it seemed that the Bhutanese students assumed we were leaders, they assumed we knew what we were doing and often in group situations they would wait for our approval of their ideas ... Often in my journal I remarked at how hard it was to get our female Bhutanese counterparts ... to interact with us in a group setting."

Because of the relationship of trust and respect that developed among the partner organizations, we were able to address this issue by adding a preparation component for the Bhutanese students before the Canadian interns arrived, including involving Bhutanese students in the selection of the community project. This dialogue with our partner is an ongoing process that continues to challenge us all, and we realize that to break free of our deeply engrained assumptions requires constant effort on both sides. What makes it possible to address these issues is that we have been able to establish among ourselves the conditions for genuine dialogue. We share a mutual belief that we all have something valuable to contribute. We have developed respect for one another, and we have created strong bonds of friendship and trust.

10.7   Building Reciprocity with Our Partners Abroad

Another aspect of the internship that can affect the ability of our students to build meaningful relations while abroad is the nature of the community activities in which they are involved. As international service learning and volunteer tourism become more and more popular (Moore 2011), we see volunteer organizations emerging all around the world and creating opportunities to meet this demand. Too often, unfortunately, projects are manufactured to keep volunteers busy and happy, and have no real value for the community apart from bringing in money (which can also generate tensions within the community around its distribution and create negative forms of tourism, such as sex and drug-related tourism). This approach can harm the community, as it fails to recognize its true needs, and it can reinforce stereotypes, such as that the community is reliant on aid (Guttentag 2009). These types of projects can also have the effect of disengaging interns as they become aware that they are doing little of importance. For example, one intern ended up spending a large amount of her time working on beautifying an ecological station where foreigners were staying, instead of contributing to a community effort to address environmental issues affecting the area. She said of the experience, "[a]lthough I think the work that's being done here is good, I also see that the majority of work is done to support life at the station."

Finding worthwhile placements and building long-term reciprocal relationships for our program require significant time and involvement by us and our partners. The partnership we have with Bhutan is a good illustration of this. It took three years of concerted effort to arrive at a point where we feel participants from both organizations are benefiting from the program. Despite this, we are conscious of the importance of constantly nurturing and adapting the internship to changing needs. I am not sure we would have been as successful without external funding to support this specific partnership. The reality is that, with the current financial restraints in higher education and without external funding, we are struggling to create similar types of relations with our other partners. To find alternative ways of doing so, our next step is to explore the possibility of partnering with Canadian non-governmental organizations (NGOs) that have developed strong links with organizations abroad, and discussing with them how an internship component could be added to projects already in place. This model is used by the Atlantic Council of International Cooperation, and we hope to learn from its experience. We believe that such a relationship would benefit both students and the NGOs. Involving students in projects created by local communities and supported by NGOs is likely to help them gain a real appreciation of the vibrancy and resilience of these communities, provide positive examples of engagement, and offer them a chance to stay involved after their internship ends.

10.8 Sharing Lives

Freire reminds us that transformational education relies on relationships fed by love, humility, and courage. He writes: "Dialogue cannot exist ... in the absence of a profound love for the world and for [human beings] ... Love is at the same time the foundation of dialogue and dialogue itself" (1972, 77–8). Freire's words resonate deeply with my personal and professional experience and with that of many of my students. One of the most powerful ways for them to build this level of commitment is by living with host families and becoming immersed in the daily routine of the community for an extended period. By sharing in community life, interns are more likely to develop an attitude of deep respect, trust, and a genuine affection for their host families as they become emotionally involved with and deeply touched by the care and love they receive. One intern's reflection on her experience in Burkina Faso in 2010 is a good illustration of this transformation:

> I learned more about poverty in the first few hours of my stay there than I had ever known in my life ... And yet, amongst all of this hardship and all of this poverty, there exists strength of character so strong I feel too weak to describe it. The people of Burkina – who opened up their homes for me, who shared with me their stories, who fed me and welcomed me into their lives, carry themselves with a dignity that I have never before witnessed. With each turn, with each difficulty I faced, with each moment in which I sought the help of another, I was met with graciousness, with kindness, with respect. People, who in my Canadian eyes had nothing, gave me everything they had to offer.

The intern's observation also illustrates how living with a host family was a humbling experience, as it pushed her to re-examine her views on poverty. By sharing in the lives of the less fortunate, interns also become conscious of what they take for granted back home, such as running water, electricity, and health care services, and they come to appreciate people's resourcefulness and determination. At Renaissance College, a fair number of students plan to pursue careers in health care after completing their undergraduate degrees. Internships appear to give students a new appreciation of the struggles of those they meet in developing countries, who often have to choose between feeding their family and getting much needed medical treatment.

10.9   Coping with the Intensity of the Experience

For eighteen-to-twenty–year-old students to establish a strong dialogical relationship with strangers belonging to a different culture in a short period of time is emotionally demanding, especially for those who find themselves in a developing country for the first time. The intensity of the experience – the harsh reality of poverty, injustice, and inequality – can take them to the edge of their comfort zone, and they soon become painfully aware of their own position of privilege. Nevertheless, being on the edge can be conducive to critical reflection and engagement as long as students have proper support to help them handle and process the experience. Our program aims to help students develop tools and networks of support that can help them cope with the emotional challenge associated with the internship. We want students to experience these support systems as safe and non-judgmental, yet critical.

At the individual level, activities such as journaling are integrated throughout the internship program, giving students the chance to examine their experience and emotions through a reflective process. We also strive to develop a relationship of trust and respect with each student. The internship coordinator is, of course, one of those connections and the students' first point of contact in times of need. It is crucial that, over the first two years of the program, the coordinator form strong bonds with all the students to permit a less inhibited dialogue to happen. The e-mail message that I received from an intern (excerpted earlier) is an example of the importance of this relationship. The small size of our program and the importance we give to community life also allow for such trusting relationships to flourish, not only between students and the internship coordinator, but also between students and other course instructors. Furthermore, a university counsellor is available for one-on-one or group consultations during their preparation, time abroad, and return.

The college also strives to foster a strong collaborative dynamic within each cohort of interns travelling together to a specific country. Group meetings and language tutorials are held, and students are encouraged to take part in social activities together. These activities all contribute to building a strong sense of belonging. Another factor that contributes to this strong group dynamic is that students take most of their core courses together before the internship and are invited to work on group projects with their travel partners.

As a class, we explore the concept of cultural adjustment, and students take part in a twenty-four-hour preparatory session, the informal nature of which helps students bond with one another and with the coordinator. Together, students prepare meals, sleep in dormitories, take part in preparatory activities, and watch movies. Past participants in the program are also invited to share their experiences with the interns at that time. The session also includes working on cross-cultural communication and cultural adaptation, as well as addressing students' concerns about their internships. I have noticed that students feel more comfortable discussing very personal issues related to the internship during and after this day-long session. Students also take part in a second twenty-four-hour debriefing session after their internship is over, which takes place off-campus and offers students a safe space to talk about their experience as a class. The session focuses almost entirely on exploring the emotional struggles the interns had abroad and upon their return, using photographs to stimulate emotions, memory, and imagination. Country-specific group debriefing sessions focusing on the dynamic of each group are also held upon return. After these, students can engage more easily in critical reflection of their experience, identify ways to become socially engaged at home, and evaluate their prior involvement in light of their experience abroad.

10.10   Conclusion

Examining and constructing the internship program at Renaissance College from a Freirean perspective has reinforced my belief that internships abroad can play a significant role in the development of students' critical awareness and ability to be agents of progressive change, as well as my conviction that the internship program needs to be positioned as an essential component of a broader educational strategy. The experience should focus on the development of students' disposition to enter into dialogical relations while on their internship. Developing such a disposition, however, requires exploring how power and privilege affect students' ability to engage in dialogue while abroad, and the dynamic between the college and its partner organizations. It also necessitates creating reciprocal relations and opportunities for students to share in people's lives. As Freire taught, critical pedagogy is as much an emotional endeavour as an intellectual one: we need to give students the support they need to deal with the emotional challenges associated with their international experience.

NOTES

1 I received funding from the University of New Brunswick Teaching and Learning Priority Fund to research the pedagogical foundation guiding the internship program at Renaissance College. Part of this chapter (with modifications) was presented at the Association of Atlantic Universities

2011 Teaching Showcase, and published online at http://www.msvu.ca/
site/media/msvu/AAU%20Proceedings.pdf.
2 According to its Web site, "Renaissance College opened its doors in
September of 2000. The College was the result of a concerted and dedicated effort by a group of faculty members and administrators from across
the [University of New Brunswick]. This group was united around the
vision of creating a new and innovative leadership program. They wanted
this new program to include the traditional ideal of a liberal arts education
combined with leading edge contemporary education theory and practical
experiential learning" (Renaissance Collge, n.d.).

REFERENCES

Butin, D.W., ed. 2005. *Service-learning in Higher Education: Critical Issues and
Directions*. New York: Palgrave.
Crabtree, R. 2008. "Theoretical Foundations for International Service-
learning." *Michigan Journal of Community Service Learning* 15 (1): 18–36.
Epprecht, M. 2004. "Work-Study Abroad Courses in International
Development Studies: Some Ethical and Pedagogical Issues." *Canadian
Journal of Development Studies* 25 (4): 687–706.
Freire, P. 1972. *Pedagogy of the Oppressed*. New York: Herder and Herder.
Giroux, H.A. 2010. "Lessons from Paulo Freire." *Chronicle of Higher Education*
57 (9): B15–16.
Grusky, S. 2000. "International Service Learning: A Critical Guide from an
Impassioned Advocate." *American Behavioral Scientist* 43 (5): 858–67.
Guttentag, A. 2009. "The Possible Negative Impacts of Volunteer Tourism."
International Journal of Tourism Research 11 (6): 537–51.
Heron, B. 2006. "Critically Considering International Social Work Practica."
Critical Social Work 7 (2): n.p.
Kiely, R. 2004. "A Chameleon with a Complex: Searching for Transformation
in International Service-learning." *Michigan Journal of Community Service
Learning* 10 (2): 5–20.
Lloyd, A.S. 1972. "Freire, Conscientization, and Adult Education." *Adult
Education Quarterly* 23 (1): 3–20.
Miller, P.M., and M.M. Hafner. 2008. "Moving toward Dialogical
Collaboration: A Critical Examination of a University, School, Community
Partnership." *Educational Administration Quarterly* 44 (1): 66–110.
Moore, E. 2011. "Guilt Trips: A Personal Perspective on the Ethical
Quandaries of Travel in the Developing World." Essay submitted to the

Faculty of Arts and Social Sciences, Irving and Jean Glovin Award Essay Competition, Dalhousie University. Available online at http://arts.dal.ca/Files/Emma_Moore_Glovin.pdf.

Ramaley, J. 2000. "Renewing the Civic Mission of the American University." John Dewey Lecture. Ann Arbor: University of Michigan.

Renaissance College. n.d. "Core Values." Available online at http://www.unb.ca/fredericton/renaissance/values.html; accessed 28 February 2013.

Sichel, B. 2006. "'I've Come to Help': Can Tourism and Altruism Mix?" *Briarpatch Magazine*, 2 November. Available online at http://briarpatchmagazine.com/articles/view/ive-come-to-help-can-tourism-and-altruism-mix/.

Tiessen, R. 2007. "Educating Global Citizens? Canadian Foreign Policy and Youth Study/Volunteer Abroad Programs." *Canadian Foreign Policy* 14 (1): 77–84.

STUDENT INTERMEZZI
Transformative learning

My experience, somebody's life

NEVENA SAVIJA

My experience, somebody's life. People do not all have equal access to rights and resources. They should, but the truth is they do not. Some people have everything they could ever ask for, and more, while others have nothing, not even clean water to drink. There is medication for HIV/AIDS that can prolong your life by quite a few years, but not every infected person in the world is given the privilege to access it. A baby born in Canada is automatically granted different rights than a baby born in Kenya; from birth, they are different. More generally, the fact is that we live in a world that is unjust, often unfair, and with the vast majority of the population sharing only a sliver of the world's wealth.

I knew this before I went to Kenya. I was aware of the reality, and I am disturbed by it now even more than I was prior to my arrival. Kenya is a beautiful land, with beautiful people and a ravishing culture, but there is a lot of pain and hardship embedded into the lives of Kenyans. The slums of Kenya appeared to my eyes as a living nightmare – and I don't mean for myself, I mean for the individuals who are born there and then have to raise their own children there. I feel as though I don't have the right to come back and state that I am bewildered and appalled by the slums of Kenya. I am just another person passing by and observing. My stay in Kenya was short, especially compared to people who call Kenya home. Sometimes, I feel as though it is not my story to tell, but on the other hand it is a story that I need to share.

I encountered streets covered with garbage and toxic contaminants, open sewage running along the sides of streets, and the inhabitants meshed in between, wherever there might be room. There were children playing and eating in these environments, or looking for something edible in the dumps, or sniffing glue to stifle their hunger and freeze the pain. There were people selling anything they possibly could on stands along the streets. The air is polluted, the water is polluted, the hospitals are overpriced for the everyday individual – and regardless, proper medical care is hardly reachable. There is not enough land and food, and there are so many people. Corruption is common, injustice is just part of life, rape in large numbers is a daily occurrence, and young, abandoned pregnant girls – the victims – are declared sinners. Of course this is the reality of the world in which we live. I know that. The pain for me came in witnessing it directly through the people I met. My heart is broken by this reality, and I find myself struggling internally to make sense of it.

Though I am far from fine with what I encountered, I was not shocked. What made the difference for me, I think, was going from being so involved here in Canada with what is going on globally to being involved abroad – and, more importantly, developing relationships with the individuals who were directly impacted. I didn't experience culture shock, nor did I have a breakdown when I was introduced to the living circumstances.

I had heartache, though, before I fell asleep each night, as I thought back to every single person I'd met that day, wondering how they are individually dealing with their pain. I would think about the little eleven-year-old boy John: how he is abandoned, beaten, and chased away by his family because he is a "rebellious child," even though I know how sweet his heart is, and I know that all he wants is somebody to hold him and show him love. I would think about fifteen-year-old Jennifer, her deafness having left her abandoned, but at a tender age still in charge of her sister's baby. The love and joy in Jennifer's heart is unimaginable, and when she laughs there is nothing that will keep a smile off of your face. These thoughts and others like them fill my head before I fall asleep and each morning when I wake up, in Kenya, and now in Canada.

I'm your average individual. As I see it, we all live in this world and somehow we are all part of what it is. Whether we contribute "more" or "less" – if such measurements can be calculated in a quantitative way – is arbitrary. We all circulate in the cycle of life; until we change it completely, it is what we are. We can't expect more than we give. We create the world and we design it, every part of it, including nature. Maybe it's all part of a greater picture, but perhaps nothing greater exists.

These were the thoughts in my head years before I decided to go to Kenya, and they will surely be the thoughts in my head for years after returning. I have merely stepped foot into a particular experience. However, it was indeed an experience. It is my own and it is unique.

When I first came back, I spent a lot of time asking myself what the point was, but now I think that it really needed to happen. The friendships that I have developed this summer will forever be a part of my heart and what keeps me aiming to accomplish more. Now, as I continue my life back in Canada, embedding myself in books, learning more and facing the realities of the world, some of these realities have faces and names.

Kenya left its mark in my life. I am the person I was before, but I also have developed increased strength and willpower to continue to fight everything that creates global inequality and fosters hardship in the lives of individuals who often have less power than I do to effect large-scale change. I realize the importance of education, and will advocate for it. I recognize that before I went to Kenya I did not sufficiently question some things that my society, including my schooling, ignored and left unexplained. Now I refuse to be complicit in overlooking and covering up social injustices throughout the world, and the role that I play in them.

Separating the wants from the needs

CONOR BRENNAN

My time in Kenya so far has been an extraordinary learning experience, from the time my feet touched Kenyan soil to the moments I think I understand the city in which I've lived this summer, only to feel humbled yet again by another unknown. I have learned a lot of lessons about myself, in the midst of some challenging situations. Yet it is a small tub of Nutella given to me as a birthday gift by friends, not any of the big moments, which has spurred my deepest reflections.

So what does Nutella reveal of my situation here in Kenya? For starters, it shows the money I have and the materialism that shapes our Canadian culture. I imagine myself "needing" chocolate, which is of course ludicrous. I have also made the assumption that people here need the same level of material wealth that has marked Canada's level of development. Nutella now makes me think of the words of an Italian man whom I met the other day at a gala NGO fundraiser: "Kenyans aren't suffering because they don't lack television, Western music, or washing machines, but we think they are because they lack this. I 'suffer' when I don't have orange juice in the morning or these fucking cigarettes every day. They aren't suffering and we should learn from them and their way of life instead of imposing ours." This shows an experienced development practitioner's thoughts given to a student coming over on an international service learning program. We waste our money while they get by with what they have. I should be learning from them how to consume, to appreciate life without needing sugar and chocolate once a week to brighten myself up. Nevertheless, the Italian aid worker still continued to smoke those cigarettes. Will I still eat Nutella?

Enjoying my Nutella by myself also highlights the individualistic Western culture which I've experienced for so long in Canada. My birthday Nutella is almost finished and no one else has touched it. That wouldn't likely happen with others here, not only because of the Kenyan sense of moderation that I've seen but also because of their love of visitors, family, and friends and the joys of sharing. They would let people share in their bounty, no matter how sparse it is.

Or at least that is how it's seemed to me so far. I've turned down enough offers to share to appreciate that attitude. I certainly recognize that I am treated better because I am white, male, comparatively rich, and the source of potential help, and that Kenyans, like others, are not immune to greed or gluttony. However, the generosity of spirit I find among Kenyans along with the sharing of their limited wealth comes from a communal outlook on life that makes me reflect on the limitations of my own culture and my own life.

With individualism sometimes comes gluttony and selfishness, and eating an entire jar of Nutella has also reminded me of these personal characteristics which, especially in this Kenyan context, now make me very uncomfortable. One spoonful would not have been enough prior to coming to Kenya, and I certainly would not have appreciated any restrictions on the amount of Nutella I could have. Yet with all the people I see here every day, and what the money used to buy this treat would mean to them, how can I justify this greed? The reality is that my Nutella binge does nothing for anyone apart from myself and the fat cat business owners in Italy. I came a long way to learn this simple lesson.

The lesson is still currently in process. While I have no intention to live the life of a Buddhist monk to compensate for my society's, and my own, materialism, I am committed to be more aware of where my money goes, and to decrease my own needs for personal comforts. After all, we vote every day with our wallet, and I want to vote for a world where equality is more commonplace, and where everybody can access the same comforts that I have. If decreasing my own amounts help, I hope I can make that decision.

So ... to see the world in a jar of Nutella? Why not? That single jar of Nutella, consumed in Kenya, has taught me quite a lot: about materialism, privilege, community, and generosity. And about what one does with them and learns from them. I hope this realization will help to change my attitude back in Canada, not just in Kenya where there is a constant reminder of the materialism that divides our two worlds.

I am also hoping to use the privileges that I have to be more generous with human connections. A study was once done where people were given one hundred dollars and split into two groups. One group spent the money on themselves while the other group was told to spend the money on others. Each group's happiness was measured before and after the activity. The happiest, not surprisingly, were those who shared their wealth, a finding that would not surprise most Kenyans. It's a lesson I hope I've learned, but acknowledging the problem and identifying the solution is only half the battle. I have a bloody, chocolaty massacre left before I truly change.

PART V

Conclusion

11 Practicalities and Pedagogies: Implementing International Learning Opportunities for Students

MICHEL DESJARDINS

11.1 Introduction

When I took up an academic position at Wilfrid Laurier University in the early 1990s, the president of the university at the time was fond of comparing Laurier to Princeton: both universities have the same enrolment, Lorna Marsden would say,[1] but just look at their endowments. Her take-away message: build up Laurier's endowments and it will be in a position to develop itself into the Princeton of the North.

This rhetoric eventually helped to generate a sound Development Office, but faculty who knew the culture of their institution, and others in Canada, were bemused by the president's message. "Get real!" was the typical faculty murmur to Dr Marsden's speeches. They recognized that Canadian universities function differently than private universities in the United States: in Canada, with few exceptions, money to support learning comes mainly from a blend of student tuition and provincial government funding, with external research funding generated from a variety of sources. Moreover, Canada does not have the tradition of private universities started and supported by capitalist largesse; indeed, Canadians in general (with a few significant exceptions, to be sure), while traditionally giving large sums to various charities, do not tend to give much to their alma maters.

We also knew that Laurier's main strength was its time-honoured dedication to apply research to teaching, including helping students contribute responsibly to their communities after graduation. "Global" was not the buzzword in those days, but building concern for others both locally and internationally was certainly part of the university's ethos. The commitment to students was palpable. "We're serious about teaching" was the mantra, enunciated with pride, and as a way to distinguish Laurier – at least in people's imaginations – from larger institutions.

Get real, and get serious about teaching: those expressions came to mind again in 2008 when I took over responsibilities as chair of Global Studies, a vibrant department in Laurier's Faculty of Arts bursting at the seams with student majors, with a well-established volunteer-abroad program for its third- and fourth-year students. Sara Matthews sketches this "Global Studies Experience" in Chapter 5, where she notes how students' international summer internships are framed by two academic courses they take on campus, one at the end of their third year, the other at the start of their fourth.

How, I wondered, was the department to manage this popular program in the midst of budgetary cuts and chronic understaffing, while taking concrete steps to turn a strong program into a model for others both on and off campus? So the department dreamed together: based on the literature, on advice from staff and faculty running similar types of programs across Canada, and on the department's own experiences in managing this program over the past decade, what could a program like this become if we had unlimited resources? And we schemed together: based on the realities of our university – for example, the distribution of the budget across faculties, the particular individuals holding administrative and staff positions, Laurier's academic plan – how could we ground these pedagogical ideals in this particular place at this particular time, with these particular constraints, people, and projections? Moving from the ideal to the realistic is both necessary and perilous.

We have not done so badly. Over the past four years, we have managed to increase the quality of our volunteer-abroad program – better than I had hoped, if not as wondrously as I had dreamed. With the strong support of our dean and the vice-president: academic, we have received significant funding to support student travel, and two of the Global Studies faculty who managed the program introduced progressive innovations, grounded in conversations with students.

But my intention here is not to present a case study of Laurier's Global Studies Experience. Rather, I want to explore some practical and pedagogical concerns I see with Canadian international learning programs in general – building on my own experiences with the Laurier program and with taking students abroad myself, on the other chapters in this book, on the literature, and on discussions I have had with other professionals in the two workshops that Joanne Benham Rennick and I organized in January 2010 and 2011 as part of the Good Global Citizenship Project that undergirds this book. Let me turn, then, to questions concerning how post-secondary institutions develop and manage pedagogically sophisticated, socially responsible, sustainable programs for students studying and volunteering abroad.[2]

11.2 Why Run International Learning Programs?

University education in general tends to be tightly controlled. A typical course syllabus will tell you everything you need to know in that regard: read this, then that, then the other thing; come to class at this particular time, and be sure not to miss anything; prepare to be evaluated and tested in these particular ways at those particular times; expect these particular topics to be presented in this exact way; and if class ends after dark ensure that you have someone to help you get home safely. Course syllabi themselves are needed as contracts, to constrain students from suing the university if their results are not satisfactory. Twenty or thirty or forty courses later, students typically get a degree in a particular discipline, having successfully met all the requirements and achieved a decent average by closely following the road map that has been carefully laid out for them.

So why do we run international learning programs in which we, as instructors and administrators, release our control, at times to a degree where we are not really sure what our students are learning, with whom they are learning it, how physically and emotionally safe they are, and what degree of havoc they might be wreaking elsewhere? Some might call this a case of bad parenting, but there are good reasons – not all of which, to be sure, might be equally acceptable to all concerned.

Let me start with a very practical economic reason: jobs, and the need to sustain universities. Universities with strong study and volunteer abroad programs now tend to attract more students, including many who are academically superior and who, in turn, are less likely to drop out before completing their degrees. Those students are more engaged and often care more about what they are learning. They are also more likely to have a positive impression of their education and become ambassadors for the university.[3] The result is clear: higher enrolment, which generates growth, and more faculty and staff jobs. Small might have been beautiful in the 1970s, especially for admirers of E.F. Schumacher, and small and biodiverse might be beautiful today for admirers of Vandana Shiva, but for Canadian university presidents in this decade it is grow or die.

Students who have participated in these international programs are also typically more attractive to employers; in fact, some students are drawn to these programs precisely because they believe that an international experience will enhance their employment opportunities. They consider the money spent to go abroad as a sound investment. Norah McRae (Chapter 6) speaks to this issue. Rather than belittle this reason, as humanists and social scientists sometimes do ("we don't prepare students to get jobs; we prepare them to think critically"), she shows students how to frame a more effective case to employers for how their international experience has made them more culturally "intelligent."

Still on this point, most of my academic colleagues, I know, would resist dedicating valuable time to a program because it creates more jobs. Although I am sympathetic to their view, my argument in this case is that *we* need to get real about the perceived value of the programs we offer. In the case of internationally enhanced programs, increased enrolment and the attractiveness of graduates in the job market come from the fact that these programs have pedagogical merit. Most of the time, students consider their international experiences to effectively complement their classroom learning, and employers clearly see the difference between students who have had these experiences and those who have not. To me this speaks to a certain quality of education that comes with including international exposure, which both students and employers honour. We need to pay attention to features in our curriculum that others value, all the more so when we ourselves give them value.

There is another practical reason for developing and enhancing international learning experiences for our students: university mission statements now increasingly support them. Scott, for example, has traced "the evolution of six major periods of university mission themes which chronologically change from *teaching* (Middle Ages) to *nationalization* (Early Modern Europe) to *democratization* (19th century America) simultaneous with *research* (European Enlightenment) to *public service* (20th century America) to the contemporary period of *internationalization*" (Che, Spearman, and Manizade 2009, 100, referencing Scott 2006, 5–6). Che, Spearman, and Manizade note that mission statements now "clearly reflect that a large number of colleges and universities are seeking to produce graduates who are, among other things, culturally aware and global-minded" (101).[4] Their data come from US sources – there is no comparable study for Canadian post-secondary institutions – but one need not look long and hard to see a similar concern in this country for "global" and "international," and, with the help of Joanne

Benham Rennick's opening chapter, to acknowledge the Euro-Christian background of many of these Canadian mission statements.

Let me offer three examples. Nadya Ladouceur (Chapter 10) identifies her college's emergence in 2000 with the University of New Brunswick's desire to create "a new and innovative leadership program ... [that would] include the traditional ideal of a liberal arts education combined with leading edge contemporary theory and practical experiential learning" (Renaissance College Web site). For its part, Laurier's mission statement (approved in 2008) "challenges people to become engaged and aware citizens of an increasingly complex world" (Wilfrid Laurier University Web site, Office of the President), and its academic plan, approved in 2010, lists "Global Citizenship" as one of its nine Core Principles (Wilfrid Laurier University Web site, Office of the Vice-President: Academic and Provost).[5] These concerns were not explicit in previous Laurier documents. Lastly, Trilokekar and Shubert (2009, 202–3) remind us of another key Canadian example: "The University of British Columbia has embraced global citizenship more thoroughly than any other. The university's 'Trek 2010,' which was launched in 2005, includes in its Vision 'prepar[ing] students to become exceptional global citizens' and states that part of its mission is to produce graduates who will acknowledge their obligations as global citizens, and strive to secure a sustainable and equitable future for all."[6]

These three examples could be replicated easily. Given the public face of Canadian institutions these days, it certainly makes sense for them to have well-running international learning programs to support their self-identity. But the cart has come before the horse. To fit our institution's new persona, many of us find ourselves scrambling to adapt programs that did not previously have explicit global components built into them – or, as in the case of Laurier's Global Studies Experience, to expand a program in ways that make us feel responsible and proud, rather than reckless. Mission statements concerning this topic rarely reflect existing resources and programs. Institutions *know* international programs are important, and advertise themselves in that way to attract students, tip their hat to their government funders, reflect faculty sensibilities, and give themselves a goal to reach; but in many cases a great deal of catch-up work needs to happen on the ground for that cart to follow the overworked Clydesdale.

International learning programs also attract educators, humanists, and social scientists who see clear links between the ideology that grounds, or could ground, these programs and what they admire most in their favourite theorists. We see this intersection, for example, in Sara Matthews's contribution (Chapter 5), which situates her own work as an educator in the context of studies by Jacques Derrida, Martha Nussbaum, and Ned Noddings. In that regard it is not surprising to see the US educator John Dewey's *Experience and Education* (1938) serve as a point of reference for some contributors to this book. As Johnston, Drysdale, and Chiupka (Chapter 3) note, Dewey's influential book "provides a strong educational rationale for international experiential learning models."

A key insight is that the most widely quoted scholar in our volume is the Brazilian educator Paolo Freire, particularly his *Pedagogy of the Oppressed* ([1968] 1970). My dog-eared copy dates from the counterculture days of the 1970s, but this Marxist thinker's book and the stories about him have never left Canadian university culture.[7] Freire continues to inspire many who are engaged in international learning programs. The contributors to this volume point to Freire's "project- or problem-driven approach to learning for its ability to fully engage the learner with their world" (Johnston, Drysdale, and Chiupka, Chapter 3), his "view of education as a lifelong journey towards personal and social transformation" (Eldridge and Smith, Chapter 7), his "conviction that learning is relational and knowledge is produced through interaction with others," which requires "humility and mutual respect" (Ladouceur, Chapter 10). Educators read Freire, students in our programs read Freire, and some international learning programs, like Ladouceur's, are framed around Freire. Taking Freire seriously is also more likely to generate the respectful dialogue needed between those of us in Canadian institutions and our non-governmental organization (NGO) community, and university partners abroad – as Ladouceur has done in her program.

My suspicion is that Freire's Marxist ideology runs counter to that of many of today's senior university and government administrators. Making international learning programs part of mainstream postsecondary education will require open and frank conversations, as well as a clear delineation of goals and purposes for these projects, as Benham Rennick (Chapter 2) notes. This is one example of where moving from the ideal to the realistic might be perilous.

In addition to a fit between theory and practice that drives some of our international learning programs, this direction is also buttressed by our national ethos. The "good global citizenship" descriptor that is increasingly linked to international learning programs is also consistent with our country's self-representation. To be Canadian, in many people's imagination, is to support a multicultural, peacekeeping ideal that, while understood in many ways, is often condensed as knowing more about others, respecting different cultures, and striving to make a positive difference in the world without leaving too many footprints.[8] These constructed Canadian goals are certainly consistent with particular forms of studying and volunteering abroad and with university programs that are set up to facilitate these activities. They are also consistent with the NGOs with which some work – including Intercordia, which, as David Peacock reminds us (Chapter 9), emerged out of Jean Vanier's humanitarian work with people with developmental disabilities. It is no wonder, therefore, that each university has champions who promote international programs on their campus. And it is no wonder that so many of our students want to volunteer abroad "to help others," despite repeated reminders from their teachers that the people most likely to be helped in these experiences will be the volunteers.

These ideals also need not be restricted to the international arena. As we have seen, both Eldridge and Smith (Chapter 7) and Bowen (Chapter 8) argue that local internships, framed around these goals, can also support a certain understanding of global citizenship. One need not spend three months volunteering with an NGO in Ghana, or a term studying in Cape Town, to be put in a state of cognitive disequilibrium – or cognitive negotiation, as DiFruscio and Benham Rennick (Chapter 4) prefer to call it – that can generate learning that re-inscribes "Canadian values." Students can also volunteer in parts of their cities or their country that are culturally quite different than their own or that cater to individuals who are culturally and socially different. With expert facilitation difference can be seen everywhere.

There is more to be said about this draw to difference, coming from the students' point of view. We set up international programs because we are educators who (sometimes at least!) listen to our students. What we hear on this front is clear and, with few exceptions, unequivocal: a good number of our students yearn to be intellectually and ideologically challenged – taken out of their bubble of safety. That challenge can come through meaningful experiences in other countries. Faced with the doom and gloom about the world that is fostered by our governments and media, students seek to make a small, positive difference. And they return from their experiences changed, exhilarated, troubled, and ready to go again; they have come alive, are full of new questions, and are further ahead than they were when they left in thinking about their own values and possibilities. Of course, nobody that I have met, at least, comes back enlightened – and a few come back worse off and more confused than when they left. No set of experiences is ever perfect; still, what happens before and after departure is transformative. How could we not want this for our students? How could we not want to set up programs that maximize this type of learning?

It is certainly not surprising, therefore, to see our leading academic associations support international learning as a form of pedagogical "best practice." A good example is the latest *Green Guide* published by the Society for Teaching and Learning in Higher Education, *Global Citizenship in Teaching and Learning*, the aim of which

> is to provoke and inspire. After reading parts or the entire book, you will be able to use a simple model of global citizenship education to guide design (or re-design) of a course or program that fosters global citizenship learning in any discipline. But to go even further, we hope that after reading this book you will have a new lens for viewing how your own actions and practices as an educator can model the attributes of a global citizen to your students. We would argue that having a global citizenship "lens" and a self-reflective stance will take you farther in your teaching practice than any given technique or tool – though we will also provide you with an array of approaches to aid in your teaching for global citizenship. Throughout the Guide we strive to flag how teaching practices which may not, on the surface, seem directly related to "global citizenship" can foster and model global citizenship. (Harlap and Fryer 2011, 13)

Another example of societal support for international experiences comes from the influential Association of American Colleges and Universities, which, in the context of promoting US education reform for three decades, has increasingly supported service learning as a high-impact educational practice and international learning as a vital part of its Liberal Education and America's Promise.[9]

Given all these reasons, then, for setting up international learning programs, it is not surprising to see universities with well-established international programs attract superb students. I think of the wonderful opportunity for students to have their entire first-year experience at Herstmonceux Castle in East Sussex, in the United Kingdom, learning with students from across Canada. This opportunity draws high school students who dream of transitioning from high school with a huge leap, not only to university but to university courses abroad that can become part of their undergraduate degree. The first-year Canadian University Study Abroad Program offers students from several Canadian universities direct access to the Bader International Study Centre at Herstmonceux.[10]

In closing this section of the chapter, let me return to Freire, with a twist that reflects the thoughts of some educators, myself included, and evokes counterculture memories of the 1960s and 1970s. Beyond using Freirean insights to consider the type of relationship that we would like to establish between ourselves and our students, and between ourselves and individuals in other countries, let us imagine Canadian educators as Freire's "oppressors" and our students as the "oppressed." Why? Because the system in which we work is not only seriously cracked; it arguably also oppresses students. It oppresses us as educators, too, but that is another matter. In a Freirean sense, we can be said to oppress students by the ways in which we traditionally teach and relate to teaching. As well, the post-secondary system in which we teach and the governments that support it can be seen to oppress students by the directions in which they have recently chosen to go.

This is not the place to develop this idea in detail, but let me sketch the main points, because I believe they have a bearing on the overall discussion. What are many of us doing wrong when we teach? We *still* typically practise the "act of depositing," or "banking," as Freire calls it, imagining students as containers and expecting them to reproduce facts and frames of thinking – even though we know, or at least we should know, that "knowledge emerges only through invention and re-invention, through the restless, impatient, continuing, hopeful inquiry" we pursue "with the world, and with each other" (Freire [1968] 1970, 58). Freire long ago encouraged educators to abandon deposit-making education and replace it with "problem-posing" education that embodies communication, respect and humility, where the teacher "is no longer merely the-one-who-teaches, but one who is ... taught in dialogue with the students" (66–7). This ideal is not often realized in current university contexts in which faculty do their best to escape their teaching "loads," where recent graduates are introduced to the guild by being socialized into thinking that success lies in getting research grants, rather than by their superior teaching, where class sizes and the ranks of administrators are both rising at dizzying speed, and where an increasing number of students are having to hold forty-hour-per-week jobs to fund an education that is becoming less and less personal.[11]

It is in this context, then, that some of us encourage students to learn by volunteering or studying abroad, in the hope that these kinds of experiences might generate the type of learning that is increasingly rare on Canadian campuses. "Go," we say, "you will be less oppressed out there" – and to ourselves we add: may you remember the lessons we have taught you and take care to minimize your oppression of others when you are away. And if we have prepared them properly and if we make the time to reach out to them when they return, our hope is sometimes realized. In short, we also run international learning programs to save our students, and ourselves.

This sort of pedagogy is perilous because the process and the results are messy, as Freire would have them. But its necessity need not deter us. The words of Anne Michaels come to mind: "Find a way to make beauty necessary; find a way to make necessity beautiful" (1996, 44).

11.3   What Is Most Important to Keep in Mind?

Joanne Benham Rennick touches all the right notes at the end of Chapter 2 when she reminds us that our international learning programs ought to remain focused on generating good Canadian citizens with a global focus and values that will promote global solidarity in the face of highly complex and contentious twenty-first-century challenges. Her insistence on global solidarity rather than global citizenship complements Thomas Homer-Dixon's notion of "ingenuity gaps," which he introduces at the beginning of his book (2000, 1):

> In this book I'll argue that the complexity, unpredictability, and pace of events in our world, and the severity of global environmental stress, are soaring. If our societies are to manage their affairs and improve their well-being they will need more ingenuity – that is, more ideas for solving their technical and social problems. But societies, whether rich or poor, can't always supply the ingenuity they need at the right times and places. As a result, some face an *ingenuity gap*: a shortfall between their rapidly rising need for ingenuity and their inadequate supply.

In the face of these ingenuity gaps, which are increasing globally, what will help – and in the end might even save us, Homer-Dixon argues – is people around the world working together to address these crises. The ingenuity is there, globally, to address most problems, but if the gaps that occur are to be filled, people from all countries will need to work and think together far more effectively than they have done so far. This is another way to think about global solidarity, and effective international learning experiences are ways to nurture that emerging reality.

In keeping with my desire to be pragmatic, let me now address two concerns that are far more prosaic in nature. International learning experiences are much more valuable to all concerned, I have come to believe, when institutions invest sufficiently in them and when students are adequately supported not only before and during but especially after their experiences. These observations are reinforced by the contributions in this book, especially in the student reflections, and the discussions we have had in the workshops that led up to this book.

11.3.1   It takes a whole university to raise an international program

International leaning programs are resource intensive. Not only does the current North American university culture's courting of internationalization and global citizenship come at a time when post-secondary institutions in this country are struggling to support their traditional forms of education, but by their very nature such programs are disproportionately expensive to run. Despite growing interest in them, in the broader university framework they attract relatively few students and cost a lot of money if they are to be done properly.[12] They must also be done properly if they are to be sustainable and if we are to take seriously our multiple responsibilities to students, to ourselves, to our institutions, to our global partners, and to the new types of global relationships we are seeking to model.[13]

I would like to expand on some of these complexities by turning my attention to study abroad programs, about which we have so far not said much in this book. International study programs are more popular and in many ways easier to manage than international service programs.[14] They are also seen as less radical by students and their families. But they still require an extraordinary degree of attention.

Study abroad, as readers of this book probably know, typically is coordinated through one or more offices on a particular campus; Laurier International does it on my campus. One or more dedicated staff are the key point persons. They are paid to establish and manage links between universities, promote the program, and prepare students to go. One need only imagine the full cost of establishing a link between, say, the University of Regina and Bangalore University, which would include at least one site visit and dozens of electronic exchanges;

or the internal political discussions that would occur surrounding possible links with a university in Iran or Malaysia. Moreover, the result, even when successful, benefits only a handful of students and perhaps a faculty member or two each year, and requires ongoing monitoring.

In addition, even with fully functioning offices that effectively manage these study abroad opportunities, some students choose to study abroad independently, at universities that do not have arrangements with the students' home university, or through other post-secondary institutions that run their own international study programs. At Laurier, only the Registrar's Office knows the full complement of students who have studied abroad in any one term, and in several cases they acquire this information only after the fact, when students request course transfer credit.

University staff not connected to an international office – departmental and decanal advisors at Laurier, for example – also spend time evaluating the nature of the courses taken abroad by their students. Is that sociology course taken in Brazil equivalent to the home university's SOC 223, and can it be used for a sociology major? And what about the online course taken in Israel by one of our students that promoted the supremacy of Israel, or the course taken at a madrassa in Cairo that devoted three weeks to learning how to chant the Qur'an (both are real cases with which I dealt two years ago as a department chair)? Faculty and staff time is taken up in departments, deans' offices, and the registrar's office with these sorts of details.

Study abroad also creates no small degree of nervousness. What happens if a student experiences abuse or trauma while abroad, or if the political situation in a country changes during this time? In fact, experienced international student advisors are often aghast at what returning students tell them, often in passing, about situations that easily could have led to very serious problems for them – "Oh yes, there was that night when my friend and I got robbed at knifepoint. But they let us go. My friend only has a small scar on her face." Does this count as a valuable experience in itself? How can a negative experience possibly be prevented?

It is also notoriously difficult to assess the nature of the learning. The type and quality of experiences that students have and create for themselves will depend on the particular university in which they are studying and the kind of course(s) they are taking. Some students will do a four-week summer course in Tuscany while others will be gone for three months in Nairobi; some will enter a university culture used to receiving international students while others will be treated as curiosities; some will work in a second or third language while others will study in English, at times even when the language of their host university is not English. And the contrasts could be multiplied. It takes skill and time to debrief students after these experiences and to assess what has been learned. Sufficient debriefing and assessment, in my experience at least, rarely happens.

In addition, the home university typically does not keep close tabs on how students are doing – even when the students have worked through their international or study abroad office to gain those international university connections. There are exceptions, to be sure. For years someone I know who performed these duties at the University of Toronto kept track of all students who were away, using a complicated computer and phone system – and for long periods of time also worked twelve hour a day, six days a week, much of it unpaid by the university. But he did this out of the goodness of his own heart ("how can I simply abandon these students?"), not as part of a pre-established university structure.

Those who promote study abroad programs to high school students tell similar stories, coupled with the difficulties those in large institutions face in not knowing all the variations available in their institutions. It is rare to find anyone in an institution who knows where all their students are studying, what has worked particularly well, which funding sources are available, and so forth. One challenge of both service and study programs is that at any one time there are many expressions of them in a post-secondary institution, but typically they are disconnected. Conjuring up Freire again for a moment, perhaps this is exactly what we are aiming for in our brave new world: relinquishing control with the expectation that new learning will happen in a novel environment because students are agents in their own education.

Practically, then, university administrators are caught between increasing the depth and breadth of study abroad programs – to attract students, support their mission statement, and address faculty concerns – while also managing budgets and tending to other high-growth areas in their institutions. I do not envy them their job. It is certainly easy to see how universities that lack champions such as the University of British Columbia's Martha Piper simply learn to live with underperforming international programs. Raising the quality of these programs and making them sustainable requires commitment and leadership from the top down, and engagement by all sectors of an institution.

11.3.2   It's not over when it's over

A message that Joanne Benham Rennick and I have heard from several international program managers and countless students – among them Cathleen DiFruscio, in this volume – is that students deserve close attention when they return from their experiences abroad, including multiple opportunities to debrief, but the attention they receive is usually inadequate. These opportunities, to be sure, apply less to students who have spent four weeks in Tuscany studying Italian art than to those who have spent eight or sixteen weeks in an orphanage in Nepal or a hospice in Ghana, but each student's international experience continues when his or her plane lands on the tarmac back in Canada.[15] At that moment an important part of the student's learning is just beginning. In fact, some research now suggests that the length of time students spend studying or volunteering abroad is less significant than the opportunities they have had, both while away and after they return, to discuss what they have experienced and to integrate those new and sometimes jarring experiences into their pre-existing knowledge base.[16] We are back, in a way, to Freire and his encouragement for educators to be in continual dialogue with those they teach.[17]

This is a different type of pedagogy. It demands deep, ongoing time commitments on the part of both students and their teachers. It cherishes messiness, it relaxes control, and it prioritizes relationships over efficiencies. New technologies, such as university online platforms and public programs such as Skype, certainly allow us to manage even those cases when students do not return directly to campus. But we need to imagine teaching in new and refreshing ways, not only extending outside our classrooms and universities, but as long-term relationships formed between several parties across the globe. How this will happen in an environment divided by academic terms and teaching units remains to be seen; progress on this front will require considerable discussion on the part of unions, faculty, administrators, and students. Our two workshops made us aware of the enormous value of having a diverse group of individuals at the table to share their experiences and to imagine possibilities. Contributors to our workshops and to this book represent a cross-section of participants in international programs, and reflect the range of perspectives and approaches we hoped would generate some valuable discussions, forcing us to listen

carefully to one another, especially when our frameworks and priorities differed. What is needed is a system or venue for monitoring and
documenting these sorts of discussions and programs at all participating universities, so that we can continue to learn from one other.

One key challenge will be to open those discussions to constituencies
that have not traditionally engaged each other on the nature and process of teaching. What does pedagogy look like when faculty are listening to and learning from staff in Student Affairs, and consulting with
community groups, students, and faculty in other parts of the world?
What do teaching "loads" look like when responsibilities are shared
and extended, to some extent resembling graduate student mentoring responsibilities? How will modern technologies affect the way we
engage international learning experiences?

Laurier's baby steps in this direction have helped me to appreciate
more of the complexities. For example, we are currently attempting to
transform a non-credit Alternative Reading Week experience that has
been run by our Student Affairs staff into a credit course in which a
seven-day Reading Week international travel component will be embedded. The novelty? The course would be taught by staff and faculty,
breaking down the artificial boundaries between one constituency of
the university that "services" students and another that "teaches" them.
We know that, in the long term, harnessing all those human resources
(and more) is likely to increase the quality of resource- and learning-
intensive international experiences, while increasing the chances that
returning students will get the support and the learning experiences
they deserve. But not a day goes by when the "get real" comment does
not rise up in my mind. Our unions are concerned ("only faculty can
teach on this campus ... who will give staff time off to carry out these
duties?"), as are some of our more progressive academics ("how is this
not voluntourism?") and students who have gone on these trips in the
past ("we liked it the way it was"). Then there is the issue of funding
and, of course, scrutiny concerning where to take students and how to
develop sustainable relationships with a community that will not rein-
scribe everything we speak against in our classrooms.

Progress on these fronts, like good global citizenship itself, as Sara
Matthews notes (Chapter 5), is "concerned with producing opportunities for dialogue across difference and for learning about the limits of
the self and the Other." The interconnections, relationships, and depen-
dence on others that the contributors to this book associate with international learning ideals start at home, on our campuses, when working
out programs that will live up to those ideals.

11.4   Closing Thoughts

It is time to get real about our international learning programs. They are here to stay, students and employers appreciate them, and they offer marvellous opportunities for innovative forms of pedagogy and learning.

If, like me, you approach a book by first skimming the introductory and concluding chapters, and you find yourself here now, my suggestion is that you start with the student *intermezzi* and read them carefully. They will tell you much about the kind of Canadian students who are attracted to international service opportunities and what they learn in the process. The rest – to paraphrase the words of the first-century Jewish religious teacher Hillel after he was asked to summarize all of Jewish revelation while standing on one leg (his answer: "What is hateful to you, don't do to others") – is explanation. Now go and enjoy ... on two legs.

NOTES

1 Both universities had roughly six thousand full-time students at the time. Laurier's enrolment has now more than doubled, while Princeton's has remained roughly the same.

2 There are many kinds of international learning experiences, only some of which I include in this chapter (see Johnston, Drysdale and Chiupka, Chapter 3, in this volume, for their overview of international learning programs). Our workshops focused on service learning types of experiences, and to those I add some discussion about study abroad later in the chapter. I do not address work and research co-op placements or the increasing number of "international" experiences that take place through various Internet programs.

3 For support for these statements, see, for example, the National Survey of Student Engagement (NSSE) report, "Experiences that Matter" (2007). The survey director, based on a large database of colleges and universities across North America, examines factors that increase student engagement and success on campus. After noting six effective educational practices (7–8), he adds his own concluding comments: "So, today when I am asked, 'What one thing can we do to enhance student engagement and increase student success?' I have an answer. I say make it possible for every student to participate in *at least two high impact activities* during their undergraduate program, one in the first year, and one later related to their major

field. The obvious choices for the first year are first-year seminars, learning communities, and service learning ... In the later years of college, study abroad, internships and other field experiences, and a culminating experience are all possible" (8). See also NSSE's Web site, "Project Deep: Documenting Effective Educational Practice," with its extensive list of articles and books (http://nsse.iub.edu/_/?cid=70).

4 They go on to say that culturally aware students "possess ... the ability to respect differences in ethnic, religious, and political perspectives while still maintaining a strong sense of self-identity" (101). This is idealistic and unnecessarily static (everyone is on a continuum); nonetheless, the criteria are sound, and there are indeed students who meet these expectations.

5 Global citizenship is defined there as follows: "Laurier students graduate with international and cultural dimensions to their learning, providing them with opportunities to understand what it means to live in a world defined by globalization. Global citizenship is not solely about geopolitical boundaries but about understanding the mosaic of world views that are framed by culture, geography, ethnicity, spiritual beliefs and socioeconomic status. Internationalization brings a global dimension to the curriculum as well as to the broader university experience."

6 Trilokekar and Shubert expand on the key role that then-president Piper played in generating this initiative.

7 Academics on both sides of the border have recently been reintroduced to Freire by H.A. Giroux (2010).

8 Trilokekar and Shubert (2009, 193) reflect "Canadian" values in this way: "The triad of knowledge, understanding, and action to create a socially equitable and just world seems to be at the core of the Canadian vision of global citizenship."

9 See Brownell and Swayner (2010) and Kuh (2008). Note also the following statement from the American Association of Colleges and Universities: "AAC&U addresses diversity, global engagement, and social responsibility as compelling educational and institutional priorities that help students and campuses engage the social, civic, and economic challenges of a diverse and unequal world. AAC&U supports colleges and universities in their efforts to create settings that foster students' understanding of the intersection between their lives and global issues and their sense of responsibility as local and global citizens. AAC&U works to increase the capacity of colleges and universities to help all undergraduates understand and engage the diversities and commonalities among the world's peoples, cultures, nations, and regions" (http://www.aacu.org/resources/globallearning/index.cfm).

10 For more information, see the Queen's University Web site at http://www.
queensu.ca/bisc/index.html. International programs can begin in unusual
ways. The Herstmonceux Castle program began with the donation of the
castle to Queen's, not because of a desire on the part of the university to
open up more study abroad opportunities for its students. One of the most
unusual cases I know for starting an international program occurred at
Arcadia University, a private university in Philadelphia. In 2003 Arcadia
"invited students to study abroad in the United Kingdom during their first
semester of college. This First-Year Study Abroad Experience ..., initially a
response to a housing shortage on campus, is now in its fifth year and has
become a central reason why many students consider coming to Arcadia"
(Hovland et al. 2009, 474).

11 On the teaching front, the work of Boyer (1990) is still important, particularly the four kinds of scholarship he identifies: discovery, integration,
application, and teaching. As Arshad Ahmad, current president of the
Society for Teaching and Learning in Higher Education, notes, "Boyer's
(1990) *Scholarship Reconsidered* has been a landmark contribution in helping
leaders to think differently about academic work. His work has sparked
major contributions from [other scholars] who conceive the work of faculty
in a broader set of overlapping areas of scholarship. This conception is
inclusive, and critical to student learning particularly when compared to the traditional hierarchy of research followed by its two poor
cousins, teaching and service" (2011, 1). Max Weber's *stahlhartes Gehäuse*
("a container that is hard as steel," or "iron cage," as it is usually translated) also comes to mind, with its image of people as cogs in a bureaucratic machine.

12 A parallel in my university would be the Faculty of Music, which is heavily subsidized by other constituencies. But nobody begrudges this faculty
its resources; there is widespread agreement throughout Laurier that the
quality of our Faculty of Music and the importance of music in a modern
university warrant this support.

13 For an example of a university that has striven to integrate many of its
academic strengths and opportunities into a coherent program that leads
students to "global competence," see Rollins's (2009) discussion about
Georgia Tech.

14 Lewin notes, in regard to the United States: "More than half of all high
school seniors express a strong desire to study abroad in college, and this
enthusiasm continues well into their first year, even if curricular or financial challenges eventually preclude many students from realizing their
dreams" (2009, xiii). Let me add that "curricular" refers to constraints that
university educators place on students.

15 See Brabant, Palmer, and Gramling (1990); Christofi and Thompson (2007); and Gaw (2000).
16 See especially Vande Berg (2009) and Yershova, DeJaeghere, and Mestenhauser (2000), which reinforce the general point that the benefits that come from learning abroad are multiplied when the experiences are guided and supported.
17 We are also in the domain of Jan Meyer's and Ray Land's (2003, 2005, 2006) theoretical framework of threshold concepts. By this they mean that there are certain learning portals through which students pass that result in new perspectives and ways of thinking about things that are also troublesome because they require giving up previous ways of thinking, previous beliefs. This stepping into the unknown requires careful guidance.

REFERENCES

Ahmad, A. 2011. "Six Suggestions for Presidents to Improve Undergraduate Education." *Newsletter of the Society for Teaching and Learning in Higher Education* 57 (Summer): 1–2. Available online at http://www.stlhe.ca/wp-content/uploads/2011/12/Newsletter57-Eng-singles.pdf; accessed 28 February 2013.

Boyer, E.L. 1990. *Scholarship Reconsidered: Priorities of the Professoriate.* Princeton, NJ: Carnegie Foundation for the Advancement of Teaching.

Brabant, S., C.E. Palmer, and R. Gramling. 1990. "Returning Home: An Empirical Investigation of Cross-cultural Reentry." *International Journal of Intercultural Relations* 14 (4): 387–404.

Brownell, J.E., and L.E. Swaner. 2010. *Five High-Impact Practices: Research on Learning Outcomes, Completion, and Quality.* Washington, DC: Association of American Colleges and Universities.

Che, S.M., M. Spearman, and A. Manizade. 2009. "Constructive Disequilibrium: Cognitive and Emotional Development through Dissonant Experiences in Less Familiar Destinations." In *The Handbook of Practice and Research in Study Abroad: Higher Education and the Quest for Global Citizenship,* ed. R. Lewin. New York: Routledge.

Christofi, V., and C.L. Thompson. 2007. "You Cannot Go Home Again: A Phenomenological Investigation of Returning to the Sojourn Country after studying Abroad." *Journal of Counseling and Development* 85 (1): 53–63.

Dewey, J. 1938. *Experience and Education.* New York: Simon & Schuster.

Freire, P. [1968] 1970. *Pedagogy of the Oppressed*, trans. M.B. Ramos. New York: Continuum.

Gaw, K.F. 2000. "Reverse Culture Shock in Students Returning from Overseas." *International Journal of Intercultural Relations* 24 (1): 83–104.

Giroux, H.A. 2010. "Lessons from Paulo Freire." *Chronicle of Higher Education* 57 (9): B15–16.

Harlap, Y., and M. Fryer. 2011. *Global Citizenship in Teaching and Learning*. STLHE Green Guide 12. London, ON: Society for Teaching and Learning in Higher Education.

Homer-Dixon, T. 2000. *The Ingenuity Gap*. New York: Alfred A. Knopf.

Hovland, K., C. McTighe Musil, E. Skilton-Sylvester, and A. Jamison. 2009. "It Takes a Curriculum: Bringing a Global Mindedness Home." In *The Handbook of Practice and Research in Study Abroad: Higher Education and the Quest for Global Citizenship*, ed. R. Lewin. New York: Routledge.

Kuh, G.D. 2008. *Top of Form High-Impact Educational Practices: What They Are, Who Has Access to Them, and Why They Matter*. Washington, DC: Association of American Colleges and Universities.

Lewin, R. 2009. "Introduction: The Quest for Global Citizenship through Study Abroad." In *The Handbook of Practice and Research in Study Abroad: Higher Education and the Quest for Global Citizenship*, ed. R. Lewin. New York: Routledge.

Meyer, J.H.F., and R. Land. 2003. "Threshold Concepts and Troublesome Knowledge – Linkages to Ways of Thinking and Practising." In *Improving Student Learning – Ten Years On*, ed. C. Rust. Oxford: Oxford Centre for Staff and Learning Development.

Meyer, J.H.F., and R. Land. 2005. "Threshold Concepts and Troublesome Knowledge (2): Epistemological Considerations and a Conceptual Framework for Teaching and Learning." *Higher Education* 49 (3): 373–88.

Meyer, J.H.F., and R. Land. 2006. *Overcoming Barriers to Student Understanding: Threshold Concepts and Troublesome Knowledge*. New York: Routledge.

Michaels, A. 1996. *Fugitive Pieces*. Toronto: McClelland & Stewart.

National Survey of Student Engagement. 2007. *Experiences that Matter: Enhancing Student Learning and Success*. Bloomington, IN: Indiana University, Center for Postsecondary Research. Available online at http://www.yorku.ca/retentn/rdata/NSSE_2007_Annual_Report.pdf.

Rollins, H. 2009. "Georgia Tech's Comprehensive and Integrated Approach to Developing Global Competence." In *The Handbook of Practice and Research in Study Abroad: Higher Education and the Quest for Global Citizenship*, ed. R. Lewin. New York: Routledge.

Scott, J. C. 2006. "The Mission of the University: Medieval to Postmodern Transformations." *Journal of Higher Education* 77 (1): 1–39.

Trilokekar, R.D., and A. Shubert. 2009. "North of 49: Global Citizenship à la canadienne." In *The Handbook of Practice and Research in Study Abroad: Higher Education and the Quest for Global Citizenship*, ed. R. Lewin. New York: Routledge.

Vande Berg, M. 2009. "Intervening in Student Learning Abroad: A Research-Based Inquiry." *Intercultural Education* 20 (supp. 1–2): S15–27.

Yershova, Y., J. DeJaeghere, and J. Mestenhauser. 2000. "Thinking Not as Usual: Adding the Intercultural Perspective." *Journal of Studies in International Education* 4 (1): 39–78.

Contributors

Joanne Benham Rennick is Assistant Professor of Contemporary Studies at Wilfrid Laurier University, Brantford. She is the former director of the Beyond Borders international experience program at St Jerome's University in the University of Waterloo. Her primary research focus has been on the influence of religion on Canadian society and institutions, and on the role of religion in society. She has written a book on the role of religion in the Canadian Forces and numerous articles on citizenship, values, and identity in Canada.

Tracey Bowen is Internship Coordinator in Communications, Culture and Information Technology at the University of Toronto. She has presented papers at several conferences on the value of experiential education in terms of developing autonomy, professionalism, and a sense of citizenry and social responsibility.

Conor Brennan is a recent graduate in Political Science from the University of Waterloo. As an Honours student, he was interested in combining international development work with electronic waste management, on which he wrote his thesis. He has volunteered in this area at a local computer recycling organization, and hopes to get a job in the future that will combine sustainable business practices with ethical waste management.

Caitlin Chiupka completed her Honours BA in Psychology at the University of Waterloo. Alongside Maureen Drysdale, she researched post-secondary experiential education from 2009 to 2011. Caitlin was involved in several practical and theoretically based research projects, including an international examination of cooperative education, examining data collected in North America and Europe. She is currently pursuing a PhD in Clinical Psychology at Suffolk University.

Jessica DeBrouwer is working for the Office of Development and Alumni Affairs at the University of Waterloo. She is a recent graduate of St Jerome's University, where she majored in Religious Studies, with the International Studies option. Currently she is a part of the Culture Plan Citizens Round Table for the City of Waterloo, working to continue to diversify the Waterloo region. In the future Jessica hopes to work with students interested in volunteering or studying abroad.

Michel Desjardins is Professor of Religion and Culture at Wilfrid Laurier University, Waterloo, former chair of Laurier's Department of Global Studies, and Associate Dean: Research and Curriculum, in the Faculty of Arts. He has taught and published in the areas of Comparative Religions, Early Christianity, Peace and Violence, the Academic Study of Religion in North America, and the scholarship on teaching and learning. He is also a Canada 3M National Teaching Fellow.

Cathleen DiFruscio is a graduate of the University of Waterloo in Honours Science and Women's Studies, and has completed studies in American Sign Language at the collegiate level. Cathleen has participated in two different international service learning programs, with placements in Nairobi, Kenya. Currently Cathleen works as a DeafBlind Intervenor, and intends to pursue studies in sign language interpretation.

Maureen Drysdale is an Associate Professor in Psychology and in the School of Public Health and Health Systems at the University of Waterloo (primary affiliation, St Jerome's University). Maureen is also a Research Associate with the Waterloo Centre for the Advancement of Cooperative Education. Her research examines adolescent school-to-work transitions. Maureen has presented at numerous professional conferences, and has published in many teaching and learning, cooperative education, and work-integrated journals and books. She is the recipient of two experiential learning research awards: The Ralph W. Tyler Award (from the Cooperative Education and Internship Association) and the Dr. Graham Branton Award (from the Canadian Association for Co-operative Education).

Jackie Eldridge is a Concurrent Teaching Education Program Coordinator at the University of Toronto, Mississauga. Her research interests address the many challenges of preparing students to become educators working in a multicultural and increasingly diverse society.

Nancy Johnston is Executive Director of Student Affairs at Simon Fraser University. She is a member of the board of governors of the World Association for Work Integrated Learning and founding member of the Canadian Association for Co-operative Education and the Alliance for Catholic Education. Nancy also led the development of an online co-op curriculum focusing on self-direction and skills transfer, and with her staff developed and launched the first co-op online learning community in North America – which was awarded the 2006 Learning Partnerships Canada's National Technology Innovation Award.

Nadya Ladouceur is the Experiential Education Coordinator for Renaissance College, University of New Brunswick, where she oversees the national and international internship programs. A graduate of the Université du Québec à Montréal (MA, Communication), Nadya was actively involved in citizenship movements and popular education in Quebec for fifteen years before moving to New Brunswick. She has also taught critical thinking, communication, and sociology at the Royal University of Bhutan.

Stephany Lau is a Wilfrid Laurier University Honours BA graduate in Global Studies. She is currently a Communications Officer at International Care Ministries, a non-profit organization that serves slums in the Philippines by teaching essential life skills to those living below subsistence level. She is stationed in the Hong Kong office, advocating for the cause and fundraising support for the organization's operations.

Lynn Matisz recently graduated from Wilfrid Laurier University with an Honours BA in Global Studies. She plans on pursuing further studies and work in the non-profit sector. She is particularly interested in working with new immigrants and refugees to Canada.

Norah McRae has been involved in cooperative education at the University of Victoria since 1992, and since 2007 she has been the Executive Director of the Co-operative Education Program and Career Services at the university. Norah is also a member of the Association for Cooperative Education for BC/Yukon, the Canadian Association for Cooperative Education, the Canadian Association for Career Educators and Employers, and the World Association of Cooperative Education. Norah has a BA in Economics and an MBA from the University of Alberta. She is currently a PhD student at the University of Victoria.

Sara Matthews is Assistant Professor of Global Studies at Wilfrid Laurier University, Waterloo. Her research interests include aesthetic responses to war and conflict, visual culture, literature and digital narrative as memory work, ethical encounters between military and civilian cultures, and teaching and learning from traumatic historical events.

David Peacock is a research associate in the Department of Education at the University of Queensland, Australia. Formerly he was the Engaged Learning Coordinator at St Thomas More College, University of Saskatchewan. In addition to coordinating community service learning and other engagement pedagogies across social science and humanities classes, he collaborated with Intercordia Canada to create student opportunities for international service learning.

Nevena Savija graduated from the University of Waterloo with an Honours BA in Environment and Resource Studies, with minors in Biology and German and a diploma in Environmental Assessment. She is passionate about international involvement and would like to pursue a future along such a path.

John Smith is Partnership Coordinator for Concurrent Teacher Education at the Ontario Institute for Studies in Education and University of Toronto, Mississauga. He teaches courses in Inclusive Education and Mentored Inquiry in Teaching. He has over thirty years of experience in education, as a teacher and administrator in the Peel District School Board and in the Ontario Ministry of Education.

Clara Yoon recently completed her Honours BA in Global Studies at Wilfrid Laurier University. She is continuing her education at the Balsillie School of International Affairs, pursuing an MA in Global Governance from the University of Waterloo. Her research interests include reconciliation and healing between the Koreas, and human rights and global justice for vulnerable sectors of society in Canada and the Koreas.

Index